DEMOCRACY MAY NOT EXIST,
BUT WE'LL MISS IT WHEN IT'S GONE

DEMOCRACY MAY NOT EXIST, BUT WE'LL MISS IT WHEN IT'S GONE

ASTRA TAYLOR

METROPOLITAN BOOKS

HENRY HOLT AND COMPANY NEW YORK

Metropolitan Books
Henry Holt and Company
Publishers since 1866
175 Fifth Avenue
New York, New York 10010
www.henryholt.com

Metropolitan Books® and m® are registered trademarks of
Macmillan Publishing Group, LLC.

Library of Congress Cataloging-in-Publication data
Names: Taylor, Astra, author.
Title: Democracy may not exist, but we'll miss it when it's gone / Astra Taylor.
Description: First edition. | New York : Metropolitan Books, 2019.
| Includes bibliographical references and index.
Identifiers: LCCN 2018029509 | ISBN 9781250179845 (hardcover)
Subjects: LCSH: Democracy—Philosophy.
Classification: LCC JC423 .T3195 2019 | DDC 321.8—dc23
LC record available at https://lccn.loc.gov/2018029509

Our books may be purchased in bulk for promotional, educational, or
business use. Please contact your local bookseller or the Macmillan Corporate and
Premium Sales Department at (800) 221-7945, extension 5442, or by e-mail at
MacmillanSpecialMarkets@macmillan.com.

First Edition 2019

Designed by Kelly S. Too

Printed in the United States of America

10 9 8 7 6 5 4 3 2 1

For Jeffrey Nye Mangum

CONTENTS

LIVING IN THE TENSION

WHAT IS DEMOCRACY? Since this deceptively simple question first came into my mind, I haven't been able to shake it. We think we understand the word, but what are we really referring to when we talk about a system in which the people rule themselves?

The word *democracy* is all around us, invoked in almost every conceivable context: government, business, technology, education, and media. At the same time, its meaning, taken as self-evident, is rarely given much serious consideration. Though the headlines tell us democracy is in "crisis," we don't have a clear conception of what it is that is at risk. The significance of the democratic ideal, as well as its practical substance, is surprisingly elusive.

For most of my life, the word *democracy* didn't hold much appeal. I was of course never against democracy per se, but words such as *justice, equality, freedom, solidarity, socialism,* and *revolution* resonated more deeply. *Democracy* struck me as mealy-mouthed, even debased. That idealistic anarchists and authoritarian leaders are equally inclined to claim "democracy" as their own only demonstrated its lack of depth. North Korea does, after all, call itself a "Democratic People's Republic," and Iraq was invaded by the U.S. Army in the name of bringing democracy to the Middle East. But today I no longer see the opportunistic use of the word as a sign of the idea's vapidity. Those powers co-opt the concept of democracy because they realize that it represents a profound threat to the established order, a threat they desperately hope to contain.

After making a documentary film, *What Is Democracy?*, I now understand the concept's disorienting vagueness and protean character as a source of strength; I have come to accept, and even appreciate, that there is no single definition I can stand behind that feels unconditionally conclusive. Though the practice has extensive global roots, the word *democracy* comes to us from ancient Greece, and it conveys a seemingly simple idea: the people (*demos*) rule or hold power (*kratos*). Democracy is the promise of the people ruling, but a promise that can never be wholly fulfilled because its implications and scope keep changing. Over centuries our conceptions of democracy have expanded and evolved, with democracy becoming more inclusive and robust in many ways, yet who counts as the people, how they rule, and where they do so remain eternally up for debate. Democracy destabilizes its own legitimacy and purpose by design, subjecting its core components to continual examination and scrutiny.

Perfect democracy, I've come to believe, may not in fact exist and never will, but that doesn't mean we can't make progress toward it, or that what there is of it can't disappear. For this reason, I am more convinced than ever that the questions of what democracy is—and, more important, what it could be—are ones we must perpetually ask.

Right now, many who question democracy do so out of disillusionment, fear, and outrage. Democracy may not exist, yet it still manages to disappoint. Political gridlock, corruption, unaccountable representatives, and the lack of meaningful alternatives incense people across the ideological spectrum; their anger simmers at dehumanizing bureaucracy, blatant hypocrisy, and lack of voice. Leaders are not accountable and voters rightly feel their choices are limited, all while the rich keep getting richer and regular people scramble to survive. In advanced democracies around the world, a growing number of people aren't even bothering to vote—a right many people fought and died for fairly recently. Most Americans will say that they live in a democracy, but few will say that they trust the government, while the state generally inspires negative reactions, ranging from frustration to contempt and suspicion. The situation calls to mind Jean-Jacques Rousseau's observation from *The Social Contract*: "In a well-ordered city every man flies to the assemblies; under a bad government no one cares to stir a step to get to them. . . . As soon as any man says of the State *What does it matter to me?* the State may be given up for lost."[1]

A cauldron of causes generates an atmosphere of corrosive cynicism, social fragmentation, and unease, with blame too often directed downward at the most vulnerable populations. And it's not just in the United States. Consider the United Kingdom vote to leave the European Union, the decision known as Brexit; the resurgence of right-wing populism across Europe; coups and reactionary electoral victories in Brazil; and the rise of fascism in India. Plato's warning about democracy devolving into tyranny rings chillingly prophetic. The promise of self-rule risks becoming not a promise but a curse, a self-destructive motor pushing toward destinations more volatile, divided, despotic, and mean.

But this book isn't about the pitfalls of popular sovereignty, though it certainly has its perils. Nor is it about the shortcomings of current liberal democratic political systems or the ways they have been corrupted by money and power—though they have been. That's a story that has been told before, and while it will be the backdrop to my inquiry it is not the focus. This book, instead, is an invitation to think about the word *democracy* from various angles, looking back through history and reflecting on the philosophy and practice of self-rule in hopes that a more contemplative view will shed useful light on our present predicament. My goal is not to negate the sense of alarm nor deter people from action but to remind us that we are part of a long, complex, and still-unfolding chronicle, whatever the day's headlines might be or whoever governs the country.

Taking a more theoretical approach to democracy's winding,

thorny path and inherently paradoxical nature can also provide solace and reassurance. Ruling ourselves has never been straightforward and never will be. Ever vexing and unpredictable, democracy is a process that involves endless reassessment and renewal, not an endpoint we reach before taking a rest (leaving us with a finished system to tweak at the margins). As such, this book is my admittedly unorthodox, idiosyncratic call to democratize society from the bottom to the top. It is also an expression of my belief that we cannot *re*think democracy if we haven't really thought about it in the first place.

One thing I've learned is that the people who are most averse to deepening democracy know exactly why they despise it (Plato, who helped invent political philosophy by railing against democracy, arguably began the trend.) A political science major told me that she doesn't value democracy much. "The phrase that inspires me," she said, "is the American dream and that ability to climb." Opportunity mattered to her and her friends more than inclusion. I expected them to see democracy and capitalism as mutually reinforcing; instead, they perceived the two to be at odds in key respects: democratic demands, whether for progressive taxation or for liberal immigration policies, would diminish their social and economic distinction.

"In capitalism, there are going to be people at the bottom," one young man enthused, confident of his place at the top and cognizant that his position was antidemocratic. Members of a privileged economic minority, these students recognized that impediments to popular sovereignty (such as the Electoral College, which handed two of the last five presidential elections to a candidate who had lost the popular vote) were necessary for the continued dominance of their class. (James Madison had as much in mind when he promoted the idea that the Senate should protect the "invaluable interests" of "opulent" landlords against expropriation by the more numerous masses.)

As much as I disagree with the students' beliefs, this right-wing position is at least the consequence of sincere, if self-centered, consideration. In contrast, many people who say they value democracy have a remarkably difficult time defending the principle in a meaningful or substantive way. Platitudes routinely eclipse more profound or personal reflection: democracy amounts to "free and fair" elections, "the peaceful transfer of power," or "freedom," pure and simple. During the process of making my film, no one I met on the street suggested that democracy was a continuous process of egalitarian inclusion and power sharing made possible by tireless agitators, even though that's a legitimate if long-winded way to define it. Nor did anyone respond with the classical description, that democracy is the rule of the people. (Though I did come across a number of men who, once they realized how little they actually had to say on the subject, told me, authoritatively, that thanks to the genius of the founding fathers America is not actually a democracy but a republic, as if that were enough to cease any further inquiry.)

We could conclude that people who struggle to speak about such an essential component of modern life are just ignorant or perhaps too distracted to be engaged, but I'm not sure it's that simple. The problem stems, I believe, from that fact that democracy is something people rarely encounter in their everyday lives: certainly not during the media- and celebrity-obsessed, money-driven circus of national elections; nor at their jobs, where they are often treated like replaceable cogs in a machine and have to keep their heads down; nor at their schools or colleges, where they are encouraged to see themselves as consumers seeking a return on investment rather than as citizens preparing to participate in the common good. For all our lauded freedoms, democracy isn't something we actually experience all that much. No wonder, then, that people can barely describe it.

Typically, democracy is considered to consist of one person, one vote, exercised in periodic elections; constitutional rights; and a market economy. On paper at least, there is no shortage of states that conform to this rather limited conception—by some estimates, eighty-one countries moved from authoritarianism to democracy between 1980 and 2002. Yet recent studies reveal that democracy, defined by the preceding attributes, has weakened worldwide over the last decade or so. According to one well-respected annual report, seventy-one countries suffered net declines in political rights and civil liberties in 2017, leading to an overall decrease in global freedom.[2] In early 2018, the *Economist* warned, "Democracy Continues Its Disturbing Retreat"—this not long after the magazine's yearly Democracy Index officially downgraded the United States from a "full democracy" to a "flawed" one.[3]

Yet democracy doesn't retreat either of its own accord or by some organic, immutable process. It is eroded, undermined, attacked, or allowed to wither. It falls into disrepair and disrepute thanks to the actions or inaction of human beings who have lost touch with or, in some cases, sabotaged the responsibilities and possibilities that a system of self-government entails. While today it's common to blame extremists for jeopardizing democracy, studies show that across Europe and the United States it is middle-of-the-road centrists who tend to hold the most hostile attitudes toward democratic practices, preferring strong and effective centralized decision making to messier, more inclusive processes. Less than half of Americans who identify with the political center view elections as "an essential feature of democracy" and only half of them, or 25 percent of centrists, agree that civil rights are crucial.[4] Apathy, or even antipathy, toward self-government and the difficult daily work it requires is one of the stones that help pave the way to a more authoritarian society. That apathy is helped by the fact that the American system was never designed to be democratic to begin with.

As with many other liberalizing nations of the late eighteenth century, the republic did not consider the majority of its residents to be members of the polity. Enslaved and indigenous people, all women, poor white men, certain immigrants, and some religious groups were denied rights, including the most basic right of citizenship, the right to cast a ballot. These founding inequities, only fitfully and incompletely redressed, continue to shape our present. As numerous academic studies show, the national agenda is set by plutocrats and well-represented interests, while the preferences of the broad population have virtually no impact on public policy. The inequalities that plague us today are not an aberration nor the result of whichever party happens to be in power, but a plausible result of the political system's very design, which in crucial ways was devised by a restricted and privileged class of men.

In the fifth century BC, the celebrated statesman Pericles famously praised the political structure of Athens: "It is true that we are called a democracy, for the administration is in the hands of the many and not of the few." Given the existence of slavery and the exclusion of women, Athens failed to meet the bar by modern standards. Yet as Plato and Aristotle noted, the overwhelming majority of people who made up the Athenian demos were not wealthy. Rule of the people, they observed, by definition means rule of the poor, since citizens of modest means are bound to vastly outnumber the rich.

This basic insight has been negated in our time as neoliberal capitalism and the massive financial inequities it creates dismantle hard-won democratic gains. Under a legal order where money qualifies as speech in the context of campaign spending and lobbying, the richest are able to purchase influence while everyone else struggles to be heard; in a system where the affluent can pass their assets to their offspring virtually untaxed, inherited wealth ensures the creation of an aristocratic class. If the last fifty years has demonstrated anything, it is that formal political equality, exemplified by the right to vote, is not enough to ensure democracy, as the wealthy have many avenues to exert disproportionate power. While earlier generations focused on expanding suffrage, today we face an arguably more formidable task: saving democracy from capitalism. Extending democracy from the political to the economic sphere is the great challenge of our age, and also the only way to protect political equality from the concentrated financial power that is proving to be its undoing.

A mere eight men—six of them American—hold the same amount of wealth as half the people on earth, their private fortunes built on mass penury.[5] The United States, perhaps unsurprisingly, is more an oligarchy than a democracy. Year upon year, the vast majority of the income generated globally flows into the pockets of the top 1 percent of the world's population, while the incomes of ordinary citizens have stagnated over the last four decades.[6] Whereas an American born in the 1940s had a 92 percent chance of outearning his or her parents by age thirty, for those born in the 1980s, that likelihood has fallen to 50 percent; in some places in the Midwest, the odds are worse. A recent Federal Reserve survey revealed that almost half of Americans are too broke to cover a four-hundred-dollar emergency expense, and they would have to sell possessions or borrow money to do so.[7]

Even more shocking, given the veneration of the achievements of the civil rights movement, is that there has been no progress for black Americans with regard to unemployment, homeownership, and incarceration since the push for racial equality reached its peak fifty years ago. As the Economic Policy Institute reports, "In 2017 the black unemployment rate was 7.5 percent, up from 6.7 percent in 1968, and is still roughly twice the white unemployment rate. In 2015, the black homeownership rate was just over 40 percent, virtually unchanged since 1968, and trailing a full 30 points behind the white homeownership rate, which saw modest gains over the same period. And the share of African Americans in prison or jail almost tripled between 1968 and 2016 and is currently more than six times the white incarceration rate."[8] The financial crisis of 2008, which wiped out half the wealth of black households, contributed to this grim state of affairs.[9] Yet, today, one of the few bipartisan issues uniting Democrats and Republicans in Washington involves repealing the meager Wall Street reforms passed following the crash.[10] There may be elections and some safeguards of civil liberties, and we should be grateful for this, but the state is hardly run by or for the people it purports to serve.[11]

The forces of oligarchy have been enabled, in part, by our tendency to accept a highly proscribed notion of democracy, one that limits popular power to the field of electoral politics, ignoring the other institutions and structures (workplaces, prisons, schools, hospitals, the environment, and the economy itself) that shape people's lives. This is a mistake. To be substantive and strong, democracy cannot be something that happens only in capitol buildings; self-rule has to be far more widespread. If we believe that democracy should serve all of society, how can we call ourselves democratic when workers juggle multiple jobs as record-breaking profits flow to owners and investors? When millions of people, disproportionately poor and people of color, are locked behind bars? When access to learning and lifesaving treatments are denied to those who can't pay? When the planet may be rendered uninhabitable so that a small number of companies can maximize revenues from fossil fuels? When the global 1 percent are on track to control two-thirds of the world's wealth by 2030?[12] We can view these issues as distinct and unrelated, or we can understand them as fundamentally interconnected, as joint symptoms of the fact that those with money, not "the many," rule.

When we to stop to ask what democracy means, we'll notice that a good number of the practical and philosophical problems plaguing us are not exactly novel; they are as old as democracy itself. The challenges are timeless: Is democracy a means or an end, a process or a set of finite outcomes? What if those outcomes, whatever they may be (peace, prosperity, sustainability, equality, liberty, an engaged citizenry), can be achieved by nondemocratic means? If democracy means rule by the people, what is the nature and extent of that rule and who counts as "the people"? We may think we are on the cutting edge, charting a socially unprecedented course, but

the fight for justice, freedom, and self-rule (and the profound difficulties of realizing these democratic ideals) necessarily entails grappling with age-old dilemmas anew.

Democracy, the classicist Danielle Allen told me, is "intellec-
tually hard." If you live in a monarchy, you can point to a picture
of the king or queen and know that that is the person who rules.
But if you live in a democracy, there's nothing to point to, in a
concrete way, that conveys the idea that the people are in charge.
"The very notion of a democratic people is an abstract conceptu-
alization," Allen explained. "You have to understand what is this
'people'? How can you have justice when you have something
making decisions that doesn't seem to quite exist?" Democracy
demands everyone wrestle with these abstract questions and
concepts.

This demand itself explains why democracy and political philosophy emerged at the same time in ancient Greece: in the absence
of a powerful tyrant or a cabal of aristocrats making decisions
from on high, democracy requires that people reason and reflect.
Thus, Athens's massive open-air assemblies obliged citizens to
ask the great Socratic question "How should I live?" collectively.
In these remarkable gatherings, thousands of ordinary people,
the demos, were expected to consider what kind of society they
wanted to live in and why. They would contemplate, discuss, and
decide on laws, punishment, and whether to go to war. In conditions of a democracy, the onus is on citizens to be inquisitive and
to question their own system of government. The political order
became an object of intensive speculation and critique. (Democracy, in other words, made Plato's antidemocratic musings possible.)[13] But what makes democracy so compelling is that it is not just
abstraction and intellectualization but also action. To be understood, self-rule must be enacted—it is thought and conduct, theory
and practice, noun and verb in equal measure.

These seeming oppositions are foundational to democracy,
which encompasses politics that are both unified and diverse, indi-
vidualistic and collective, that mix egalitarianism with hierarchy

and autonomy with constraint. More than oppositions, these are paradoxes, contradictory elements that, while liable to clash, must coexist. The most famous paradox of all, the product of Jean-Jacques Rousseau, is of the chicken-or-egg variety, addressing the problem of creating democratic subjects, people who incline toward and are capable of democracy. "For an emerging people to be capable of appreciating the sound maxims of politics and to follow the fundamental rules of statecraft, the effect would have to become the cause," Rousseau mused. "The social spirit which ought to be the work of that institution, would have to preside over the institution itself."[14] Put more plainly, the question is what comes first: the society and institutions that mold democratic citizens, cultivating and educating them, or citizens who are able to create such a society and institutions? The paradox is that democracy appears to require, in advance, the very structures and sensibilities on which it needs to rely in order to emerge, persist, and thrive.

Democracy is rife with these sorts of occasionally discordant yet indivisible dualities: it always has to balance freedom and equality, conflict and consensus, inclusion and exclusion, coercion and choice, spontaneity and structure, expertise and mass opinion, the local and the global, and the present and the future. There can be no unambiguous resolution on one or the other side of the binary.

What follows is an inquiry into democracy as a balance of paradoxes, an exploration of opposites, a framework I've chosen in hopes of jolting us out of more well-worn paradigms. No doubt I've failed to include some important paradoxes; by design, this book could never be conclusive; as philosophy, it asks more questions than it answers. But one absence in particular is worth mentioning: the rich versus the poor. I see no reason to accept the gulf between the haves and the have-nots, the owning class and the laboring class, as an inherently necessary paradox or an insurmountable fact of society, especially given our technological capabilities and productive capacities.

This brings us to a definition of *contradiction*: for Karl Marx, a contradiction is a conflict within capitalism (the antagonism between private property and common wealth, for example) destined, at some date, to be resolved in such a way as to usher in a new economic regime. Marx saw democracy as "the solved *riddle* of all constitutions" because in a democracy, "the constitution appears as what it is, the free product of men."[15] In contrast, the paradoxes I've identified do not stand in opposition in a Marxist sense, because they are necessary and irresolvable facets of democratic life. Though I believe that the process of democratization involves moving toward an equitable distribution of power and resources (what some call socialism), I doubt all riddles will ever be perfectly solved. I aim to show that existing economic inequality intensifies certain sides of the paradoxes I've highlighted, increasing instability and suffering. Still, it is my view that even without capitalist exploitation, democracy would remain messy and conflicted, full of what Plato called "variety and disorder" (which, despite being democracy's first and most acute critic, he regarded as part of its charm).[16] Should we ever achieve a fully economically and socially egalitarian society, we'll still have to strive to balance spontaneity and structure, for example, or grapple with how best to weigh our present-day desires against future needs.

By teasing out these conflicts, we might gain better insight into why the challenge of self-rule is so great. Indeed, what motivated me to undertake this project was an urge to understand why democratic principles are so difficult to put into practice, a quandary my work as an activist makes me intimately familiar with. Democracy cannot be reduced to a system of laws to abide, a set of "indicators" to meet, or a ten-point proposal to enact but is instead something more emergent and experimental, a combination of order and flux rooted in both procedure *and* principle, modes of production (how we organize the creation of goods necessary for our survival) *and* popular sentiment. As we shall see, for democracy to continue and transform, the two poles represented by the paradoxes explored in these pages must be held in thoughtful, delicate tension.

Tension—that's the key word. Consider democracy's dark history, from slavery and colonialism to facilitating the emergence of fascism, from the omnipresent threat of nuclear annihilation to the danger posed by climate change. Think of all the bad decisions made by democratic humanity: the disastrous referendums, the selfish attachment to bigoted beliefs, the stubborn refusal to evolve even when our lives depended on it. All this makes democracy a "leap of faith," as the philosopher Cornel West calls it, one that requires "living in the tension," the tension of paradoxes unresolved and arguably irresolvable. The history of democracy is one of oppression, exploitation, demagoguery, dispossesion, domination, horror, and abuse. But it is also a history of cooperation, solidarity, deliberation, emancipation, justice, and empathy. Which side do we fall on, where should the emphasis land? In the final hour, is democracy a lost cause or our last hope?

"There's always going to be mountains of evidence to convince you that you must be losing your mind if you believe this demos is going to make good decisions," West told me. "But on the other hand, you say, lo and behold, so many of the best ideas about how you treat human beings, best ideas about justice, often come from the very folk you thought you had no grounds for trusting in their ability to think and reflect. Cuts both ways. Living in the tension. I think that's the key."

I don't believe democracy exists; indeed, it never has. Instead, the ideal of self-rule is exactly that, an ideal, a principle that always occupies a distant and retreating horizon, something we must continue to reach toward yet fail to grasp. The promise of democracy is not the one made and betrayed by the powerful; it is a promise that can be kept only by regular people through vigilance, invention, and struggle. Through theory and practice, organization and open rebellion, protecting past gains and demanding new entitlements, the inspiring potential of self-rule manifests, but it remains fragmentary and fragile, forever partial and imperiled. In the end, living in the tension, embracing the incongruities and possibilities of democracy without giving up, is the message of this book.

CHAPTER 1

FREE TO BE WINNERS AND LOSERS

(FREEDOM/EQUALITY)

IN 1989, WHEN the Berlin Wall fell, people everywhere cheered the dawn of a new democratic age. The free world had triumphed over the unfree and was now in ascendance. The liberal doctrine of individual rights, periodic elections, and consumer abundance appeared both irresistible and unstoppable. Socialism, painted as a bleak and blinkered condition where individualism and opportunity were suppressed in favor of state-sponsored sameness, was condemned as a condition of equality run amok, while capitalism, an inherently unequal economic system, was increasingly taken to be synonymous with democracy or freedom.

Some historians say the Cold War began in 1947 with a speech by President Harry Truman in which he used the word *free* or *freedom* an astonishing twenty-four times in a mere eighteen minutes; the word *equality* was not uttered once.[1] By 1989, *freedom* and *equality*, two terms central to the theory and practice of democracy, occupied opposite ends of a bipolar political spectrum after decades of a slow rupture. Ideals that throughout democratic history had been intertwined in complex, fruitful ways were severed; concepts long allied had become enemies. This was an unprecedented inflection point in the history of democratic governance. Moreover, the eclipsing of Marxist alternatives in 1989 also, counterintuitively, inaugurated aspects of democracy's decline: deregulated markets and transnational policy making began to ramp up income inequality and undermine attributes of national sovereignty on which a liberal-democratic, welfare-state system depends. Thus this dawn of a new democratic age in fact inaugurated the degradation of democracy in key ways.

The consequences of severing freedom and equality have been profound. Although distinct and occasionally discordant, freedom and equality were regularly envisaged as virtues that could positively reinforce each other when held in proper balance. Over time they have been reconfigured as wholly incompatible, with one term jeopardizing the other. While equality was recast as a threat to liberty, freedom became reduced to the right to be left alone—what some philosophers, following Isaiah Berlin, call negative liberty, or "freedom as non-interference." Capitalism's resounding 1989 victory concluded this shift, with the locus of freedom moving firmly to the marketplace. Contemporary freedom is, above all, the freedom to compete in the economy without intervention from meddling government, and to get ahead or fall behind trying. It means, in other words, being free to be unequal. "Freedom breeds inequality," the celebrity conservative talk show host William F. Buckley pronounced to a television audience of millions in 1968, articulating a perspective that would soon become commonplace. "Unless you have freedom to be unequal, there is no such thing as freedom."

Flashback another couple of hundred years, and we can see how novel, and strange, this formulation is. This blunt dualism, the pitting of freedom and equality in a zero-sum game, stands in stark contrast to earlier modes of understanding. The slogan of the French Revolution, in 1789, married *freedom* and *equality* to a third term: *liberté, égalité, fraternité*. The two ideals, bonded by brotherhood—not sisterhood, as visionary feminists, including Olympe de Gouges, noted at the time, an insight for which she paid with her life—reinforced each other, a trinity of virtues that required the end of aristocracy and a class leveling to stand a chance of being enacted.

In the revolutionary formulation, influenced by the writings of the philosopher Jean-Jacques Rousseau, individuals become both free and equal through the exercise of common citizenship (what could be called collective freedom or, following Berlin again, positive liberty). It was a remarkable shift in perspective. Since the dramatic demise of ancient Athens over two thousand years prior, democracy had been associated with freedom spun out of control, with anarchy and mob rule; to present democracy as a desirable alternative to stifling aristocracy and a guarantor of basic liberties was unorthodox, to say the least. Thus, the French Revolution, like the end of the Cold War, was a democratic watershed, this one marking the moment when the idea of political equality entered the popular imagination and when the word *democracy* was rescued from the disrepute that had long stalked it.[2]

Today, one corner of the *liberté, égalité, fraternité* triad reigns undeniably supreme. Freedom, and freedom alone, is the paramount value, the concept on the tip of everyone's tongue, while equality languishes as the less celebrated counterpart, and brotherhood can barely be discerned. While making my documentary I asked dozens of people what democracy meant to them. "Freedom" was the standard and often instantaneous reply, as though that clarified matters and the concept's meaning was self-evident.

The people I met usually defined *freedom* as the chance to exercise choice and get ahead. For some—typically people from marginalized backgrounds—freedom was defined as the absence of fear. (In this, they echo the musician Nina Simone, who told an interviewer, "I'll tell you what freedom is to me. No fear.") For twenty-one-year-old Salam Magames, a Syrian refugee I met in Greece from war-torn Aleppo, freedom contains both elements: "Freedom means that a human being gets all their rights." And, she added, "We just want to put our head on the pillow without having nightmares that someone will come and kidnap and assault us."

No one, not a single soul in the United States or elsewhere, told me that democracy meant "equality."

If I had prodded, perhaps the people I spoke to would have professed a commitment to the principle that human beings are intrinsically equal. Maybe they simply took this equality as a given—an innate quality every individual automatically possesses simply by virtue of being born human. And yet I don't believe that equality went unmentioned merely because it was taken for granted. For most of history, hierarchies were assumed to be not just legitimate but natural (how else could monarchs, aristocrats, racists, and misogynists hold on to power?). Equality emerged as an intellectual concept much later than the idea of freedom, which means its roots are not as deep or as robust as we might think. And equality is rarely used for propaganda purposes, which means it is less quick on the lips: we visit the Statue of Liberty, not the Statue of Equality; and in the early oughts, we built a Freedom Tower and were served freedom fries, not equality ones; we fight for our civil liberties, not civil equalities. Equality—which has been called "the most controversial of the great social ideals"—just isn't as hyped.[3]

Freedom and *equality* have never been self-evident, impartial terms, but are constantly evolving, invoked and refashioned to serve the desires of conflicting groups and interests, their dominant meanings challenged by those with dissenting perspectives. Thanks to these struggles, more people than ever believe that human beings are roughly equivalent on some metaphysical level. That may be the case, but we are hardly the same. Democracy has to cope with incredible human variation, a process that can require treating people unequally in order to ensure the possibility of something approaching just outcomes. Someone like Salam, who has been made homeless and traumatized by war, may need extra degrees of assistance and support in order to be equally free. In these seemingly special cases, we can see a truth of the human condition that in fact applies to every single person on earth. Freedom is not a state of independence but a state of *inter*dependence, one in which our unique needs are met by the society in which we live, in order that we might all have a fair chance of flourishing. In a democracy, what that means in practice will always fluctuate. The tension between freedom and equality, though often exaggerated, is real: an excess of one can endanger the other, but at the same time neither value can be expressed in isolation.

If we want to understand our present confusion over the relationship between equality and freedom, we have to look all the way back to ancient Athens, that mythic birthplace of democracy that was built on the economic bedrock of bondage. Athenians were not ashamed of the existence of slavery, which was typical for city-states and empires of that era. Rather, what they were proud of, what set them apart, was their system of directly democratic self-rule, a unique situation in which the *demos*, people, held *kratos*, power.

There are reasons to question Athens's formative place in the democratic pantheon. One can highlight the existence of other proto-democratic traditions, for example in regions that correspond to modern-day Turkey, Egypt, Syria, Iraq, and, as we'll see, the Americas. Nevertheless, and despite Athenian society's many shortcomings—slavery, misogyny, xenophobia, and imperialism (terrible characteristics modern societies have yet to be fully cured of)—there's no denying that the city-state was remarkable in many respects.[4] The Athenian system of direct democracy consisted of a wide range of institutions, laws, customs, and concepts aimed at enabling all citizens to enjoy *isonomia*, or equality before the law—an equality founded on *isegoria*, or "equal freedom of speech," the right to both speak and be heard in the Assembly and to rule and be ruled in turn.

The innovations of the Athenian system were legion, from a complex and virtually incorruptible jury system to the practice of ostracism that cast out would-be strongmen; from rotation by lottery as opposed to election for key public offices (on the grounds that elections were not democratic enough, as the well born and well spoken tended to win) to payments for civic service to cover lost wages for those who could not otherwise attend. Athenian craftsmen used marble and bronze to empower citizens and curb corruption in ways modern engineers with silicon chips and wireless networks would do well to learn from.

Ancient Athens's signal breakthrough, however, was that it gave real political power to poor people—so much power that one esteemed scholar has likened it to a "dictatorship of the proletariat."[5] The Assembly of Athens was open—in practice, not just in theory—to tens of thousands, hardscrabble farmers and wealthy landowners alike. In that all-powerful body, and also in the courts that determined the fate of the community and its members, the lower classes occupied the space of free and equal citizens, not passive subjects. "Neither is poverty an obstacle, but a man may benefit his country whatever the obscurity of his condition," Pericles maintained.

The obstacle of poverty was first circumvented at a point widely regarded as one of the birth moments of Western democracy. In 594 BC, in response to a crisis that had farmers selling themselves into foreign slavery because they could no longer pay their debts, an aristocratic poet turned social reformer named Solon instigated the first significant step toward the inclusion of the working poor in political life. "All the common people were weighed down with the debts they owed to a few rich men," Plutarch's account of this period reports. Though Solon declined to redistribute land and impose strict quality in living standards as some of his supporters hoped, his "shaking off of obligations" involved canceling payments and returning the enslaved Athenians to freedom while outlawing the practice of debt bondage. He also tackled criminal justice, repealing the laws established by the former tyrant Dracos, whose "draconian" code made almost every crime—even stealing a single fruit or vegetable—punishable by death. Disappointing those who urged him to seize control and become a tyrant himself, Solon instead created a new social order, laying the foundation for a system in which impoverished citizens could fully participate in the governing institutions of the city.[6]

Given the history of debt bondage and the constant threat of invasion from neighboring city-states such as Sparta the Athenians evolved to become supremely wary of domination, whether perpetuated by fellow citizens or external enemies (although male citizens dominated other social groups within, through slavery, and without, through imperial conquest). Freedom from external domination meant cultivating military might, but avoiding internal threats involved cultivating equality of political power among citizens so that no individual or group, no matter how charismatic, rich, or highborn, could reign supreme. Such were the convictions of the people who invented not just the word *democracy* but also *demagogue* and *oligarchy*.

During the two centuries of democracy that followed Solon's reforms, Athenians remained committed to the insight that the polity would disintegrate into civil war and chaos if economic inequality undermined the standing of poorer citizens. The classicist Danielle Allen distilled the logic for me as follows: "Freedom requires political equality; political equality requires social equality and economic egalitarianism. You line the concepts up that way, and freedom and equality fit together like hand in glove." It doesn't take the brilliant mind of a Pericles to see that differentials of wealth invariably translate into imbalances in political power. The dichotomy between freedom and equality that is so common today would have been nonsensical to the ancient Greeks. After all, the interdependence of the two ideals had been affirmed at the very inception of their social order through the reforms of Solon.

In some ways, ancient Athens was very much like the early United States. Both ostensible cradles of government by the people were founded on institutionalized unfreedom and the fervently held belief that some human beings did not qualify as political equals and could be ruthlessly exploited. Indeed, it was the visible presence of slavery that led people in both societies, Athenian and American, to deeply, and perhaps pathologically, value and romanticize the ideal of liberty as the antithesis of bondage.

American legal scholar Aziz Rana calls this core contradiction the "two faces of American freedom." "All men are created equal," the American Declaration of Independence famously declares, those equal men endowed with the inalienable right to pursue liberty alongside life and happiness. But the upper-class owners of human chattel who penned and signed that document counted each enslaved African as three-fifths of a person, denied men without property and women the right to vote, and committed genocide against native people while illegally speculating on stolen land.

For early American settlers, democratic ideals "gained strength and meaning through frameworks of exclusion," Rana explains, the emancipatory and oppressive features of American life tightly bound.[7] Liberty and economic independence—for a limited elite class—required free land and forced labor, perpetuating the dispossession of indigenous people and the institution of slavery (freedom meant the freedom to settle and to enslave). On this corrupt foundation, the colonists who counted as full political citizens, as members of the democratic demos, constructed a conception of "republican freedom" that "provided a truly expansive vision of collective life—in which self-rule entailed actively asserting one's authority over economic, political, and religious institutions." For that fortunate subset of men, freedom and equality were complimentary. The republican conception of liberty upheld civic participation as essential to freedom. Self-rule, in turn, required a degree of economic equality among the citizenry lest political equality be undermined. That meant settler citizens should be propertied men, with land of their own, not itinerant menial laborers who were subservient and therefore incapable of self-government. (In his *Commentaries on the Laws of England*, from the 1760s, Sir William Blackstone propounded this view, insisting that men without property, lacking independence, would threaten the "general liberty.")

Rana's conception of the Janus-faced nature of American freedom adds a new dimension to the standard narrative of American independence we all learn in school. Children are taught about the thirteen colonies that rose up against an oppressive monarchy under the famous rallying cry "No taxation without representation," but the reality was, of course, more complex. Though they had a variety of grievances, settlers were motivated to revolt against British control at a moment when their privileged position within the empire was shifting. As imperial administrators sought to manage far-flung subjects—whose ranks now included French and Spanish colonists, indigenous people, Caribs, and Bengalis—white-skinned Protestant colonists regarded any sign of increased tolerance and diversity (that is, increasing equality) as a threat to their special status and the freedom that that special status conferred. When the Crown issued the Royal Proclamation of 1763, gesturing toward protecting the territorial rights of tribes with whom it had treaties from further encroachment, American settlers were aghast, for their model of freedom and equality depended on an expanding frontier. This indignation was the glue that united small-time farmers and wealthy land speculators such as George Washington, who were affronted that taxes were being levied to pay for British troops to halt settler appropriation of Native American land. According to sociologist Michael Mann, independence from imperial prerogatives typically correlated with increased settler violence against natives: "the stronger the democracy among the perpetrators, the greater the genocide."[8]

Meanwhile, successful legal challenges to slavery mounted on British soil, such as the celebrated 1772 *Somerset* decision declaring slavery odious and incompatible with English common law, only added to the settlers' sense of imperial persecution. American revolutionaries protested that they were, in fact, the true slaves, to an absolute and arbitrary power across the Atlantic, with such cries of oppression emanating the loudest from slaveholding colonies.[9] Seen from this perspective, the American Revolution was arguably conservative, aimed as much at maintaining the status quo than ushering in a radically different, more democratic epoch in which the racially excluded might have a chance to reap the benefits of freedom and equality's coexistence.

The settlers succeeded on their terms. The continuation of slavery and the post-revolution grab of indigenous territory ensured a degree of economic egalitarianism unknown in the mother country. Schemes such as the Georgia Land Lotteries, in which the U.S. government forced Native American communities from their homelands and distributed parcels to European settlers, made the fabled yeoman farmer possible. Even as they unabashedly protected the property rights of the prosperous, the founding fathers supported redistributive policies that would be anathema to most officeholders today, recognizing that massive imbalances in wealth could undermine the fragile republic. Thomas Jefferson, for example, successfully brought an end to Virginia laws of entail (which limited inheritance to a family line) and primogeniture (the passage of property to the eldest son) in order to break up large estates and ensure a more middling distribution of land and wealth so as to prevent the emergence of a "future aristocracy." The tremendously popular pamphleteer and "father of the American Revolution" Thomas Paine went even further, arguing that every man and woman should get a basic grant of income, in the form of a lump sum and then an annual stipend, financed by inheritance taxes through a national fund, to eliminate economic servitude and promote a more resilient vision of republican freedom and equality.

Unfortunately, Paine's influence on political developments after the republic's founding was hindered by his abolitionist views, which meant his proposal for social security and a basic income went untried. Instead, freedom's two faces were conscripted to further entrench hierarchies based on skin color while providing cover for growing inequities of wealth and power within the white community. In 1860, Georgia governor Joseph E. Brown vividly described the way slavery made it possible for patricians and plebeians to envision themselves as equals, though one lorded over a vast plantation while the other lived in relative squalor.

Among us the poor white laborer is respected as an equal. His family is treated with kindness, consideration and respect. He does not belong to the menial class. The negro is in no sense of the term his equal. He feels and knows this. He belongs to the only true aristocracy, the race of white men. He blacks no masters boots, and bows the knee to no one save God alone. He receives higher wages for his labor, than does the laborer of any other portion of the world, and he raises up his children, with the knowledge, that they belong to no inferior cast; but that the highest members of society in which he lives, will, if their conduct is good, respect and treat them as equals.[10]

To ward off empathy between the exploited, envy and awe of the upper classes was encouraged alongside a vicarious experience of superiority to racialized populations; white workers earned what the brilliant historian and scholar W. E. B. Du Bois would later dub a "psychological wage" that helped them accept their meager monetary one. That white people were not held in bondage proved they were free, and that they were white made them superior to those who were not, and thus equal to whites who were their material betters.

We might flatter ourselves that such logic was abolished along with slavery, but it lives on, reverberating through the pronouncements of right-wing populist politicians in the United States and Europe who, claiming to represent "the people," boost plutocrats by pitting downwardly mobile insiders against scapegoated outsiders, be they racial minorities, immigrants, or refugees. "Just watch the interlopers from the world come and install themselves in our home," intoned Marine Le Pen, president of France's far-right National Front Party (now called National Rally) to her followers. "They want to transform France into a giant squat. But it's up to the owner to decide who can come in. So, our first act will be to restore France's frontiers." In 2018, a caravan of more than seven thousand men, women, and children seeking sanctuary in the United States that began in Honduras, one of the most impoverished and violent countries on earth, was portrayed in the conservative media and by Republican leaders as an invading army determined to commit crime and steal jobs, not human beings pursuing their legal right to seek asylum and have a chance at a decent life. The hollow freedom and equality of exclusion still serves as cover for vast social and economic disparities.

Abid Muhajir, a twenty-one-year-old Afghan and asylum seeker I met during his long, hazardous trek to Germany across the Aegean and through the Balkans, vehemently challenged the idea that democracy is synonymous with freedom. He was staying on the outskirts of Athens, at a derelict airport that had been transformed into a camp holding nearly four thousand men, women, and children. "Freedom? What freedom do I need here?" Abid said. "Freedom of what? Hurting somebody? Freedom of killing somebody? This is also freedom, a negative we also have."

I was taken aback by the passion and vividness of his response. Until that moment, Abid, a former English teacher (though he was able to attend school only through the second grade), had been soft-spoken. He apologized profusely for his strong opinion, as though he risked offending me by pointing out freedom's downsides, before explaining why he felt the way he did. As a member of a persecuted ethnic and religious minority, he had seen the violence of unfettered freedom firsthand when he was growing up in Quetta, Pakistan, where he and his mother had sought refuge from the Taliban in their home country. "The problem that we have is that we are Hazara," Abid explained. "They say, 'They are Hazara, they are from Afghanistan, they don't have right to live here, let's kill them.' In front of my own eyes, I witnessed many of the people who were killed. Because we are Shi'a Muslims, they kill us, they shoot. Wherever we go, we are the target." The exercise of brutality without restraint had made Abid skeptical that freedom was an unalloyed good. "In my opinion, justice means rules . . . if you have rules, this is the limit, if you cross this limit, you will be found guilty, you will be sentenced, you will go to prison. I need rules, justice. Such things are called democracy. Democracy doesn't mean freedom for everything, I think."

I thought about Abid whenever I passed a statue outside the University of Toronto law school. The statue is simple enough at first glance: a ten-foot-tall monument featuring a lion and lamb on opposite sides of a level plank, their eyes meeting. Though one is large and fearsome, the other small and docile, the sculpture grants them the same weight—thus its name, *Equal Before the Law*. Initially, I found the piece to be a charming, if idealized, portrayal, given the fact that the powerful possess tremendous advantages within the legal system as it exists: lions can typically afford better lawyers than lambs, and keep them on retainer longer. Or, as poet and novelist Anatole France observed, "The law, in its majestic equality, forbids the rich as well as the poor to sleep under bridges, to beg in the streets, and to steal bread." But many walks later, I noticed a literal twist. The plank supporting the lion and lamb is not perfectly straight, like some balanced seesaw, but askew, bent at a sixty-degree angle. The law, the statue seems to be saying, cannot achieve equality by being applied neutrally, but must account for a range of differences in order to achieve a just outcome. That contortion, that complex balancing act, is called justice—or, in Abid's formulation, democracy.

Abid's comments were a powerful reminder that freedom for some can mean domination for others, since all are not equal. Freedom of what? Abid rightly inquired. And, we could add, for whom? Likewise, we might ask: Equality of what? And among whom? Human beings may possess an equal, intrinsic value, but the fact that we are not makes matters perpetually complex. Even when we bracket differentials of socioeconomic status and life experience, there are differences in gender, age, physical and mental ability, health, and so on. We cannot treat children, the elderly, or disabled people the same as able-bodied adults and reasonably expect to arrive at equitable results. Equality doesn't just exist, it must be enacted, a process that entails recognizing people's varying abilities and needs. Or to put it another way, democracy cannot be a lion and a lamb deciding what to have for dinner, for that would mean imposing a destructively simplistic conception of equality on two unequal beings and elevating a single type of freedom over freedom's other incarnations.

In his magisterial sociological history, *Freedom in the Making of Western Culture*, Orlando Patterson lays out three kinds of freedom: personal, civic, and sovereign. The last is the freedom to do whatever one pleases to an individual or group; it is the freedom of absolute power, the freedom of the tyrant, the slave owner, and the robber baron, and it is this form of freedom that the commitment to equality and rights has to be strong enough to check. No wonder, then, that it was the abolitionists who advanced civic freedom—the capacity to participate in public life—by institutionalizing the concept of equality before the law in the United States, which had no precedent in antebellum jurisprudence. They did so, in part, by extending civil liberties or fundamental rights to all citizens.[11] Today, one of the main ways democracies keep would-be lions in check is through the concept of rights, those equally distributed entitlements designed to prevent overzealous institutions from encroaching on our individual freedom. (In contrast to the republican vision of freedom through civic engagement and collective self-rule, this liberal conception of freedom emphasizes autonomy, the rule of law, and constitutional protections; these two traditions, republican and liberal, while not necessarily opposed, are distinct.)[12]

As Patterson shows, there has always been a struggle for freedom from above and below. "Who were the first persons to get the unusual idea that being free was not only a value to be cherished but the most important thing that someone could possess?" Patterson asks. "The answer, in a word: slaves." Personal freedom, in particular, began as a longing for domination's end, for someone else's destructive, sovereign freedom to be shackled. Those first slaves who dreamed of freedom were not who you might expect.

They were, Patterson reveals, women. Women suffered captivity long before it made economic sense to subjugate their male counterparts in substantial numbers. Only when men began to be enslaved as frequently did freedom begin to be recognized as a concept worth taking seriously.

Throughout history the ideals of freedom and equality emanate intensely from the ground up, with the most authentic and expansive dreams conjured by those who were most emphatically excluded. This is true of the first women held as chattel as well as in ancient Athens. There, the most radical exponents of freedom were not Plato and Aristotle, both of whom despised democracy and the liberty and equality it entailed, or even Pericles, who eulogized the city-state's system of self-rule, but two men who had endured slavery: Diogenes of Sinope and Epictetus. Diogenes, the founder of cynicism who lived in the streets and slept in a large urn, was arguably the first proponent of a kind of irreverent freedom of expression we now might associate with the counterculture of the 1960s. (*Cynic* comes from the Greek word for "dog,' a creature Diogenes admired for its lack of inhibition.) Flouting convention, Diogenes treated everyone equally, which is to say, cheekily: he famously told Alexander the Great, one of his many admirers, to move aside and stop blocking the sunlight. Epictetus, whose reputation also exceeded his humble circumstances, was an early proponent of stoicism. He believed in cultivating inner or spiritual freedom that could be maintained regardless of one's external circumstances and the vicissitudes of fate. Material quality matters less when freedom is conceived as a state of mind.

In the modern era, we see the promise of democracy as a marriage of freedom and equality most vividly articulated at the grassroots, especially in social movements aimed at promoting economic and racial justice, from the civil rights movement in the United States to the battle to end apartheid in South Africa. The African National Congress's 1955 Freedom Charter was devised over years by organizers going from door to door and asking black South Africans how they wanted to be governed. The resulting document stirringly conveys their ambitious mission to seek both racial and economic justice.

> We, the People of South Africa, declare for all our country and the world to know: that South Africa belongs to all who live in it, black and white, and that no government can justly claim authority unless it is based on the will of all the people; that our people have been robbed of their birthright to land, liberty and peace by a form of government founded on injustice and inequality; that our country will never be prosperous or free until all our people live in brotherhood, enjoying equal rights and opportunities; that only a democratic state, based on the will of all the people, can secure to all their birthright without distinction of colour, race, sex or belief; And therefore, we, the people of South Africa, black and white together—equals, countrymen and brothers—adopt this Freedom Charter. And we pledge ourselves to strive together, sparing neither strength nor courage, until the democratic changes here set out have been won.

As Marxists, the founders of the ANC understood that in a country as socially and materially unequal as South Africa, freedom would not be achieved by the ending of the apartheid regime alone. A radical redistribution of resources was required. However, the planks that insisted that South Africa's substantial mineral wealth be owned "by the people as a whole" and that "all other industry and trade shall be controlled to assist the well-being of the people" were abandoned when the ANC took power in the early nineties; policies designed to fairly apportion a country's resources through nationalization were deemed incompatible with the market-driven approach of the new, post-1989, unipolar free world. In the words of Ronnie Kasrils, who served on the ANC's National Executive Committee and the High Command of the party's armed underground wing, the fact the ANC "took the levers of political power, but not the economic levers" was a strategic blunder from which it could never recover. To be free, people needed access to housing, education, health care and work in addition to political rights. Today, South Africa remains one of the most unequal places on earth; it's not entirely clear if the country qualifies as a democracy at all.

In the United States, forward-looking individuals have attempted to push a reluctant nation down a path similar to that mapped out in the Freedom Charter, making incremental but essential progress. During Reconstruction numerous efforts attempted to foster class solidarity across the color line, like the seven-hundred-thousand-strong Knights of Labor, which fought to create a multiracial cooperative commonwealth. Decades later, civil rights activists pushed for economic and political rights, a line from a rousing spiritual—"freedom is a constant struggle"—ringing out as one of the movement's mottos. Today we all know the famous 1963 March on Washington, an event that essentially invented the tradition of the mass protest march in America, but rarely call it by its official name: the March on Washington for Jobs and Freedom.[13] In 1966, two of its lead organizers, A. Philip Randolph and Bayard Rustin, both socialists with deep links to trade unions, proposed a Freedom Budget centered on increased spending for jobs and urban development.

Integrated lunch counters, organizers recognized, were of limited value if black citizens lacked the money to order a meal. "Equality with whites will not solve the problems of either whites or Negroes if it earns equality in a world stricken by poverty and in a universe doomed to extinction by war," Martin Luther King Jr. wrote in his final book, *Where Do We Go from Here: Chaos or Community?*, which calls for a new coalition aimed at winning "power for poor people." More recently, the Movement for Black Lives issued a platform detailing policies aimed at promoting racial liberation that put economic justice front and center: "We demand economic justice for all and a reconstruction of the economy to ensure Black communities have collective ownership, not merely access." These efforts have all envisioned the federal government as a potential custodian of freedom, not just a threat to liberty.

In the mid-sixties, it seemed that the political establishment was catching on. Under immense pressure from activists at home and Communists abroad (whose propagandists made hay of America's failure to live up to the basic democratic tenet of equality by condoning segregation), Lyndon B. Johnson adopted the cause of civil rights as his own and promoted a blueprint for a Great Society. In 1965 he intoned:

> Freedom is not enough. You do not wipe away the scars of centuries by saying: Now, you are free to go where you want, do as you desire, and choose the leaders you please. . . . This is the next and the more profound stage of the battle for civil rights. We seek . . . not just equality as a right and a theory, but equality as a fact and as a result.

Johnson dared to connect freedom not just to equality of opportunity, but also to equality of outcome, or result. Within a few short years, though, the Great Society project was already in disrepair, and the war in Vietnam was one of many wrecking balls. Fighting communism in the name of freedom abroad took precedence over creating the conditions for true and equal freedom at home.

What that true and equal freedom might look like can be glimpsed in fragments of conversation from 1964's Freedom Summer. Organizers with the Student Nonviolent Coordinating Committee asked black children in Mississippi what freedom meant to them. The answers varied: "going to public libraries"; "standing up for your rights"; "having power in the system"; a "state of mind." As the historian Eric Foner notes, these children obviously "did not adhere to standard 1950s assumptions about freedom," including Berlin's celebrated distinction between "positive" and "negative" liberty. "Freedom meant both of these and more—equality, power, recognition, rights, opportunities. It required eradicating a multitude of historic wrongs—segregation, disenfranchisement, exclusion from public facilities, confinement to low-wage menial jobs, harassment by the police, and the ever present threat of extralegal violence."[14] It was precisely this kind of multidimensional conception of freedom that powerful interest groups dedicated themselves to suppressing, and they did so by attacking equality.

"Today, there is no meaning of equality and freedom other than the meaning that you see in the market," political theorist Wendy Brown told me, confirming the completion of the severing that began in 1989. "But the market itself is a domain of inequality. It's a domain of winners and losers. And winners and losers are therefore the natural outcome of a fully marketized democracy."

Of course, we can still comprehend and value other, more expansive definitions of freedom and equality. We can recognize that a baseline of equality is needed for people to freely make democratic decisions, and that if they are impoverished or otherwise disadvantaged, they can more easily be disenfranchised or coerced. But the point is that these kinds of competing interpretations, no matter how lucid, do not shape our lives to the same degree.

Consider the fact that so many people are willing to tolerate Gilded Age levels of inequality—they may not like the situation, but they endure and hope to improve their lot. That is possible only because a market notion of justice currently prevails, and in the marketplace, not everyone comes out on top. We are told, by employers, companies, politicians, teachers, and pundits, that if we end up at the bottom of the heap, while a small handful wind up billionaires, it is our fault alone.

In the 1930s, a magazine editor observed that two opposing concepts of liberty were doing battle. What he called "freedom for private enterprise" faced off against "socialized liberty," which he defined as "an equitably shared abundance." During that period, President Franklin Delano Roosevelt attempted to claim both equality and freedom for a liberal agenda. In a 1941 address Roosevelt famously outlined what he called the Four Freedoms:

freedom of expression; freedom of worship; freedom from fear; and freedom from want. With the nation gearing up for World War II, isolationists read the speech as little more than a cynical justification for foreign intervention; free-marketeers, meanwhile, dismissed it as a ploy to use the war effort to bolster flagging New Deal liberalism. Neither criticism was totally wrong, but the speech also represented an attempt to offer a richer conception of freedom appropriate to a post-agrarian, fully industrialized society—one that underscored the state's responsibility to provide a minimum of material well-being and thus acknowledging, at least implicitly, the importance of economic equality to liberty.

This implicit aspect was made explicit when, three years later, Roosevelt used a State of the Union address to make the case for an economic bill of rights that would, among other things, guarantee to all people regardless of "station, race, or creed" the right to a useful and remunerative job; a decent home; adequate medical care and the opportunity to achieve and enjoy good health; adequate protection from the economic fears of old age, sickness, accident, and unemployment; and a good education. "This Republic had its beginning, and grew to its present strength, under the protection of certain inalienable political rights—among them the right of free speech, free press, free worship, trial by jury, freedom from unreasonable searches and seizures. They were our rights to life and liberty," Roosevelt intoned, his voice broadcast live across the country by radio from the White House's Diplomatic Reception Room. "As our Nation has grown in size and stature, however—as our industrial economy expanded—these political rights proved inadequate to assure us equality in the pursuit of happiness. We have come to a clear realization of the fact that true individual freedom cannot exist without economic security and independence."

"Necessitous men are not free men," Roosevelt told an America for whom the memory of Great Depression–era poverty was still fresh. Influenced and aided by his ingenious secretary of labor Frances Perkins, the nation's first female cabinet member and the principal engineer of the New Deal, Roosevelt reshaped liberal democracy.[15] Yet although egalitarian principles resonated with a wide public, Congress, dominated by northern industrialists and southerners committed to maintaining Jim Crow, could never fully support FDR's quest to constrain those he dubbed "economic royalists" in order to expand freedom for everyone else. The Democratic Party's racist powerbrokers demanded that the new social safety net keep segregation in place; black people, women, and immigrants were blocked from reaping the benefits of key government programs. In the end, the New Deal was severely compromised and Roosevelt's Four Freedoms, despite being central to the government's wartime propaganda efforts and immortalized in a series of iconic paintings by Norman Rockwell, failed to guide the development of the nation.[16]

Instead, a retrenchment gained steam. Under the guise of anti-communism and economic rationalism, bigoted Dixiecrats, powerful businessmen, and conservative intellectuals conspired to undo New Deal progress, sunder freedom from equality, and yoke freedom to their cause. For these reactionaries, the threat of equality loomed large: workers with access to sufficient economic resources are free to disobey their employer (just as a woman with sufficient means can leave an abusive spouse). In 1947, the year Truman made his famous speech launching the Cold War, Congress passed the Taft-Hartley Act, breaking the power of trade unions, which were beginning to push not just for better wages but for the "abolition of the wage system" entirely (segregationists also fretted over the prospect of labor organizers fostering inter-racial working-class solidarity). *Business Week* lauded the bill as a "New Deal for America's Employers": it outlawed sympathy strikes and secondary boycotts and ushered in the era of "right to work,"[17] the catchphrase for a policy designed to take rights away from working people and allow owners to extract more profit.

In his popular book and documentary series *Free to Choose*, Milton Friedman, a prominent architect of neoliberalism, compared the economy to a game of baccarat in a casino; who would come back to play if the champion didn't get to cash in his chips and take other people's money?[18] ("There's nothing fair about Marlene Dietrich's having been born with beautiful legs we all want to look at," Friedman writes, rationalizing disparate outcomes as a fact of life, but "millions . . . have benefited from nature's unfairness."[19]) In this light, the huge gulf between the haves and have-nots we see today is a sign not that the system is broken but rather that it's working. When freedom is nothing but the liberty to pursue your own interest and enhance your own value, equality becomes the right to throw your hat into the ring and to emerge victorious or fail trying.

Friedrich Hayek was even more antagonistic toward equality in his 1960 work *The Constitution of Liberty*, a book that would find eager readers in Margaret Thatcher and Ronald Reagan. Because freedom is "bound to produce inequality in many respects," any effort to mitigate inequality's effects had to be abandoned lest overall liberty be decreased. (Such efforts, Hayek insisted, while carried out under the banner of social justice, were in fact motivated by nothing other than envy.) One could easily amass mountains of empirical evidence challenging the now-pervasive faith that freedom and equality are inversely proportional to each other, like weights on a scale. Human beings, throughout our fraught history and into the present, have sadly often found themselves neither free nor equal: consider the case of black men and women living in the antebellum South or today's citizens of North Korea (the Democratic People's Republic of Korea, as the country is officially called). But it's more difficult today, thanks to decades of concerted efforts to erode equality and reconceptualize freedom, to prove the corresponding case: people can have more of both, and that the values, however distinct, are not inevitably rivalrous but often complementary. Not, to be clear, because there aren't plenty of examples of such complementarity, but because economists such as Friedman and Hayek and the movements they helped spawn have taught us not to recognize or appreciate them.

Hayek and Friedman both harken back to and idealize an earlier era, when laissez-faire liberalism allegedly ruled the economic day and men could truck and barter free from state interference. The development of industrial capitalism and the rise of waged factory work empowered an emerging class of economic elites to begin to alter the meaning of freedom. Where the early American settlers connected freedom and equality to economic and political independence and democratic self-rule (for a restricted group and propped up by slavery and stolen land), across the pond a new focus on "free labor" redefined freedom as the ability to contract one's services in the marketplace without overt coercion. People weren't enslaved or indentured, after all—they were employed, even if they toiled day and night in a mill or mine, earning only a pittance and packed into an urban slum.

After the Civil War and during the Gilded Age, southern planters and northern industrialists seized on the idea of freedom as waged labor, or what they called "liberty of contract." What they championed above all was their sovereign freedom to seek maximum profits, unencumbered by land redistribution, taxation, minimum wage, child labor laws, government regulations, or trade unions. In the post–Civil War South, courageous figures such as Ida B. Wells decried the stifled promise of emancipation and the lie of free labor, exposing lynchings and other forms of racial terror as modes of economic control deployed to keep black citizens trapped in what Frederick Douglass called "the twilight of American liberty."

Since the mid-twentieth century, conservative strategists have made a concerted effort to erase decades of reform while rehabilitating laissez-faire capitalism's image. They have achieved this in two primary ways. First, as William F. Buckley demonstrated with zeal on network television, they condemned egalitarianism in any form as an attack on freedom. (Buckley's close associate the 1964 presidential hopeful Barry Goldwater said he aimed to create not an "integrated society" but a "free society," in which individuals enjoyed "the freedom *not* to associate," and though he lost the election his campaign helped usher free market, anti-statist, racially divisive politics onto the national stage.) Second, they redefined equality in a way that justified radically disparate outcomes.

According to this logic, equality is why affirmative action is discriminatory and progressive taxation is repressive (both violate the principle of equal treatment) and why voter identification laws are fair (it doesn't matter if marginalized communities are disproportionately prevented from voting because, technically, the rule applies to everyone). The two positions were tidy corollaries. If advancing equality via affirmative action or progressive taxation is portrayed as an unjust curtailment of liberty, it follows that "color-blind" policies or a flat tax that treats everyone the same, regardless of their background, qualify as equity—maintaining, in other words, equality before the law while ignoring equality of opportunity or outcome. This is how equality has been twisted to mean leaving vast imbalances of power firmly in place, lest the freedom of the unfathomably wealthy or racially privileged be impinged.

These novel ideological formulations, however, weren't quite enough on their own. While equality was being decanted from liberty, a dash of social Darwinism was added to the mix—a toxic cocktail the historian Nancy MacLean has dubbed "economic eugenics." Americans were told they had to choose between freedom and survival of the fittest *or* equality and survival of the unfittest. "To rail against the accumulation of wealth is to rail against the decrees of justice," the prominent social Darwinist and Yale professor William Graham Sumner snarked in his 1883 book *What Social Classes Owe to Each Other* (the answer: nothing). Where eugenicists were convinced that they could breed superior humans by manipulating bloodlines, hardcore capitalists simply maintain that those who can't afford necessities such as food and shelter don't have any right to them, which effectively means they don't have the right to subsist. For some libertarians, dying is preferable to receiving taxpayer-financed health care because any assistance from the government is a form of domination. Survival of the fittest has mutated into survival of the richest.

This market-triumphalist paradigm, which made freedom for private enterprise the paramount form of freedom, became normalized common sense. But it did not organically take root in the public imagination: instead the right invested tremendous sums to rebrand freedom for its side. The marketplace of ideas evolved into a *literal* marketplace and pushing freedom at the expense of equality didn't come cheap. Journalists and scholars have documented the existence and machinations of a network of corporate-funded think tanks and policy shops, such as the American Liberty League founded in 1934 to oppose the New Deal, set up to doggedly promote the gospel of "free people and free markets," of prosperity and opportunity through economic deregulation and the privatization of public goods. A single conservative think tank, the Heritage Foundation, spends nearly $30 million a year "advancing conservative principles."

At the center of this astonishingly expensive and effective enterprise is the recognition of the power of ideas to shape reality. Today, the definitions of *freedom* and *equality* employed by the political right are simple enough to be widely understood, but also flexible enough to be adapted to circumstance. Conservatives have at their disposal a handy conceptual tool kit, one that rationalizes and further entrenches the status quo of wildly concentrated wealth while appearing to safeguard freedom and equality. Thus, former Speaker of the House Paul Ryan could tweet, "Freedom is the ability to buy what you want to fit what you need. Obamacare is Washington telling you what to buy regardless of your needs," without wondering, as Senator Bernie Sanders pithily replied, "What good is the freedom to buy the health care you want if you can't afford it?"

Faced with this onslaught, many contemporary liberals retreated, ceding the rhetoric of freedom to the right. Today, there is no clear, concise consensus on the meaning of freedom or equality for progressives to fall back on. And so, while right-wingers have waged a war for the rich under the captivating cover of liberty, the left has shrunk from core values, too often resorting to wonky policies and superficial fixes in place of clear principles. Mainstream liberal political figures downplay equality, preferring instead to speak in the language of diversity and inclusion, aiming to make the economic hierarchy less stratified by getting people of different races, ethnicities, genders, and sexual orientations into positions of power. Although they do not connect enterprise to the cause of freedom in the way of conservatives, they nonetheless exalt the private sector and the entrepreneurial spirit.

While conservatives spin things such as welfare, single-payer health care, and environmental protections as assaults on freedom by a smothering "nanny state," a good many liberals respond with privatizing efforts of their own that are distinguished by degree, not kind: subsidies to private insurers instead of an expansion of public health care programs; school vouchers for privately owned charter schools, not defending public education; a modest carbon tax in place of green infrastructure; and so on. For decades, centrist liberals have failed to advocate for robust social programs and regulations as a means to enhance both freedom and equality. Nor have they confronted how markets actually limit individual opportunity and choice, ultimately making us unfree. Without government intervention in the economy, citizens remain wholly at the mercy of employers and corporations whose bottom lines determine our wages, hours, and benefits (or lack thereof), not to mention the quality of the air we breathe and the water we drink.

Even the welfare state we owe to the New Deal was conceived not on the grounds of freedom or equality but of security. (Equality was always elusive given the fact black people and women were purposefully barred from core government programs.) It offered a safety net but no opportunity for self-rule; "recipients" of welfare are objects of government assistance, not agents in shared governance and collective decision making. In keeping with the Progressive Era's approach to reform, assistance was dispensed from on high, through public channels but not participatory ones. Security was disconnected from a deeper, democratic purpose, becoming an end in itself and not a means to a stabler, more independent, engaged citizenry. And today, as the social services first implemented during the New Deal are dismantled at the behest of big business, security has been stripped even of its economic component. When current leaders speak of security, they don't mean protecting citizens from destitution, let alone empowering them to participate more fully in public life. They mean keeping the United States safe from dangerous outsiders: Islamic terrorists, job-stealing immigrants, and desperate refugees.

Similarly, FDR's Four Freedoms have been reconceived for a neoliberal era. The European Union officially champions a transnational economic vision founded on what have come to be known as the Four Freedoms, although these are freedom of goods, freedom of capital, freedom of services, and freedom of labor. This compact reduces human beings to their status as workers and promises them no more than the right to pursue the goods, capital, and services, which have also been liberated. These are the freedoms deemed essential to those who seek to found a single market, not a democratic society.

A free society, in contrast, would require a very different kind of freedom of labor, and a metamorphosis far more profound than the New Deal allowed. Marx and Engels, for example, imagined a kind of liberty that would require the self-emancipation of an international working class, a truly democratic society of equals. Like Rousseau before him, Marx refused to set freedom and equality in opposition. Collectivizing the means of production, he insisted, would provide the material basis for human freedom, and that freedom would take two forms: collective *and* individual. In contrast to his reputation, Marx was as much a theorist of leisure as he was of work: and so, where capitalists promoted wage slavery under the cover of "free labor," Marx insisted on the importance of free time. In a socialist society, where people work to provide for their needs and well-being and not to increase profits and enrich the boss, there is no reason to relentlessly grow the economy or amass private fortunes.

Real communism, then, would not be a crude leveling, but rather full equality, a way to liberate every individual to experiment and develop their true capacities. As Engels wrote, "The possibility of securing for every member of society, by means of socialized production, an existence not only fully sufficient materially, and becoming day by day more full, but an existence guaranteeing to all the free development and exercise of their physical and mental faculties—this possibility is now for the first time here."[20] Security, understood as equal access to the means to meet one's needs, would be a basis for social freedom, not something we have to sacrifice liberties in order to achieve.

Should we ever exit the market's zero-sum game for an economy of cooperative production and shared prosperity, challenges and questions will, of course, remain. When would equality go too far and when would freedom need to be constrained? How will we organize education and training, for example, to create a common culture and knowledge base while also balancing people's differing abilities and interests with society's need for certain forms of expertise? Even if opportunities for meaningful labor and leisure massively expand, there will still be plenty of work that must get done. Goods will need to be manufactured and trash taken out and somehow safely disposed of—which brings us to the challenge not just of necessary or unglamorous tasks but of ecological limits, perhaps the most significant restraint on our utopia of egalitarian liberation. Should capitalism as we know it cease to be, the conflict between freedom and equality will linger on.

Throughout history, freedom has often been symbolized as a woman. In paintings and statues, in cartoons and on coins, the emblem of liberty is unmistakably female, often young, buxom, and brave. Though women slaves, as Patterson points out, were likely the first to invent the concept of personal freedom, the vivid propagandistic portrayals and idealization stand in stark contrast to the lack of credit women received for their conceptual innovation, not to mention their subordinate social position through the ages.

Since first contact with the so-called New World, indigenous Americans have been subject to a similar dynamic of idealization, subjugation, and conflicted representation. Looking back on the early days of the American endeavor, the ideal of freedom as self-rule that formed the basis for the republic was greatly inspired by the very native people the settlers dispossessed. Indigenous contributions to the development of political theory have been mostly written out of the history, the transatlantic flow of ideas downplayed in comparison to accounts of material flows of natural resources, goods, and human bodies. Yet the American Indian was, and still is, used as a symbol of liberty (while also being reduced to generic stereotypes). The revolutionary colonists who dumped tea into the Massachusetts Bay in protest in 1773, for example, did so dressed as Mohawks. Settlers fetishized and appropriated indigenous freedom, even as they also sought to suppress and eradicate it.

While some European chroniclers characterized indigenous people as barbarians who deserved to be exploited or annihilated outright, other explorers, missionaries, soldiers, and colonists rendered the land and people in near-paradisiacal terms. One of the first and most influential figures was Peter Martyr d'Anghiera, who in the late fifteenth century sent reports of a place where individuals lived as the "most happye of all men," free from tyranny and toil, masters and greed, laws and judges. "Myne and Thyne (the seedes of all myscheefe) have no place," all things being held in common.[21] "They hold that the earth belongs to no individual, any more than the light of the sun," marveled another observer in 1615.[22]

After an encounter with three indigenous Americans traveling in France in the mid-1500s, the philosopher Michel de Montaigne noted that the guests could not comprehend why people submitted to the rule of a "beardless child" instead of nominating someone with more experience and wisdom. They also perceived there were men amongst us full-gorged with all sorts of commodities, and others which, hunger-starved and bare with need and poverty, begged at their gates," and marveled that "the needy could endure such an injustice, and that they took not the others by the throat, or set fire on their houses."

Such themes were not as rare as one might expect. When commentators used indigenous cultures to hold a mirror to European society the picture was not always flattering. One affronted writer denigrated colonizers for their cruelty toward those who "exceed and excel all other peoples in kindness, warmth, and humanity," while many objected that Europe was the home of the real barbarians. The absence of social hierarchy was frequently commented on: "They have neither kings nor princes, and consequently each is more or less as much a great lord as the other."[23] The pull of the New World and its egalitarian social arrangements on the European imagination was immense, inspiring best-selling books, blockbuster works of theater, and new avenues of political thinking affirming what would come to be called the "myth of the noble savage." While the popular stories and plays of the period were romanticizations typically based more on European wish fulfillment than on actual fact, they had a profound intellectual impact. The message of a better mode of life, even if founded on misunderstanding or stereotype, threatened the royalist status quo, which is why leaving the colonies to live among Indian tribes was a crime punishable by death.

Influenced by contact with the indigenous people of the New World and their political theories and practices, a radical concept of liberty began to circulate: liberty as equality and masterlessness. "It is the Indian custom to deliberate," William Penn wrote to the Free Society of Traders in August 1683. "I have never seen more natural sagacity." The fact that native leaders, whom outside observers routinely mistook for "kings," did not rule absolutely but took the council of their people astonished those accustomed to monarchal arrangements. Here, for the first time, settlers saw freedom and equality, democracy, in action.

Transmitted back to Europe, these stories and concepts helped fuel a democratic revival by providing vital inspiration for philosophers, including John Locke and Rousseau and their writings on the social contract. But where Locke placed property rights above all and argued that indigenous people deserved to be deprived of their homeland because they did not maximize returns and "improve" the soil the way British agriculturalists would—there's a reason the American founding fathers loved him—Rousseau's impressions led to very different conclusions. His famous *Discourse on the Origin and Basis of Inequality Among Men* was the culmination of centuries of reports that equated freedom and equality with the indigenous populations of the Americas. Man, Rousseau insisted, was born free and equal in the state of nature. It was the introduction of private property that corrupted everything.

> The first man who, having enclosed a piece of ground, bethought himself of saying *This is mine*, and found people simple enough to believe him, was the real founder of civil society. From how many crimes, wars and murders, from how many horrors and misfortunes might not any one have saved mankind, by pulling up the stakes, or filling up the ditch, and crying to his fellows, "Beware of listening to this impostor; you are undone if you once forget that the fruits of the earth belong to us all, and the earth itself to nobody."[24]

For Rousseau, this lost Eden posed a challenge to the present while undermining the newly emergent myth of progress—European civilization was not some higher stage or advancement over prior "primitive" cultures. Forward momentum could go in reverse, with positive attributes forgotten or suppressed in the frantic quest for improvement. Modern civilization, not original sin, was the source of man's defilement.

To promote true virtue, Rousseau imagined new models of self-rule, merging impressions from the Americas with rose-colored memories of humble assemblies in his home city of Geneva. In the

right kind of world, Rousseau believed, everyone would participate in the general will together, willing for themselves as a people
in common, which would result in perfect equality expressed
through the perfect freedom of self-government. The people, not
the king, were sovereign, and their liberty manifested through reciprocity, not coercion. A generation later, after his reveries informed
the French Revolution and helped rehabilitate the concept of
democracy, that word—one America's aristocratic founders were
not too fond of—then traveled back across the ocean yet again
to transform the very land from which the shoots of Rousseau's
dream of freedom and equality had originally sprung.[25]

Over the same period, settlers were influenced by direct and
sometimes daily contact with indigenous societies. The League of
Six Nations, or what is often known as the Haudenosaunee or Iroquois Confederacy, would leave an indelible mark on the American democratic system and political philosophy, deeply impressing
Benjamin Franklin and Thomas Jefferson and, later, inspiring figures such as Friedrich Engels and the first wave of suffragists.
(When *The Communist Manifesto* was originally published in
1848, Marx and Engels declared, "The history of all hitherto existing society is the history of class struggles," but after reading about
the Iroquois, Engels added a footnote to the 1888 English edition:
"That is, all *written history*."[26])

Here, then, is a dynamic that seems to transcend time and
place. Over and again, people marked as inferior, expendable, or
alien profoundly shaped and advanced our understanding of freedom and equality—indigenous people are no exception. Western
political traditions are the product not of any single linear heritage,
but of a unique and often contradictory amalgam constructed
over centuries and indelibly marked by outsiders whose creativity,
suffering, perseverance, and foresight expanded the democratic
polity. The widening of citizens' rights through the nineteenth,
twentieth, and twenty-first centuries has not simply been the
inevitable fruition of seeds planted centuries ago by far-seeing
founding fathers or the perfection of enlightenment ideals, but a

repudiation of their truncated vision in favor of something more vital. With each successive push, women, racialized people, indigenous people, colonized people, disabled people, queer and transgender people, trade unionists, socialists, and other visionaries have not just spread but transformed the concepts of freedom and equality, giving them substantive meaning while revealing their necessary interconnections. Angela Davis has pointed out the extraordinary and underappreciated role children played in the civil rights movement, braving police dogs and firehouses and integrating classrooms and other spaces—for example, fifteen-year-old Claudette Colvin who refused to give up her seat on a Montgomery, Alabama, bus nine months before Rosa Parks made headlines doing the same. And today's teenagers are continuing the tradition by leading the charge against gun violence and climate change, highlighting how the freedom of weapons manufacturers and oil companies to profit jeopardizes the security of our schools and planet. "You are not mature enough to tell it like it is," another fifteen-year-old, Swedish environmental activist Greta Thunberg, told world leaders at a recent climate summit. "Even that burden you leave to us children."

Every step of the way, the disparaged and dispossessed have placed those contentiously aligned terms, *freedom* and *equality*, at the center of the unfinished and unpredictable path toward that alluring but elusive horizon of self-rule. It has fallen to them to broaden our democratic vista, in part because the marginalized are positioned to see truths the powerful cannot, or choose not to perceive. So democracy from below persists, strengthening the very connection between freedom and equality that the powerful aim to shatter to ensure that most people are neither.

CHAPTER 2

SHOUTING AS ONE

(CONFLICT/CONSENSUS)

ON A WARM September morning in 2011, I made my way to Manhattan's Financial District. A few months prior, a call had been put out through activist networks to "occupy Wall Street," and I thought I'd see what was going on. It was an explosive year for social movements, with the Arab Spring uprisings and the Movement of the Squares across Europe, and there were signs that discontent had reached American cities. Earlier in the year, Wisconsin's Capitol had been occupied by citizens for weeks, alongside demonstrations that drew upward of one hundred thousand people united against state budget cuts and attacks on labor unions. Protest was in the air.

I went downtown that afternoon more out of curiosity than conviction. Don't get me wrong; I agreed with the basic premise behind the event. Three years after the 2008 financial crisis, the only social movement to have achieved national prominence in response to the crash was the right-wing Tea Party, which peddled a bizarre victim-blaming narrative about the nation's financial woes. (A common theory held that African American mortgage holders were responsible for the crisis, not the lenders who had been shown to have committed systemic fraud.) While the Tea Party efforts grew, there was barely a dissenting peep from the left. Unlike in Iceland, where financial executives went to prison, the

American banking sector got a multitrillion-dollar bailout, with Wall Street taking massive taxpayer-funded bonuses while millions of Americans lost their jobs and homes to a dire recession and an unprecedented wave of foreclosures. The hubris of the industry alone got me on board with Occupy Wall Street. Something was terribly wrong with the system. I just wasn't sure camping out was the most effective response.

Still, if nothing else, Occupy's mere presence provided a jolt, reminding the public of a basic truth: the rule of the people is incompatible with the rule of the rich. Whatever the movement's shortcomings, that rudimentary assertion restored inequality to the national agenda, from which it had long been banished. The simple slogan "We are the 99 percent," and the corresponding naming of the now-infamous 1 percent, got Americans talking about class in a way that hadn't happened in my lifetime. Our society and economy, Occupiers said, were being run for the few, not the many; unfettered capitalism and democracy are at odds, hardly the inseparable allies we had been led to believe. The diagnosis resonated; across the country, in cities and towns large and small, thousands of encampments popped up like mushrooms attracting people from all walks of life. Occupy's remedy, however, was difficult to enact, in part because it was vaguely defined. The only cure, the movement maintained, was a deeper, more substantive, more authentic, more "real" democracy.

The rallying cry of "real democracy" resonated around the globe in wildly different contexts, uniting activists in Egypt and Bahrain against authoritarianism with optimistic students gathered in Hong Kong under the Umbrella Movement and comparatively privileged citizens of Europe and the United States, places that supposedly represent the most advanced liberal democracies on earth. While the rebels of Egypt's Tahrir Square or Turkey's Taksim Gezi Park may have been calling for basic human rights and fair elections, a core constituency of anarchists at Occupy Wall Street understood real democracy to mean running everything by consensus. People would make decisions for themselves, without delegating tasks to representatives, and everyone was to be included in the decision making, no matter how painstaking. Unanimity was the aim. A primer shared on Occupy's New York City General Assembly website explained, "Consensus is a creative thinking process: When we vote, we decide between two alternatives. With consensus, we take an issue, hear the range of enthusiasm, ideas and concerns about it, and synthesize a proposal that best serves everybody's vision."

Occupy's early days were intoxicating, likely because and not in spite of this intense idealism. I went to Zuccotti Park on the first day and stayed the afternoon, only to find myself coming back compulsively. It was not your average protest. In place of standing in the streets shouting at strangers, we sat and debated among ourselves. Like a postmodern, tech-savvy version of the Athenian agora, we gathered in small, impromptu circles to discuss economics or philosophy or in formal, regularly scheduled working groups, which focused on everything from managing the nascent community's growing food and laundry needs to interfacing with the media. The well-stocked volunteer-run library became an international symbol of the Occupy movement, a metaphor for its insistence that democracy requires engagement with ideas, with both action and reflection.

The General Assemblies, which handled decision making for the overall group, were gigantic, and open to anyone off the street. They were also often strangely beautiful, with voices echoing in the dusk through the "human microphone," the repetition of statements as a way around the city's prohibition on other forms of amplification. Some evenings, standing in the dark with hundreds of others, repeating what a stranger had said so others at a distance could hear it, I felt as if I were a part of some great living, breathing poetry. But even as I was almost moved to tears and appreciated being part of such a unique social experiment, I never believed I had joined a credible example of a better form of government. I had read enough about the history of protest movements to know that the assembly would break down.

Eventually it did. Occupy at least adopted a system of "modified consensus" with a fallback to a two-thirds majority vote, so that a single person could not derail an entire meeting, but the consensus-seeking participatory ideal was untenable nevertheless. Even before the park was cleared in mid-November 2011, the General Assembly showed signs of cracking up. Early heated discussions over the drum circle in the far corner of the square foreshadowed troubles to come; the majority wanted the drumming to be less relentless, while a handful of tireless musicians defended their right to play, declaring their rhythms to be the "heartbeat of the movement." ("Don't call yourself my heartbeat!" I remember one woman yelling in response; I was a fan of the fellow who'd made a sign that read, "I Care About Democracy More Than I Hate This Drum Circle.") The flaws were intrinsic to the decision-making structure that had been adopted. The long evening meetings favored those who had free time, making equal participation a challenge for people with demanding work schedules or families to care for. Because there were no membership requirements, people exercised rights without corresponding responsibilities, with random visitors to the park raising their hands to support plans they had no intention of helping to carry through.

Worse, disproportionate weight was given to small groups of dissenters. There was no way to exclude anyone from Occupy's decision-making demos, even those who wielded power in bad faith. As the weeks turned into months and the weather became cold, a shrinking turnout at the assembly meant that a small, irascible group could obstruct perfectly reasonable proposals, with consensus devolving into tyranny of an unaccountable minority and the gears of the machine gummed up for no good reason. Squabbling overtook reasoned deliberation. One night, after the park had been cleared but before the movement's organizing body had disbanded, the atmosphere was tense. I stood in the shadows, watching the mood sour further, until a fistfight broke out. I can't even remember what caused the confrontation, but knew the time had come to give up the ghost. The consensus-based system, promoted as a cure for the ills of mainstream democracy, had turned out to be unbearable, arguably more unstable and a good measure more ridiculous than the original disease.[1]

During Occupy, it often struck me how little those of us gathered actually knew about political theory or the intricate workings of the state. Perhaps if we had been better informed, glaring pitfalls could gracefully have been averted as we attempted to create our own governing structure—not that our ignorance was necessarily or wholly our fault. American democracy allows most citizens precious few opportunities to participate meaningfully in democratic processes outside marking a ballot every two or four years. What Occupiers did know, in their bones, as they faced home foreclosures, overwhelming student debt, mounting medical bills, insecure employment, and impending climate catastrophe was that they had very little influence over matters that concerned them. This sense of dispossession was felt not only in response to unaccountable, unresponsive structures of government but also in the workplace, schools, and communities. These gut feelings were eventually affirmed by academic studies and best-selling books, which quantified the astonishing economic dominance of the 1 percent and showed that regular people, in contrast to their wealthy and corporate compatriots, have negligible influence over public policy.[2] In 2015, even former president Jimmy Carter claimed that the United States had become an oligarchy—a system ruled by an elite few.

In my sympathetic reading of Occupy, understandable disgust with an unjust system led to an overreaction, a casting away of the proverbial baby with the bathwater. Occupiers were tired of elections as paid-for, celebrity-focused spectacles, so they did away with representation altogether; they were sickened by a judiciary that, in the previous year's *Citizens United* decision, had equated campaign donations with free speech and opened the floodgates to political spending, so they refused to consider mechanisms that would curb the power of the assembly; they were appalled by existing social and economic hierarchies, so they embraced a form of radical equality that was unsustainable in practice; they were frustrated by government secrecy, so they adopted an ethos of radical transparency, live-streaming or tweeting proceedings no matter how sensitive or outrageous.[3] The founders of Occupy aspired to do something profoundly different, to build a new, more authentic cooperative society. They believed that a commitment to consensus (as opposed to a winner-take-all approach that delivers total control to a group with 51 percent of support regardless of the preferences of the other 49 percent) was paramount, the most revolutionary plank of their bid to remake democracy from the ground up.

At the time, I never paused to question the assumption that consensus symbolized a complete break with the status quo, a radical alternative to politics-as-usual. I took for granted that the model was so egalitarian and onerous, so demanding and inefficient, that no legitimate established institution ever touched it. I was mistaken. I eventually discovered, for example, that the UN General Assembly justifies the use of consensus in language that would have fit right in at Zuccotti Park.

> When you adopt resolutions by a vote, you only need to get a simple majority to agree on the text of a resolution. You don't need to care about or try to understand the perspectives of the minority who disagree. This process is divisive. When you adopt resolutions by consensus, you have to be concerned about the viewpoint of everyone and engage in negotiations that often result in compromises so that different points of view are taken into consideration. This process is inclusive.[4]

Voting, the document continues, is a "way of operating stuck in the past." But consensus is not only forward-looking, it's also pragmatic: "Because the General Assembly's resolutions are recommendations and not legally binding on Member States, reaching consensus has evolved as a way to ensure the widest possible implementation of GA decisions." The aspiration to unanimity, it turns out, is far more mainstream than I or most Occupiers realized. The pursuit of consensus is not a fringe phenomenon, but an enduring ideal, and one that pervades many of the political theories and structures that in turn shape our lives.

How, one might reasonably ask (especially in this world of political polarization and media divisiveness), could anyone possibly think that a system contingent on all participants agreeing is a workable idea? From a certain clear-eyed, realist's perspective, aiming for consensus seems patently ridiculous. Just take a quick glance at the Internet. People squabble and curse one another, even in the comments section of cute cat videos. Such is human life. Given our propensity to bicker, it seems reasonable to accept that our best bet for achieving a functional society is to devise a system that accounts for the constant conflicts of interest and tries to create space for constructive competition, allowing groups to have a fair chance of exerting influence or winning the day.

The proponents of consensus at Occupy, and in the movements that informed it, took a radically different view. It's not that they thought people were all saints or all wanted the same thing. Rather, they insisted that each individual mattered as much as any other and should have a meaningful voice, not just a vote. The anarchists I know—and I know many, and while I don't count myself as one, I often admire them—believe that the common habit of expecting other people to do the work of democracy on our behalf via elected representatives is not the apex of democracy but, in fact, the system's undoing, because it encourages passivity, cynicism, and worse. To committed anarchists, who tend to be intensely civic-minded and conscientious, *democracy* is a verb, something that doesn't take place just in Ottawa or Brussels, but that must be practiced wherever people are—an ongoing process, not a finished product.

In whatever they do, whether it's opening cafés or bicycle shops, cooperative bookstores or factories, alternative schools or mutual aid societies, anarchists are prepared for conflicts to flare up among participants, but believe that they can be overcome with time and patience. It may be hard work and slow going—there's a reason for the joke about freedom being an endless meeting—but it will be worth it in the end, because everyone will be heard and be invested in (or at least understand) the result, however unpredictable.

Consensus, the anarchist anthropologist David Graeber has written, comes down to two principles: "everyone should have equal say (call this 'equality'), and nobody should be compelled to do anything they really don't want to do (call this 'freedom')." That's why, under a consensus model, a single individual (in the case of absolute consensus) or a specified percentage of the whole (in its modified version) has the power to block, or veto, any proposal. It's this veto power that, in theory, compels the group to find a solution that everyone finds acceptable. But as I saw vividly at Occupy Wall Street, in actuality, the reckless exercise of the veto is also the model's fatal flaw.

When I expressed my doubts about the efficacy of consensus, Graeber offered a counterargument. Consensus, he told me, has a practical component, at least within specific settings. If you and a few dozen people are plotting a protest in a park (say you are planning to occupy Wall Street), no one really has much power over anyone else. One individual can't withhold another's wages or threaten imprisonment to keep the group in line. Under such circumstances, giving everyone an equal say through consensus is not some pie-in-the-sky fantasy, but an honest reflection of the existing power dynamic. And, because it acknowledges and respects participants' autonomy, it helps keep them engaged and committed.

It's true that small groups of friends collaborating on projects often use a de facto consensus, a system typically adopted by default—I've certainly operated that way many times in collaborative settings. But while it can work well for those who share a strong bond and clear aim, this friendship model of decision making is exceedingly difficult to scale to a large gathering of strangers, let alone an entire modern, complex, industrialized society. In her 1980 book *Beyond Adversary Democracy*, political scientist Jane Mansbridge set out to explore why this is the case. Using her experience as a member of various collectives associated with the New Left of the 1960s and early '70s as a leaping off point, Mansbridge wondered why the era's ideal of "participatory democracy" was so hard to achieve in practice, even (or especially) when the goal of unanimity was held dear.

Through detailed ethnographic study, she concludes that there are two types of democracy that uneasily coexist and that must be distinguished so they can be properly balanced. On the one hand, there is what she calls "adversary democracy," which is based on the assumption that people have conflicting interests (this is the democracy of winner-take-all elections and majority rule). On the other, she identifies "unitary democracy," which assumes common interests and deliberates face-to-face (this is the model of anarchist meetings and New England town halls). While the former model dominates, the urge for the latter runs deep. Every polity, Mansbridge observes, contains both conflicting and common interests, and so requires both adversary and unitary institutions. When people's wants and needs generally align, unitary institutions can help cultivate and expand fellow-feeling; however, when a situation ceases to be friendly and needs and desires diverge, the unitary model can actually produce more anger and bitterness than its adversarial counterpart: "If there is no solution that is in everyone's interest, more debate will not usually produce agreement"—instead it results in additional frustration and strife.[5] Mansbridge concludes that "the failure of unitary democracies often derive from their refusal to either recognize when interests conflict or to deal with those conflicts by adversarial procedures." Some clashes will never lead to consensus, no matter how long the meeting seeking resolution lasts, yet in Mansbridge's nuanced view that does not mean we should cease striving to cultivate unanimity whenever possible.

"Democratic society, at its most profound, is one of conflict, but one in which there is no one who does not dream of social unity (however they may conceive of it)," the French social theorist Marcel Gauchet said. The American founders were hardly immune. Eighteenth-century thinkers "often postulated that society should be pervaded by concord and governed by a consensus that approached, if it did not attain, unanimity. Party, and the malicious and mendacious spirit it encouraged, were [sic] believed only to create social conflicts that would not otherwise occur," historian Richard Hofstadter has observed.[6] The men who drafted the Constitution fit this mold, fearing nothing more than conflict, or what they dubbed the "spirit of faction."

Most famously, in *Federalist* no. 10, James Madison, writing under the name Publius, decried the pernicious consequences of faction while locating the source of social strife in man's very nature.

A zeal for different opinions concerning religion, concerning government, and many other points, as well of speculation as of practice; an attachment to different leaders ambitiously contending for pre-eminence and power; or to persons of other descriptions whose fortunes have been interesting to the human passions, have, in turn, divided mankind into parties, inflamed them with mutual animosity, and rendered them much more disposed to vex and oppress each other than to co-operate for their common good. So strong is this propensity of mankind to fall into mutual animosities, that where no substantial occasion presents itself, the most frivolous and fanciful distinctions have been sufficient to kindle their unfriendly passions and excite their most violent conflicts.

For Madison, freedom itself was the source of faction, but because constraining the liberty of citizens was an unacceptable price to pay for peace (for that would mean a return to tyranny), the only recourse was to try to mitigate the damage. A well-formed system, complete with checks and balances and the separation of powers, he believed, could curb faction's more destructive effects and yield social unity. "We are attempting by this Constitution," Alexander Hamilton declared in 1788, "to abolish factions and to unite all parties for the general welfare." Functional consensus could be forged from chaos.

The trick would be to have so many competing elements that they canceled one another out. As Voltaire writes in his *Lettres philosophique*, "If there were only one religion in England, one would have to fear despotism; if there were two, they would cut each other's throats; but they have thirty and they live happy and in peace." A consonance of conflicting elements could be achieved, and civil war averted, the result in line with poet Alexander Pope's picture of an Edenic forest:

> Not chaos-like, together crushed and bruised
> But, as the world, harmoniously confused:
> Where order in variety we see,
> And where, though all things differ, all agree.

Ironically, then, the first political parties in America, the Federalists and Anti-Federalists, were created by men who, in Hofstadter's vivid formulation, "looked upon parties as sores upon the body politic." Men with quite varied political ideologies and ambitions were united in their disdain of parties, which they believe played people against one another to serve their own partial interests. "[T]he division of the republic into two great parties," said John Adams," is to be dreaded as the greatest political evil under our Constitution." But the eventual development of political parties, and the endless battle between Democrat and Republican to which we are today daily subjected, does not quite mean that conflict prevailed and the dream of consensus was abandoned.

Instead, a new understanding of conflict developed: that of legitimate opposition. In this innovative framework, rival parties remained bound by what could be called a constitutional consensus: competing interests accepted certain principles and rules as fundamental and nonnegotiable in the contest for power. "It is understood, on one side, that opposition is directed against a certain policy or complex of policies, not against the legitimacy of the constitutional regime itself," Hofstadter writes in *The Idea of a Party System*. "Opposition rises above naked contestation; it forswears sedition, treason, conspiracy, *coup d'état*, riot, and assassination, and makes an open public appeal for the support of a more or less free electorate. Government, in return, is constrained by certain limitations as to the methods it can use to counter the opposition."[7]

These are ideas we take for granted today—of course, candidates from different parties can duke it out to have their turn at running things—but there was a time when this paradigm was untested and terrifying, for the young republic had few positive models from the Old World to draw upon, only ruinous religious sects. The fledgling Federalists and Anti-Federalists aimed to completely vanquish the competition and absorb their enemy's members; neither aimed to take alternate shifts at the White House or secure a rotating regime of predictable, ordered conflict. It would be decades before parties were seen as not a necessary evil, but a necessary good, the most efficient and logical means of organizing masses of people to promote their interests effectively.

Today, at the national, state, and local levels, the two parties engage in electoral tug-of-war while bound by a constitutional consensus. These "free and fair" elections are the hallmark of American democracy, a system of controlled conflict—barely controlled, it seems, if one looks at Congress today. But the common image of political parties with their horns tangled in interminable struggle doesn't convey the whole picture. Too often, a more fundamental solidarity goes ignored, a bipartisan consensus that has never been explicitly articulated, let alone put in writing, but that undergirds the whole arrangement. While third parties exist on the margins of American politics, the two main political parties would prefer to represent the extent of legitimate opposition in America, and they support mutually beneficial policies to reinforce their dual dominance and keep other potential competitors at bay. This tacit agreement is as fundamental to American political life as our revered Constitution (which makes no mention of parties), but it goes far less remarked upon.

The day after the election of Donald Trump, I spoke to African American studies professor Omar H. Ali, who has written extensively about the history of independent parties dating back to the Civil War. "When Trump says the elections are rigged, there's actually something to what he's saying, but not in the way he's talking about," Ali told me. Republicans and Democrats, the two entrenched political parties, are private, not public, entities that reap enormous benefits through the laws and regulations they create. The two parties may seem like facts of the political landscape, a kind of governmental infrastructure, but they are in fact special interests whose politics are ultimately about self-preservation.

"Through structural ways to keep themselves in power, such as closed primaries, ballot-access restrictions, who is included in the presidential debates, the redistricting of congressional lines—all of this stuff is done in a very bipartisan way that benefits either the Democratic or Republican Party," Ali reflected. "There are all kinds of ways in which it's become normal for the parties to use their offices to advance their partisan interests. Even though they fight like cats and dogs, at the end of the day, they kind of lock arms together to keep themselves in power."

The American system stands out among liberal democracies in this respect. "Perhaps the clearest case of overt partisan manipulation of the rules is the United States, where Democrats and Republicans appear automatically on the ballot, but third parties and independents have to overcome a maze of cumbersome legal requirements," Pippa Norris, director of democratic governance at the United Nations Development Program, has written.[8] Legal restrictions (which were erected state by state, often to ward off left-wing challengers gaining popularity in the polls) mean third parties face an uphill battle just to get on the ballot. Should they manage such a feat, they still will not be eligible for the federal subsidies available to the two major parties, and the country's first-past-the-post system typically dooms them to play the role of spoiler.

In Ali's words, "Those who make the rules, rule." Today, tens of millions of citizens who consider themselves independents are shut out of the first (and often critical) round of voting, which helps protect the seats of incumbents associated with the two parties and sets the stage for a reality in which nearly every major public office in the nation is occupied by either a Democrat or a Republican. Echoing the founders but with a more democratic twist, Ali believes that the power of the two main parties must be reined in by the people they ostensibly exist to serve. The stranglehold of bipartisan consensus should be broken to make space for other parties and political perspectives—in other words, for even more legitimate opposition and democratic conflict.[9]

Democracy depends on faith in the system, and always has. Yet the nature of this faith has transformed over time. In ancient Athens, citizens respected the decisions made by the Assembly, even though attendance was haphazard, and trusted a host of other systems that delegated roles by way of a lottery, because they believed the gods of the city had a behind-the-scenes role, directing the apparent randomness through which life-altering decisions were made. When Jean-Jacques Rousseau revived a vision of democratic participation and civic freedom in the eighteenth century, he relied on a faith in human nature that shocked those who believed in the existence of original sin and man's fallen disposition.

Rousseau maintained that humans were, by nature, good, while the institutions of modern, commercial society had a corrupting influence. When humans came together to run themselves, he argued, they could reach for and channel what he called the "general will," a higher consensus that transcended individual needs and wants in order to guide the well-being of the community. Later, those known as deliberative democrats would posit that sustained, reasoned debate was the key to achieving a "rational consensus" in the public sphere. (Both perspectives are challenged by the insights of psychoanalysis, which posits the human condition as one of perpetual inner conflict. With our unconscious and repressed urges, we hardly know ourselves and can hardly be relied upon to want what's good for us, let alone to detect a general will. With irrationality built into the structure of our psyches, there's little wonder reason rarely wins the day.)

Though I never heard anyone at Occupy Wall Street directly invoke Rousseau, his faded fingerprints could certainly be detected. The deliberative tradition also left a palpable mark, as people hashed things out in meetings large and small, animatedly discussing matters for hours on end. (For the record, I also never heard anyone discuss psychoanalytic theory.) But beyond these phantom influences, the use of consensus processes in activist circles has more recent, direct origins. The practice can be traced back to the Society of Friends, or Quakers, who have a history of involvement in social justice causes such as abolition and who believe that a shared spiritual conviction facilitates accord. Consensus, in this devotional setting, involves opening a space for a higher power to make itself felt. I would wager that the scrappy activists participating in Occupy's General Assembly did not all believe that the Holy Spirit was guiding the group. Nonetheless, Quaker techniques have been widely adopted.

Longtime activist and author L. A. Kauffman has written about what she calls the "theology of consensus," challenging the wisdom of using consensus methods within social movements. Early on she tried to warn the enthusiastic assembly of Occupy Wall Street that their efforts would crash on consensus's rocky shores, but the approach was already entrenched, and her advice went unheeded. "If the forty-year persistence of consensus has been a matter of faith, surely the time has now come for apostasy," Kauffman wrote following Occupy's demise. "Piety and habit are bad reasons to keep using a process whose benefits are more notional than real."[10]

Kauffman's original research, documented in her book *Direct Action*, hinges on the year 1976, when the group the Clamshell Alliance, also known as "the Clam," began a campaign against a proposed nuclear power plant in New Hampshire. Two staffers from the American Friends Service Committee, a peace and justice organization affiliated with the Quakers, suggested consensus as a way to run the group, not knowing the method would spread far and wide. "*Under consensus, the group takes no action that is not consented to by all group members,*" the group's action manual explained.[11] As Kauffman notes, civil rights and labor organizations have long tried to build internal agreement among diverse participants or members, but the Quaker approach sought something more profound: not just unanimity, which can be superficial and pragmatic, but a unity springing from a deeper, spiritual place. Their method renounced voting in order to find what the Quakers call the "sense of the meeting"—the harmony of a higher, religiously inflected truth, which sometimes could be discovered only by sitting in silence to allow the sacred to reveal itself. Over time, consensus processes would became increasingly common within secular, political subcultures, the religious conviction that underpinned the Quaker quest for unity falling to the wayside in meetings where raucous debate replaced reverential quiet.

Unshakeable confidence, in God or the gods, in humanity's innate goodness, or in our capacity to rationally define a common good, guided some of the experiments in direct democracy and consensus, with mixed results. For the American founders, the faith that seeped into their framework was more scientific than divine, despite the Declaration of Independence's invocation of a Creator. Their scheme to curb conflicts through "checks and balances" related to new mechanistic concepts, conjuring the counterpoise and equilibrium of the physical world, not the harmony of a metaphysical one. The gears of government should turn as elegantly as those of a clock, reflecting a faith that conflicting social forces can be balanced, like the forces of nature, and that a constitutional device could be devised that, through a hierarchical system of representation, what the founders dubbed a republic—as opposed to direct self-rule, or a democracy—could siphon desirable elements, the so-called natural aristocracy, to the top and filter out the riffraff. (The total disenfranchisement and disregard for the rights of slaves, women, and unpropertied men constituted only the first stage of purification.)

For Madison, who has come to be known as the father of the Constitution, this filtering process was one of the legendary document's primary aims—and it was understood that those who rose to the top would necessarily be the well-to-do. Much has been made of *Federalist* 10's reference to the need to control what Madison calls "the mischiefs of faction" and the fact that Madison pins the cause of faction on human nature and human freedom. But what he asserts as faction's primary source, inequality, has drawn less attention, even though it's far more revealing of the article's real argument and purpose: "The most common and durable source of factions has been the various and unequal distribution of property. Those who hold and those who are without property have ever formed distinct interests in society."

As a member of the former group, Madison justified material inequalities as the inevitable outgrowth of some people being more talented and capable than others.

> The diversity in the faculties of men, from which the rights of property originate, is not less an insuperable obstacle to a uniformity of interests. The protection of these faculties is the first object of government. From the protection of different and unequal faculties of acquiring property, the possession of different degrees and kinds of property immediately results; and from the influence of these on the sentiments and views of the respective proprietors, ensues a division of the society into different interests and parties.

The Constitution's role, then, was to protect property owners from faction. Or, phrased differently: the minority had to be protected from "the superior force of an interested and overbearing majority." Madison feared direct democracy because in such a system, the poor, who are always more numerous than the rich, would rule, and inevitably push for things such as paper money, the abolition of debts, an equal division of property, and "any other improper or wicked project." Such are the things of which nightmares are made if you are a member of the 1 percent.

Today, we speak endlessly about protecting the rights of minorities, and we recognize that principle as intrinsic and indispensable to the American system. When we hear the word *minorities*, we imagine people of color; women; lesbian, gay, queer, and trans individuals; or the disabled. The concept has, thankfully, evolved into something more profound and inclusive than the founders could ever have imagined. While it's certainly true that the founders were concerned with protecting religious and political dissidents, we rarely comment on the irony that the initial overwhelming concern for the rights of minorities stemmed from the fact that a small group of wealthy, pale-skinned, land-hungry, slaveholding aristocrats were jealous of their fortunes—a faction if ever there was one. (Electing a real estate mogul president is in perfect keeping with the American tradition: when George Washington took office in 1789, he was one of the nation's largest and richest landowners and had a history of illegally speculating on unceded indigenous territory.) The primary goal of government, Madison said, is "to protect the minority of the opulent against the majority."

It is deeply disturbing that a man as uncommonly intelligent as James Madison could not recognize that the true victims of majoritarian tyranny were black people, whose enslavement found broad support among the larger white population, and not the minuscule percentage of upper-class men who held them as chattel. Resistant to such insight, and discounting the humanity of those they enslaved, the founders sought assurance that the remaining mass of poor white men would not seek to dispossess them of their advantage. Forging a constitutional consensus offered an appealing solution. Checks and balances provided cover, masking the conflict that flows from unjust material relations. The bluntness of *Federalist* 10 is striking: the propertied classes (the landowners, manufacturers, merchants, and creditors) must be kept safe from the less fortunate hordes, even if that means constraining the power of the majority.

The founders certainly knew that other ways to solve this dilemma could be devised.[12] Madison, for example, may have praised Socrates in *Federalist* 55 ("Had every Athenian citizen been a Socrates, every Athenian Assembly would still have been a mob"), but that didn't stop him from ignoring the wisdom offered by philosophy's most famous gadfly—or rather, the wisdom attributed to him by his student Plato.

In the *Republic*, the founding text of Western political philosophy, Plato provides a blueprint for his ideal city. A just city, his fictionalized Socrates argues, requires that its inhabitants be divided into three groupings based on natural abilities, including a class of rulers. While Plato has been met with derision for proposing a "philosopher king," the *Republic* is not an argument for a single enlightened dictator, even if it is deeply hostile to democracy as we understand it. Instead, Plato describes a complex system in which lovers of knowledge, male and female philosophers, rule, an idea that is understandably offensive despite being more gender inclusive than Plato is usually given credit for. (Plato was no feminist before the hour, but at least two women are known to have studied at his academy, though almost nothing is remembered of their thought or lives.) Crucially, however, these rulers had to be absolutely indigent, having no property whatsoever. It was their task to ensure a middling distribution of resources and to prevent both wealth and poverty from destroying the city and breaking it in two, pitting the rich against the poor in civil war. In other words, Plato proposes what Madison insists cannot be done: eliminating the primary cause of the mischiefs of faction, economic inequality. Instead, Madison preferred to limit democracy.

Here we come to a core question: What kinds of conflicts are fundamental and unavoidable? What conflicts can only be reduced and what can be resolved? Madison confidently asserts that there will always be rich people and poor people, because some people are by nature more adept at accumulating wealth than others. Today, this view is generally accepted: liberal technocrats believe that while inequality may be a problem, the only solution is to manage the divide, mediating disputes through market-friendly policies that still hold supreme one's right to property. The conflict between rich and poor, according to this Madisonian perspective, is eternal, a fact of human life that cannot be wished away.

But there is hardly consensus on this matter. The protesters at Occupy Wall Street (precisely the sort of aggrieved, indebted majority faction Madison feared) insisted that the 1 percent are not a natural minority but a class propped up by rules that have been written in their favor since the nation's inception. But by turning inward, toward consensus and the project of prefiguring the world they wanted to see on a small scale, the Occupy movement radically underestimated the degree of conflict required to win even modest economic reforms (even though the state's willingness to use force to squelch dissent was often on glaring display, including the night the Manhattan encampment was cleared by a veritable army of police officers in military-grade riot gear while helicopters buzzed overhead). The demands of working people have always been met by intense resistance, from the mercenaries hired to subdue and even kill labor activists struggling for the eight-hour day in the nineteenth century to the professional strike-breakers called to intimidate workers asking for a living wage today. As the famous liberal billionaire Warren Buffett remarked in 2011, there is indeed a class war, and his side is waging and winning it.[13]

Antagonism between rich and poor may be fundamental to our society as it currently exists, but that is because of how we choose to structure the economy. Class conflict is inherent to capitalism, but it does not follow that it must always and forever plague democracy, since economic inequality undermines the principle of political equality upon which democratic systems are founded. Yet it is no surprise that Madison and the other founders accepted divisions of wealth as a permanent feature of the political landscape, for to accept otherwise would have meant forsaking their own privilege and power.

The founders declined to address the true nature of economic conflict in favor of a false consensus—no doubt, the Constitution would have been very different if slaves, indigenous people, women, and poor men had been granted an opportunity to add their input—but we don't have to make the same mistake. Until there is a total transformation of the system and a forging of a new social compact, one that doesn't deny the existence of human difference and disagreement, but that refuses to accept that the opulently rich are a minority who deserve to have their interests protected at all costs, the ruling and working classes will be trapped in a struggle from which there is no escape. At minimum, a truly democratic consensus would have this as a first premise: American democracy cannot survive, it cannot even credibly exist, when the top 1 percent of households owns more wealth than the bottom 90 percent combined, as it does today.[14]

The kind of political system one designs depends on where one puts the emphasis: conflict or consensus? Where Marx saw social life shaped by underlying material relations, he believed that common ownership of the economy and a radical commitment to equality could eliminate class conflict and unleash human freedom and creative potential. Where the romantic Rousseau believed that a kind and genial polity was possible, he revered the idea of small-scale assemblies guided by the consensus-inspiring general will. The seventeenth-century thinker Thomas Hobbes, in contrast, saw conflict in the darkest of lights: inherently selfish individuals are prone to violence and disorder. Because day-to-day existence in the state of nature was, as Hobbes famously put it, "nasty, brutish, and short," human beings, out of self-interest and a desire for security, consented to join society and hand control to a strong sovereign (what Hobbes dubbed the Leviathan) who would quell conflict from on high and impose consensus by force. Hobbes calls this submission "more than consent, or concord; it is a real unity," a unity that necessitates sacrificing freedom. For Hobbes, who lived through the English Civil War, and for whom the state of nature was not some hypothetical past but a metaphor for the sort of social breakdown he had witnessed firsthand, such a price would have been well worth it.

The antidemocratic impulse to forsake liberty for security, for the consensus of despotism, is hardly something we've outgrown, despite liberal democracy's steady expansion. Fear loosens our grip on core principles, a tendency President George W. Bush played on expertly. Citizens surrendered civil liberties in service of a War on Terror that still hasn't come to an end. Yet even with this folly firmly in mind, one can't wholly dismiss out of hand the Hobbesian desire for a strong sovereign, especially among those who have lived in a failed state, and not just one that is failing to live up to its democratic potential. (Coming from the United States and Canada, I'll admit there are harsh realities I've never had to endure.) Pulled as we all are between persistent hazards and the possibility of harmony, the question is whether political theory's competing and contradictory insights into the role of conflict and consensus can be productively combined.

One group offers a surprising and thought-provoking model: pirates. As professional pillagers, pirates were no strangers to deadly conflict, but they also built a model of a different kind of society, one complete with robust democratic structures, economic fairness—pirates devised what some say are the first systems of universal health care and unemployment insurance—and considerable racial tolerance. According to Marcus Rediker's book *Villains of All Nations*, "Black Sam Bellamy's crew of 1717 was 'a Mix'd Multitude of all Country's,' including British, French, Dutch, Spanish, Swedish, Native American, African American, and two dozen Africans who had been liberated from a slave ship."[15] Flying high on the mast, the Jolly Roger flag symbolized not just an embrace of outlaw status but also a rejection of nationalism: when asked of their origin, buccaneers would reply that they came "From the seas."

"That leadership could derive from the consent of the led, rather than be bestowed by higher authority, would have been a likely experience of the crews of pirate vessels in the early modern Atlantic world," John Markoff writes in the essay "Where and When Was Democracy Invented?" In contrast to the standard navy and merchant ships of the day, which were effectively autocracies—captains had absolute authority over crew, made far more money, and could accuse anyone who resisted them of mutiny—pirate life was remarkably egalitarian. "The pirate ship was democratic in an undemocratic age," observes Rediker and his frequent collaborator Peter Linebaugh. "Pirates distributed justice, elected officers, divided loot equally, and established a different discipline. They limited the authority of the captain, resisted many of the practices of the capitalist merchant shipping industry, and maintained a multicultural, multiracial, multinational social order."[16] One captive marveled at the lack of hierarchy onboard a pirate vessel—"they are, on Occasion, all Captains, all Leaders."[17] Pirates, he also noted, loved to vote.

Ship constitutions show that pirate crews made collective decisions in regular assemblies, exercised divided and limited powers, enjoyed rights specified in contracts (ship articles, for example, specified shares of booty and rates of compensation for on-the-job injury), and chose their leaders. Thus captains were not tyrants but elected officials whose authority and compensation were highly circumscribed; their daily rations were the same as the average sailor and they pocketed a reasonable amount of plunder compared to the rest of the crew, getting double for their trouble—unlike today's CEOs, who make 271 times the average worker's wage. Most significantly, they held absolute power only during the chase or combat. (As one observer noted, "They permit him to be Captain, on Condition, that they may be Captain over him." At any moment a captain could be deposed for cowardice, cruelty, or, as was the case on at least one ship, being "too Gentleman-like.")[13] In other words, only during periods of high-stakes conflict did the slow-moving quest for a workable internal consensus grind to a halt in favor of efficient despotism. When a conflict subsided, the captain became just another ordinary crewman again, with the common council firmly at the helm.

While it seems a bit awkward to extrapolate civic lessons from freebooters marauding on the high seas, it also seems fair to give credit where it's due. Pirate ships were some of the first workplace democracies on record, the literal embodiment of the solidarity implied by the old proverb "We are all in this boat together." And in terms of lessons for larger systems of government, the maritime radicals got some complex things right. First, they acknowledged the presence of external conflicts and allowed for the fact that it might be useful to have competent leaders during periods of extreme duress. Second, they diminished the potential for internal conflict by ensuring a basic separation of powers and enabled equal participation in decision making by guaranteeing a baseline of economic and social equality. Crewmates, in other words, had both economic and political rights. The pirate model, it seems, creatively incorporated aspects of adversary and unitary democracy, adroitly reflecting Mansbridge's insights while adding a dash of Madison and Marx to the mix, too. Little wonder, then, that the era's imperial and merchant powers, fearing the mutineers would "soon multiply," insisted that the seafaring rebellion be squashed.

When I asked philosopher Cornel West what would have happened if ending Jim Crow or integrating public schools had been put to a vote, he didn't miss a beat. "They never would have passed," he said (before adding that school integration still falls dramatically short in practice). Had the civil rights activists of the mid-twentieth century had to wait for unanimity to see a change in the law of the land, they likely still would be fighting their case today. (It's no surprise that John C. Calhoun, the nation's seventh vice president and an outspoken champion of slavery, was one of the most forceful advocates of government by consensus, a system he believed would grant a tiny slaveholding minority the right to block change and carry on keeping others in bondage—presuming, of course, that enslaved people would continue to be disenfranchised and not permitted to issue vetoes of their own.)

Given all this, some simple facts are important to note. After centuries of agitation and resistance, black people in the United States finally secured formal legal equality not because the Constitution's enlightened system of checks and balances or safeguards against faction protected them. Nor did it happen because, through long meetings and patient rational deliberation, former white supremacists came to see the error of their ways. The Civil War and the civil rights movement were both sustained, bloody conflicts. Progress was won because a determined, inspired minority fought, sometimes to the death, for a deeper, more real democracy against the majority's will and its circumscribed conception of the American republic.

What's more, that minority was, in fact, a minority of a minority, as only a small percentage of black Americans actively committed to the cause of civil rights. At the time, the majority of Americans objected to their actions: for example, 61 percent of Americans polled disapproved of the Freedom Riders, who risked their lives to pressure the federal government to end unconstitutional segregation on interstate buses, and 74 percent thought demonstrations ultimately hurt the activists' cause.[19] (Similarly, only a minuscule percentage of women demanded the right to vote; the large mostly female memberships of many anti-suffrage groups reflected mass opposition to the franchise.) Adding another layer of complexity, under mounting pressure from social movements and shifting public sentiment, the counter-majoritarian institution known as the Supreme Court made the minority's claims into law: schools had to be integrated, voting rights had to be respected, and equal opportunity upheld. Such was the new consensus, instigated and imposed by tiny minorities below and on high, whether or not the majority assented.

The simple moral is that consensus and conflict have different meanings depending on the context. Neither can be understood as purely virtue or vice. What appears to be destructive conflict from one perspective is seen as a heroic democratic struggle from another's. Take Madison's example of debtors impinging on creditors' rights to be repaid. If looked at from another angle—say, the perspective of a single mother who was unfairly issued a subprime loan by Wells Fargo and lost her house (as was the case with thousands of low-income black homeowners in Baltimore), or a student whose college debt payments will be so high that she's afraid to take the financial risk of getting an education—better terms for debtors, even the total discharge of their obligations, becomes an issue of social justice and fair play.

The same goes for consensus. Despite the fact that consensus processes have been adopted by idealistic anarchists around the world, they can also be found in plenty of established institutions with a range of consequences. Juries, for example, require unanimous verdicts, a principle developed in England in the fourteenth century. As the role of juries was to pronounce the truth and speak with the voice of the country, and because there was only one truth and one nation, consensus became a prerequisite. Indeed, given the gravity of legal decisions, unanimity seems an appropriate bar. What's more, through a process known as jury nullification, jurors have the authority to acquit, a form of veto designed to act as a check on an abuse of state power. Modern jurors could decide to find defendants not guilty and thus prevent convictions in cases where they believe the law is unjust (for example, in the case of drug offenses or other victimless crimes), just as they did in the mid-1800s, for example, to defy the Fugitive Slave Act or, later, to resist Prohibition. However, jurors rarely know this right to nullify exists.[20]

If consensus can sometimes be used to promote just outcomes, it can also uphold unjust circumstances, as Calhoun well knew. The most glaring example is the way the requirement of consensus is employed to maintain the immense and arguably undemocratic power held by the U.S. Senate, a body that grants two seats to every state regardless of its population. Thus, the 2 percent of Americans who live in the nine smallest states possess the same power as the 51 percent who reside in the nine largest, a structure that dramatically increases the influence of voters who tend to be white and rural. Whereas other parts of the Constitution can be changed with the approval of two-thirds of both the House and Senate and three-fourths of the states, the Constitution stipulates that "no state, without its consent, shall be deprived of its equal suffrage in the Senate." Any change to the principle of equal state representation in the Senate is forbidden without the states' "unanimous consent." And why would Wyoming, with a population that barely exceeds half a million souls, willfully give up parity with California and its population of nearly forty million?[21]

This leads us to the deeper issue: not whether conflict itself is good or bad, or whether consensus is pragmatic or a pipe dream, but what interests are at stake and who stands to win or lose in any given situation. A conflict may flare up pitting women who need reproductive health care or gay individuals who want equal rights against Christians who see abortion and homosexuality as unforgivable sins; disabled people who want access against business owners who resent being forced to pay for accommodations; community members who need drinkable water against a corporation disposing of waste near the local aquifer; or millionaires who want a tax cut against teachers at a failing public school. In each of these cases, the positions are irreconcilable. We have no choice but to take sides and battle it out.

In a democracy, conflict is essential, not aberrational. But conflicts are often hidden under a veneer of consensus, or what the Italian political theorist Antonio Gramsci described as hegemony, the everyday ideas and cultural habits that make power structures and pecking orders appear natural and immutable. Consensus can be implicit—the unstated but ubiquitous understandings that affirm the dominance of certain social groups over others while making inequality seem inevitable. Hegemony, then, is a kind of constraining common sense. This is why the philosopher Jacques Rancière equates democracy with what he calls *dissensus*. Democracy, in his formulation, is the disruptive and unpredictable process through which an existing consensus is challenged so that a new consensus can be forged, outbursts of antagonism leading to revised agreements and accords. For Rancière democracy is not a set of procedures or institutions but a spontaneous expression and interruption, an affront to established norms that unsettles social hierarchies and obstructs business as usual.

Let's imagine, for a second, that dissensus erupts and a more egalitarian consensus is forged. It's interesting to imagine what kind of disagreements might persist. Marx imagined that "the *genuine* resolution of the conflict between man and nature and between man and man" was possible, and he called this situation communism ("the true resolution of the strife between existence and essence, between objectification and self-confirmation, between freedom and necessity, between the individual and the species"). While it sounds wonderful I'm less sanguine. Even if class conflict disappears we will still find plenty to argue about. What methods best determine the good of a community? What development projects and whose needs should be prioritized? Who makes which decisions and how? As long as we remain human, we'll battle with each other and ourselves thanks to our reliably conflictual natures. Do we want what's good for us or what feels good? Shall we live selfishly or serve others? Will we indulge our immediate desires or plan for the long-term?

Conflict springs eternal. Nevertheless, we should be wary when people are too eager to insist that specific conflicts or conditions are permanently intractable, whether they are referring to a "clash of civilizations" between East and West; a primordial tension between races and an inexorable tendency toward white supremacy;

a perpetual battle of the sexes and heteronormative assertion of male dominance; or Madison's everlasting war between those with property and those without. History shows that religious, racial, gender, and material relations are malleable. While some societies have been rent by religious and ethnic conflagrations, others have demonstrated that peaceful pluralism is possible. Anti-blackness and white supremacy, however constitutive of the modern experience, are not timeless truths but, as many scholars have shown, outgrowths of racialized categories that are relatively recent inventions. Likewise, while misogyny has yet to be stamped out, relationships between men and women have become far more egalitarian, and gender more fluid, in a remarkably short time span (even if there's still far to go).

Finally, especially in an age of machine-enabled abundance, there's no compelling reason why enormous disparities in wealth should continue to exist—it is not some unyielding universal law but the contingencies of capitalism, and the greed and hubris of the class it privileges, that stand in the way of a more equitable distribution. Those who declare these disputes and disparities eternal, hardwired into humankind's selfish nature, are probably invested in one side of the status quo. A new democratic consensus, which might one day resolve some of these old antagonisms (even if other disagreements and disputes would inevitably emerge in their place), will come about only through conflict—through the very sort of struggle and discord the powerful would prefer to see suppressed.

CHAPTER 3

REINVENTING THE PEOPLE

(INCLUSION/EXCLUSION)

A TINY HIMALAYAN country precariously perched between China and India, its small population dwarfed by the bordering superpowers, Bhutan is a place few foreigners visit. Geographically and culturally isolated, the country is often presented as an uncorrupted Buddhist Shangri-la—a paradisiacal image bolstered by the government's embrace and promotion of its Gross National Happiness index. Befitting its blissful reputation and breathtaking vistas, Bhutan's transition to democracy had an almost fairy-tale quality. Press accounts told a story of a wise king who understood the world was changing and that his country would have to adapt.

The time had come to nurture "a vibrant democracy" in the "the womb of a strong and peaceful monarchy."[1] And so, in 2007 after announcing his plan to abdicate the throne, King Jigme Singye Wangchuck commanded his subjects to become citizens and practice self-rule. With a single pronouncement, over half a million people obediently embarked on what the *New York Times* called a "fire drill for democracy."[2] Gently nudging his charges into the modern era, the king's administrators organized mock elections. Four "dummy" political parties were distinguished by color: Blue Thunder Dragon, Green Thunder Dragon, Red Thunder Dragon, and Yellow Thunder Dragon. (The thunder dragon, or "Druk," is Bhutan's national symbol.) Each party had a platform

Blue stood for free health care, education, and anticorruption, Green for ecological sustainability, Red for industrial development, and Yellow for custom and conventional values. Represented by the official royal color, the Yellow party posed a question—"Do you believe in the preservation and promotion of our rich cultural heritage and tradition?"—and triumphed at the polls, scooping up forty-six out of forty-seven constituencies.[3] "If you had a referendum, even today, Bhutan would reject democracy. That's the ground reality," one aspiring leader remarked. At that time, most Bhutanese wanted what they had before: a stable and powerful monarchy.

Thrust into political life, the average Bhutanese felt bewildered, and so did many of those tasked with running for office. "We're not starting a party because we have an ideology. We're not starting a party because we have a vision for a better Bhutan. We are starting a party because the King has ordered us," explained Tshering Tobgay, the future prime minister.[4] "[The people] are being given democracy without having to fight for it. In any other country it would be the other way around." According to Tobgay, Bhutanese subjects had no choice but to accept whatever was handed down from on high: "We are his like children and now he is asking us to grow up. We must trust the wisdom of his judgment. Some people may be worried today but when democracy begins to happen for real they will look back and realize the King was right."[5]

Ten years on, it's not entirely clear their preferences have really changed. Ahead of elections in 2018, the local press was reporting a sense of fatigue. When one newspaper asked people to reflect on what had been "lost and gained" during the first decade of democratic government the responses were lukewarm. "Ughhh," replied one candidate for office. "We have lost trust, friends, and families. What have we gained? I don't know . . ."[6] Someone else paid tribute to Bhutan's constitutional monarchy, emphasizing royal over representative wisdom: "We are lucky to have access to His Majesty the King for guidance and hence our democracy has a better beginning than most countries."[7] Describing the national mood, a newspaper editorial noted: "Two rounds of parliamentary elections and a decade into Bhutan's transition to democracy, we have agreed to associate politics and the processes of democracy, especially elections, as dirty, divisive and all about money."[8] Only one voice, that of Tobgay himself, offered qualified enthusiasm. "People have been pushed out of our comfort zone" and forced to "take responsibility as citizens," he said. "In some ways, being removed from this comfort zone can be considered a loss. But it is good for Bhutan."[9]

Good or bad, the decision had been made by fiat and could not be overturned. As political theorist Stephanie DeGooyer reveals in "Democracy, Give or Take?," a fascinating essay interpreting these events, Bhutanese citizens were compelled to accept the "gift" of democratic responsibility most of them didn't want.[10] So regardless of popular misgivings, Bhutan continues on its path to modernization. Schoolchildren learn about the virtues of self-government in class, while the royal family have been reconfigured as glamorous figureheads dispossessed of any real claims to sovereignty. Citizens are beginning to speak the language of rights and figuring out how to have a free press—one that frequently reports on the fact democracy is not all it's cracked up to be.

The official story of Bhutan's transition to democracy is one of a remarkable transfer of power devoid of conflict or disturbance, a benevolent and beloved monarch peacefully entrusting his people to rule themselves. But as DeGooyer reveals, there is another, more troubling, version of events yet one that is also more truthful.

Decades before the king made his seemingly enlightened decree to dissolve the absolute authority of his lineage, there were in fact, people demanding democracy in Bhutan: the ethnic and religious minority known as the Lhotshampas, or "southerners." Though they had been recruited to Bhutan from Nepal as craftsmen as far back as the early 1600s, the Hindu Lhotshampas were treated as second-class citizens.[11] A source of cheap labor, they were also easy scapegoats, frequently discriminated against and eventually painted as a demographic and cultural threat. In 1989, new laws denied them the right to speak their own language, practice their faith, or wear their traditional clothes. The community rose up, protesting that they could do all of these things and still be Bhutanese, while an outspoken minority called for an end to absolute monarchy and began pressing for democracy. It was the Lhotshampas who formed the country's first political party in 1990, the Bhutan People's Party, which was quickly branded a terrorist organization.

The crackdown quickly became a horrific campaign of ethnic cleansing. In what is, proportionally, one of the largest forced exoduses in history, over 110,000 Lhotshampas—one-sixth of the country's entire population—were compelled to flee. Though most had called Bhutan home for generations and counted members of the majority Buddhist community as friends and neighbors, the Hindu Lhotshampas, with their Nepali heritage, were deemed foreign, alien, unwelcome. Their homes and land, which had become more valuable over the years, were seized. Stripped of the citizenship some, but not all, the Lhotshampas had been granted in 1958, people were threatened with rape, torture, imprisonment, and worse.

Distant family of the rebels, people who had never spoken up or made trouble, were taken away and never heard from again. Suddenly stateless, tens of thousands crossed the border to Nepal where the government established seven camps to provide basic shelter but refused to integrate them. The Lhotshampas were outcasts, "illegals," not counted among "the people" of Bhutan nor Nepal. The underbelly of Bhutan's famous embrace of Gross National Happiness, it turns out, was an assumption of homogeneity as an essential component of civic contentment. The dark side of the king's edict, "One Nation, One People," manifested even during that initial mock election. As the results came, Indian troops opened fire on Lhotshampas attempting to reenter Bhutan to protest their exile, leaving a teenager to die of blood loss and injuring dozens of others.[12]

This version of Bhutan's shift from monarchy is quite unlike the appealing fable and far more commonplace: a fight for a more inclusive democracy driven from below, the charge led by those who occupy the social ladder's bottom rungs. The more accurate account hinges on one of the central tensions of democratic theory and practice: inclusion and exclusion. Who is included in the demos of democracy? Who counts as part of the people and who is cast out or even killed? Even in periods of relative political calm, the conflict between democracy's promise of universal inclusion and its unavoidable limitations lurks below the surface anywhere the people are said to rule.

At the heart of democracy is an abstraction, "the people" an entity that is empowered to rule but does not tangibly exist. The United States Constitution reflects this fundamental incoherence when it identifies three distinct populations inhabiting the same continent: "People" or those entitled to rights and freedom; "other persons," or the enslaved; and Indians, who possess tribal sovereignty and are excluded from the body politic. Despite, or because of, this fundamental conceptual ambiguity, every democratic community no matter how large or small, has to struggle to define itself and its limits. Self-government is a perpetual negotiation over who is included and who is excluded, who is us and who is them. The boundaries of the demos expand and contract, and "the people" can be invoked to serve different and often conflicting aims.

"To have democracy there has to be a we. You have to know who *we the people* are. It can't just be a kind of vague universal thing," Wendy Brown told me in our interview. I felt myself cringe in response, wishing it weren't so. The ugly, bigoted history of exclusion makes it tempting to reject all exclusionary boundaries as inhumane and unjust. At the same time, such sweeping universalism risks making democracy either incoherent, since nearly eight billion people cannot practically make decisions together, or imperial, for it implies a single system governing everyone, everywhere.

"For us to say we're going to engage in a democratic process we have to decide who's in and who's out of that process," Brown continued. Decisions must be made *by* and accountable *to* a specific people to be democratically defensible. Communities having a say over the decisions that affect them necessarily entails exclusions (there's no need for me to weigh in on Nordic library budgets or the priorities of worker-run factories in South America). The challenge, Brown notes, is that most limits have been premised on terrible forms of discrimination, hierarchy, and ways of "naming who's human and who's not human." Wealth, skin color, gender, sexual orientation, physical and mental ability, religion, nationality, ethnicity, immigration status, criminal history, and career choice all have been or are still being used to justify denying some people full equality. "I'm not defending any of that," Brown said, "but democracy has to have bounds. It has to have a constitutive we."

Faced with this eternal perplexity, some insist that, at least at the level of the nation-state, the matter is solved. Since the nineteenth century, ethno-nationalists the world over have maintained that "the people" is a stable self-evident entity, bound by blood and soil, who hold a legitimate claim on the right to rule over a specified territory, the borders of which must be defended. This view replaces the demos, a politically defined people who come together to govern a state, with an ethnos, an ethnically defined people said to embody the spirit of a nation; where the demos is invented and contingent, the ethnos purports to be organic and eternal.

This sleight of hand passed for regal sagacity in Bhutan in the years before the mass expulsion of the Lhotshampas: that "real" Bhutanese share a patrimony reflected in their Buddhist beliefs, traditional customs, and language the absence of which marks others as interlopers. Next door in India, Hindu extremists claim a divine right to rule over people of other faiths and lower castes. A resurgence of exclusionary ethno-nationalism spans the globe:

in 2018 the Israeli Knesset enshrined in law that the right of national self-determination is "unique to the Jewish people" alone; in Turkey, President Recep Tayyip Erdoğan questioned the legitimacy of his critics ("We are the people. Who are you?"); in Brazil, President Jair Bolsonaro ran a campaign insulting and threating black people, women, and homosexuals; in Europe, right-wing parties, some with Nazi roots, are mobilizing around anti-immigrant platforms; in England an older Anglo-Saxon majority wants to take its country back (Nigel Farage, member of the European Parliament and vice chairman of Leave Means Leave, praised Brexit as a "victory for real people" as though everyone else was unreal); in the United States predominantly white conservatives want to make their nation great again by curbing immigration and banning visitors from the Middle East.

It is tempting to see these populist outbursts as aberrant, regressive detours along liberal democracy's ever-more inclusive march, but the history of self-rule is a catalog of the struggle to define the collective. Group identities are necessary yet hazardous; they bind and divide, nurturing solidarity and belonging alongside suspicion and estrangement. Complicating this struggle is the fact that any attempt by a demos to define its boundaries intrinsically carries the possibility of self-destruction The philosopher Jacques Derrida uses the term *autoimmunity* to refer to such attacks on the political body by the political body in the name of the political body. Democracy, he contends, contains the germs of its own undoing: "democracy protects itself and maintains itself precisely by limiting and threatening itself."[13]

In ancient Greece exclusion, not openness, was the norm. Those fortunate to be neither enslaved, female, nor foreign jealously guarded the privileges of membership. As James Miller points out in his book *Can Democracy Work?* the apex of Athenian democracy corresponded with a series of reforms that redistributed public wealth on an unprecedented scale: the Assembly instituted daily pay for the armed forces, public works projects to employ artisans and craftsmen, and the establishment of a fund to pay citizens a per diem for serving on the courts and in the council. At the same time, the Assembly made citizenship even more restrictive: boys had to have a native-born mother and a native-born father to qualify as Athenian.[14] New heights of economic egalitarianism came with new measures of exclusion. As we shall see, rarely can the politics of belonging be neatly disentangled from economic concerns.

In democratic Athens the urge to exclude was formidable but never racialized. Athens' elite classes justified their superior status and the existence of slavery through other means—race and racism, as we currently understand them, did not yet exist. It was enough that might made right; superior strength provided reason alone to conquer and control.[15] Meanwhile, when leading thinkers of the ancient world classified human beings they did so according to climate not skin tone; relative humidity or aridness was believed to account for the temperaments of varied populations, as Hippocrates mused in his *On Airs, Waters, and Places*. The United States broke ground by binding the democratic project to theories of racial difference, which offered pseudo-scientific rationales for the Atlantic slave trade, colonialism, and a range of citizenship restrictions.

In 1897, decades after the Civil War and two years before he became governor of New York, Theodore Roosevelt took for granted that self-rule was the provenance of a supposedly superior white race: "The whole civilization of the future owes a debt of gratitude greater than can be expressed in words to that democratic polity which has kept the temperate zones of the new and the newest worlds a heritage for white people." But as historians including Nell Irvin Painter and David Roediger have masterfully demonstrated, who counted as white was perpetually in flux. When they landed on the docks Irish, Italian, Slavic, Hungarian, and Jewish immigrants were not considered white—yet whiteness was a destination their progeny could reach, even if the process was fraught. Only by becoming white could complete inclusion in the nation's polity be achieved and the full benefits of citizenship enjoyed.

Across the ocean in Paris, the title of the revolutionary 1789 Declaration of the Rights of Man and of the Citizen put the tension between democracy's universalism and particularism on display: where the rights of man are expansive and all-inclusive, the rights of citizens, in contrast, are constrained and exclusionary. The declaration's stirring opening article—"Men are born and remain free and equal in rights"—was equally provocative and ambiguous, a line destined to spark intense debate in part because it brought the hypocrisy of racial exclusions to the fore. To whom did the inspiring dictum apply? To all men regardless of citizenship, national origin, or race?

With that, additional questions rushed forth: What about women? How about the destitute and propertyless? Jewish and Protestant religious minorities? Members of disreputable professions, such as actors and executioners (whose services, unbeknown to all, were soon to be in high demand)? As time went on, the questions only keep coming: What about children and teenagers? The disabled? What about gay, lesbian, queer, trans, and nonbinary people?—and, as we'll see, eventually extended beyond the human: What about animals? Rivers and trees? What about robots and other forms of artificial intelligence? Perhaps one day, depending on what scientists discover in outer space, we'll even have to ask about real, as opposed to resident, aliens. Should we ever encounter them, will extraterrestrials be free and equal in rights? Will they be included as citizens in the demos?

The Declaration of the Rights of Man opened the door to these questions because if rights are universal, then restrictions require explanation and the disadvantaged have been given grounds to resist their marginalization.[16] No wonder, then, that revolutionary fervor spread to the French colony then called Saint-Domingue, now known as Haiti, where the enslaved rose up to lead a revolution with a democratic mandate more profound than their French rulers dared to offer. It was in Haiti that the world's first multiracial democracy was born. Against tremendous odds, the most socially excluded and ruthlessly exploited liberated themselves from a nightmarish system that obsessively divided the population into 128 divisions based on parentage, each intermediate step between "pure" black and "pure" white meriting its own designation (mulatto, quarteron, marabou, sang-mele, and on and on), all so a pale-skinned minority could live in leisurely opulence while their human property toiled and perished.[17]

Historians often portray the Haitian Revolution as a fulfillment of enlightenment ideals first articulated in France: enslaved men and women took up the mantle of equality and freedom and, by protesting their exclusion, helped realize the inherent universal potential of democratic principles. This interpretation risks giving Europeans too much credit while selling Haitians short. In a thoughtful reconsideration, scholar Adom Getachew argues that while the Haitian Revolution would not have happened without its French predecessor, it charted a new course and took democracy in unprecedented directions, and not just because it was the only successful slave revolt in history.

The Haitian Constitution of 1805, for example, not only abolished "all distinctions of color," it also elevated blackness as a generic political category. "Haitians shall henceforth be known by the generic appellation of blacks," the Constitution declared, whatever shade their skin or parentage. Thus blackness signified a socially transformative solidarity at the heart of a new conception of the people. The young nation's borders were permeable, open to any victim of racist terror. Asylum was offered to "all Africans and Indians, and those of their blood," with naturalization after a year of residency (Simón Bolívar, the leader of Latin American independence, and his generals took up the offer twice during their campaign to liberate Venezuela). In contrast to white supremacy, which upheld a form of freedom that could be secured only through the colonial oppression of others, blackness was reconceived to embody a new kind of freedom—freedom secured through collective action against colonial oppression—and novel forms of belonging and citizenship.

This vision of multiracial and international solidarity posed a profound challenge and alternative to Europe's truncated conception of democracy. Seen in this light, the Haitian Revolution was not a battle to join a preexisting democratic order, but something far more radical: an uprising that understood inclusion as a means to vanquish racist practices of domination and to advance the individual and collective autonomy of subjugated people.[18] From their small island territory, Haitians offered a transnational vision of democratic justice aimed at overthrowing slavery wherever it could be found, setting their sights on a "a previously unimaginable world in which both slavery and colonial rule would finally be transcended."[19] Generations of Haitians were forced to pay the price for their predecessors' uniquely successful and truly visionary rebellion. The country was punished with permanent debt peonage: 150 million francs, later reduced to 90 million (an amount estimated to be around forty billion in today's dollars) demanded by France for appropriated plantations and military expenditures. More recently, Haitians seeking asylum in the United States to escape the brutal Duvalier dictatorship, an anticommunist ally, found themselves repatriated by the tens of thousands. (Guantánamo Bay first opened as an offshore detention center to hold ill and impoverished Haitian refugees.[20])

At the revolution's best, the goal was not merely inclusion but transformation. Slavery, after all, was not just a problem of exclusion, which was itself a means to an end. Exclusion enabled domination of enslaved people by white masters; domination enabled exploitation; and exploitation facilitated profit. From colonialism through contemporary immigration debates, the cruelest exclusions typically serve an economic purpose.

As Barbara and Karen Fields point out in their brilliant study *Racecraft*, the chief business of slavery in the Caribbean and the American South was the production of cotton, sugar, rice, and tobacco for profit, not white supremacy for its own sake. The passage of 1882's Chinese Exclusion Act and the "repatriation" of more than one million Mexicans and Mexican Americans during the Great Depression provide more recent examples of racialized exclusion serving a strict economic calculus. ("In the case of the Mexican, he is less desirable as a citizen than as a laborer," the U.S. congressional Dillingham Commission reported in 1911.) And let us not forget that the Lhotshampas, invited to Bhutan as a hardworking underclass, were ousted when their land began to become more valuable than their labor. These are but a handful of examples in a seemingly endless litany of exclusions that, while devastating to some, were lucrative to others.

Rightless people, after all, are easier to exploit, which is why companies encourage the importation of cheap foreign labor and push for immigration laws designed to create an underclass of temporary workers who have few protections and live in fear of deportation. In response, domestic workers and their unions too often respond by blaming foreigners for stealing jobs and driving down wages instead of pinning blame on employers (though empirical research shows no definitive correlation between immigrant labor and depressed earnings for native workers).[21] The old socialist dream of solidarity between the "exploited and oppressed masses of all lands," as Eugene Debs phrased it, is hard to achieve when material insecurity pits vulnerable groups against each other, creating conditions under which the comparatively secure—who may be citizens but not particularly privileged ones—feel threatened by those who occupy the social hierarchy's lower rungs.

It should come as no surprise, then, that an ethno-nationalist resurgence has taken place against our current backdrop of Gilded Age inequality and neoliberal austerity. The shocking discrepancy between the obscenely affluent and the barely scraping by—the extremes of abundance and poverty—are never far from view when the question of who counts as "the people" becomes pressing. Economic extremes turn the debate over the boundaries of the demos into a struggle between winners and losers, who is on top and who on the bottom, who exploits and who is exploited.

Capitalism creates a pyramid-shaped society, with less room the higher one climbs, but that is not the shape a democratic society has to take. Typically we speak of inclusion in terms of identity and diversity, not class—but class is key, in part because it exposes inclusion's limits. We can aim to increase diversity by including various marginalized groups—racialized populations, women, trans people, the disabled and so on—in society's uppermost echelons, but it makes far less sense to speak of including the poor, because if they were on top they would no longer be poor. A more democratic world is not one where the extremely rich are more diverse but one where the pyramid levels and no one has to struggle to survive.

One young American woman I spoke to told me of her enthusiasm for Donald Trump's call to build a wall along the southern border with Mexico. "If we don't have a border, we don't have a country," she said. "It's not that we want to keep everybody out, but we need to do better ourselves," meaning people like her had to feel economically secure and successful before immigrants could be welcomed into the fold.

We tend to think of walls as a means of keeping people at bay, but as this young woman reminded me, they also keep things in. Walls hoard resources and opportunity for some at the expense of others and have served this function since the earliest days, as Rousseau famously speculated in his *Discourse on the Origin of Inequality*. His fabled fence was erected to serve a possessive purpose—if this is mine, it cannot be yours. But where Rousseau was critical of this mercenary move, John Locke was enthusiastic, effusively praising fences. In his view, parceled plots of land and a system of private as opposed to communal ownership distinguished colonial "civilization" from "savagery," the "wild Indian" who "knew no enclosure" so their land existed for the taking.

Capitalism was born of enclosure, a process that ripped people from their land and communities and made them dependent on the market. The resulting individualism, taken to its extreme, erodes the very idea of the people. Instead of being a demos, a collectivity asserting our political sovereignty and deciding how to live together, we are left on our own—liberated or isolated depending on how you see it—searching for a path to the top, even if we have to climb over others to get there.

In sixteenth-century England, and later in America, talk of "the people" emerged as a carefully crafted rhetorical tool. Protestant upstarts wielded the concept like a weapon to dismantle the authority of monarchs who claimed to possess a divine right to rule. "A new ideology, a new rationale, a new set of fictions was necessary to justify a government in which the authority of kings stood below that of people or their representatives," writes historian Edmund S. Morgan in his classic account *Inventing the People*. Aspiring representatives invoked the idea of popular sovereignty to topple English kings—and to justify their own rise to power and prominence as a new and privileged political and religious class. The events in Bhutan flipped the script: it was the king who invoked the people to justify his own resignation.

But first he worked to construct a people who he believed would not threaten the new social order he established—the Lhotshampas, with their more inclusive democratic vision, had to be crushed. In Bhutan, as in England centuries before, "the people had to be tamed, its operation and meaning established in such a way as not to threaten the government of the few" before "the divine right of kings could be safely interred."[22] The rhetoric of popular sovereignty may appeal to elites, but they also recognize the risks. Seeking a veneer of democratic legitimacy but loath to let the people actually rule, they face a strange inversion of Rousseau's famous paradox: their challenge is creating a docile citizenry out of a democratically spirited one.

One evening in Charlotte, North Carolina, I sat drinking tea with thirty-year-old T. P. Mishra and his seventy-four-year-old father at their small ranch-style home. T.P.'s father had arrived from Nepal only a few weeks before we met, nearly a decade after his son came to America with little more than the clothes on his back.

In 1992, when T.P. was a small child, the family was violently evicted from their land in Bhutan and condemned to limbo. For over twenty years they lived in a Nepali refugee camp, where a single outdoor faucet provided water for over two hundred people and school classes took place under the shade of a tree. Against these odds, T.P. and his brothers found a way to start a newspaper when they were teenagers. Today their website, the Bhutan News Network, is the primary source of information for the Bhutanese refugee diaspora. T.P. runs the media service on a volunteer basis and makes his living as a caseworker at the local Refugee Resettlement Agency, where he guides new arrivals through a process he knows firsthand.

T.P. had never heard the full story of his family's painful exile, and he took my visit as an opportunity to ask his father some searching questions. What had happened in the months before they were forced to leave their homeland? Some people of Nepalese origin had been permitted to stay in Bhutan, on the condition that they gave up their culture and collaborate with the authorities, and while they lacked equal rights, they did not have to endure expulsion. Had his father ever considered this route? Did he regret protesting? Speaking Dzongkha, the official language of Bhutan, T.P.'s father was firm. "No, not at all. I knew what I was doing."

He paused to take a sip of tea, waiting for us to indicate that he should go on. "I was ordered to send the girls from the village to the army camp. I couldn't do that." He told us of his time in prison, of being tortured (his fingers were pierced with needles; he was forced to drink urine; he was beaten so badly he lost his hearing in one ear, the pain radiating through his head to this day) He saw people shot, their limbs broken. After he spent ninety-one days locked in a cell, a friend who was a village official and member of the Buddhist elite, or Drukpa, managed to secure his release from prison, though he had been sentenced to three years. Such a relationship was not so unusual.

For a long time, T.P.'s father explained, the Lhotshampas and

Drukpas lived in peace as neighbors, coexisting side by side in what many believe is the most beautiful country on earth. "It was good at first," he said. "But when the agitation was at its peak, it started becoming bitter. They called Nepali *Jyaga* and *Gyange*, meaning that we were dumb and ghosts. Some of Drukpas favored us while others did not. When there is an agitation in a country, people get divided into those who want the change and those who don't." He was in favor of democracy when most were not. His son asked him to define democracy. "This is the system which allows rights for all: children, women, the disabled, the old, the youth." He supported the struggle because he believed he and his family had the right to be themselves.

I asked T.P. to translate a question for me. "There is democracy in Bhutan now, but the people who wanted it are no longer there. How does this make you feel?" The old man scoffed. "One hundred thousand Nepali people have been chased away. The country is not as populated as it was before. They have given democracy. But who have they given it to? To the bears of the forests or to the trees?" He summed up, waving his hands in disgust at the memory of all he and his people had endured. "There is no problem giving democracy to docile people." Bhutan's king gave the gift of democracy only after the ones who originally wanted it had been brutalized and banished. With the rebellious Lhotshampa expelled, politicians could adopt one of the most progressive, human-rights-respecting constitutions in the world without having to worry about unintended consequences, since those most in need of protection had been expunged.

Though proud and grateful to live in the United States, father and son still dream of Bhutan. Decades on, the government refuses to recognize the exiled Lhotshampas' citizenship claims and none have been granted permission to return. The refugees continue to protest from outside their homeland's borders, hoping to force the state to acknowledge what transpired so that a formal process of truth and reconciliation can commence. Scattered around the world, but linked by T.P.'s wired network, Bhutan's original democrats demand the right to be included in a political system they fought and suffered for but from which they have been excluded. Perhaps one day, under pressure from activists and the international community, Bhutan will admit the error of its ways and readmit those who were banished. That's what the Mishras hope. Only then, they insist, will the country finally become the democracy it claims to be.

What about the democracy the United States claims to be? A few months after we sat drinking tea, T.P. and I saw American democracy up close, in all its conflicted glory. At eight in the morning on Election Day in 2016, we met in the parking lot of a suburban elementary school, about thirty minutes outside Charlotte. Earlier in the year T.P. had been allowed to naturalize as an American citizen; he was going to cast a vote for president for the first time in his life. "I never had a country I could claim as my own," he said, full of pride. "And this is my country now, and it is my moral obligation to participate in the democracy."

As we approached the school, a middle-aged Republican candidate pressed campaign materials for his reelection to state legislature into my hand. I recognized the name. Dean Arp was known for his support of that year's notorious "bathroom bill," which denied trans people the right to use gender appropriate restroom facilities and had inspired boycotts of the state. He was also a vocal supporter of the incumbent governor, who had been grabbing headlines with promises to ban Syrian refugees from North Carolina. He asked what media outlet we were with, and I answered the National Film Board of Canada.

While T.P. went inside to vote, my crew and I began to set up outside. As my camerawoman adjusted her settings, the candidate began taking photos of us and promptly uploaded them to social media. The images, which showed us standing idly on the sidewalk with a car parked nearby, were alarmingly captioned. "The media" was on site intimidating a "conservative, pro-life" voter—

the person in the car, judging by its bumper sticker—and we were foreign, to boot. I tried to assure the man that we were doing no such thing. As required by law, I had notified the polling officials of our presence and they had approved my request to shoot. But he and his followers were implacable. The comment threads grew increasingly distressed, locals expressing alarm and outrage. No one seemed to notice that it was the acting state legislator and candidate for office, not us, who had taken a photo of this specific conservative voter's vehicle and then made it public for all to see.

An older woman raced over. "Are you the people I saw on Facebook?" she asked, eyeing me suspiciously. "You say you're from Canada. You sure are a long way from home." I didn't try to explain that my parents lived ninety minutes away and that people could both be from Canada—or anywhere else, for that matter—and still be connected to North Carolina.

Scrolling through the angry online comments when he returned, T.P. was reflective. He detected more than an undercurrent of racism in the candidate's reaction—if his skin had been white perhaps the response would have been different. But we understood that what had happened was not just one person's idiosyncratic or bigoted reaction, but a symptom of widespread agitation. Republicans in North Carolina had been spreading rumors about mass voter fraud, about immigrants being bused in to vote illegally, and about other ploys supposedly aimed at tilting the playing field in favor of Democrats; Trump, meanwhile, had warned his supporters to remain vigilant at the polls, insinuating that if he lost the election illegitimate ballots would be the reason. The message was clear: white Republicans, not racial minorities, were the real victims of voter suppression, the real people under attack. In such a quiet bucolic setting, my crew and I were this particular candidate's best bet for conjuring up a nefarious transnational liberal conspiracy to stifle the conservative vote and help foreigners infiltrate and undermine America.

We made some jokes, but the hostility had shaken us. As we

wrapped up, T.P. told me he was worried about what would happen to his clients at the resettlement agency if the Republicans won: the families that would not be reunited, the threat of deportation, the stress that comes from being stigmatized. He knew firsthand that the process of vetting asylum seekers is intense and thorough, and that concerns about the threat to security posed by refugees is overblown. By embracing divisive xenophobic rhetoric—whether directed at trans people, immigrant voters, or refugees—the American people, he felt, were playing with a flame that had already engulfed his life.

It's a spark to which many modern democracies have succumbed. Certain conditions ignite what sociologist Michael Mann has called "the dark side of democracy," which takes the tendency to define "the people" in racial and ethnic terms to its murderous, genocidal extreme.[23] In 1951 another former refugee, Hannah Arendt, published *The Origins of Totalitarianism*, putting her lived experience as a Jewish victim of Nazism into sweeping historical and theoretical context. Arendt lived as a stateless exile from the age of twenty-seven to forty-five before naturalizing as an American. In her analysis, the dehumanizing horrors of World War II cannot be understood without taking European imperialism into account. The racist ideology that developed to justify the colonial "scramble for Africa" and the quest for power and profit would eventually come home to roost.

In the book's most famous chapter, Arendt described citizenship as "the right to have rights." We tend to think of human rights as a given, something that people possess regardless of nationality. But human rights can lose their powers of protection if detached from citizenship. There is, Arendt wrote, "nothing sacred in the abstract nakedness of being human."[24] Being excluded from the category of citizen leaves individuals profoundly exposed, despite their inclusion in the universal category of human being.[25]

What this proves, Arendt contends, is that rights are not inborn and "inalienable." Instead they are agreed upon, or "socially constructed," as academics like to say. We possess rights only when we are counted as members of a particular political entity that recognizes and ensures them, which is why Edmund Burke quipped that he'd rather have the rights of an Englishman than the rights of man. Paradoxically, citizenship—legal inclusion in a demos— is required if our human rights are to have any chance of being respected.

On paper and institutionally, human rights are better defined today and more robustly upheld than when Arendt found herself without a passport in occupied France. The 1948 Declaration of Human Rights lays out our inalienable entitlements, what we deserve by virtue of being born—including the right to a nationality and the right to seek (but not to be granted) asylum. Yet the problem of rightlessness remains and is all the more acute in recent years. According to the United Nations High Commissioner for Refugees, nearly 1 percent of the planet's population—65.3 million people—is either "an asylum-seeker, internally displaced or a refugee." But even this staggering figure does not quite convey the true scope of human uprootedness: almost 250 million people are international migrants, the majority on the move out of necessity more than choice. These figures will only increase as climate change makes densely populated regions uninhabitable. (Legally, there is no such thing as a climate refugee. Human rights law currently distinguishes between those fleeing war or direct persecution by oppressive regimes, who qualify as "legitimate" asylum seekers and refugees, and those seeking to escape poverty and other forms of hardship, who are deemed "economic migrants" and can be kept out.)

While speaking the inclusive language of human rights, today's ostensible democracies practice exclusion in the extreme, militarizing borders and vetting individual cases as though refugee status were a scarce privilege and not the universal legal entitlement it actually is. This much was clear in 2015, when more than a million men, women, and children, overwhelmingly from warwrecked Syria but also from Afghanistan, Iraq, Sudan, and Eritrea, risked the journey across the Aegean and Mediterranean Seas to arrive on European shores. (Generally speaking, it was the relatively affluent who managed to reach the Italian and Greek coasts; those too poor to cover the costs or pay smugglers' extortionate fees got stranded along the way.[26]) The new arrivals became a political flashpoint in Europe and North America, even though the beaches of the United States and Canada cannot be reached by inflatable raft.

Exclusion can be a profitable business, financially as well as politically. Responding to the migrant crisis with a strategy described by investigative journalist Apostolis Fotiadis as "militarization and externalization," European governments redirected massive budgets away from aid and development to border security, biometrics, and surveillance. Military suppliers and security companies seeking lucrative government contracts have a vested interest in playing up the specter of one million immigrants, although the number is hardly enormous spread over a continent with a population of some half a billion souls. Politicians, sensing opportunity, exaggerated the "refugee flood" to position themselves as protectors of a beleaguered people threatened by outsiders.[27]

By this logic, the fact a mere eleven Syrian asylum seekers were admitted to the United States in the first three months of 2018 could be cast as a tribute to national security and a sign of toughness, not a travesty.[28] (Meanwhile, politicians blithely ignore the fact that most hailed from regions American foreign policy played a role in destabilizing.) But where the War on Terror provides cover for the exclusion of refugees under the guise of protecting "democratic" ways of life, during the Cold War the opposite was true.[29] That period's geopolitical calculus encouraged leaders to welcome people persecuted by democracy's alleged enemies. Sheltering asylum seekers from the Soviet Bloc burnished capitalism's image and possessed the desired political symbolism.

After the failed Hungarian revolution of 1956, the United States, Canada, and Western Europe welcomed tens of thousands of "freedom fighters" fleeing communism (my maternal grandfather among them). Beginning in 1975 nearly one million people from Indochina resettled in the United States alone, in addition to those accepted by Canada, Europe, and Australia. Similarly, following the rise of the socialist Sandinistas in Nicaragua, many Nicaraguan refugees were allowed in, but not Salvadorans or Guatemalans, who came from countries run by authoritarian leaders and counterinsurgents backed by the United States.[30] And of course Cubans who denounced U.S. enemy Fidel Castro with their feet were granted asylum when they touched American soil.

Building on this trend of using people in need of sanctuary as political pawns, today's leaders promote what we might call a "velvet rope" approach to citizenship: the denial of access is taken as proof of the existence of an elite and desirable status. (Exclusivity has always been a remarkably cheap way of inflating a good's perceived value, and the same holds true for citizenship, even as social services are slashed and other benefits of national membership eroded.) Meanwhile, citizens who would prefer to include the vulnerable in their ranks rarely have the opportunity to effectively express or act on their preferences. The system of Private Sponsorship in Canada offers an unusual exception by allowing small groups of at least five individuals to sponsor refugee families, on the condition that they commit to providing substantial financial and emotional support to strangers for at least a year. Since 1978 participants have facilitated the arrival of an estimated three hundred thousand refugees in excess of the government's baseline human rights commitments. Where demagogues foment fear, this unique program fosters solidarity, allowing citizens the uncommon ability to extend rights to the rightless.

For over three decades I lived in the United States as a permanent resident—a "legal," as opposed to "illegal," alien. (Though my father is American, by the time of my birth he had lived in Canada for too long to automatically pass along his citizenship to me.)

Most people who become American have to naturalize, a strange word that implies the existence of "natural" people and "unnatural" ones. I assumed such a metamorphosis would be my fate, until the lawyer I hired made a discovery. Through an obscure provision, it seemed I had inherited status through my grandfather, an American border patrol agent stationed in Winnipeg, Manitoba, at the time I was born. Typically *jus sanguinis* and *jus soli*, the right of blood and the right of soil, are the two main rationales of nationality law, but ultimately it was my grandfather's job working for the federal government that made the critical difference in my case.

Still, I was required to attend a ceremony in downtown Manhattan that would mark my acceptance of my birthright. Along with a dozen or so others I swore an oath in front of an American flag. The woman leading the oath warned us not to lose our certificates of citizenship, as they were costly to replace—and the price, she joked, was only going up. The ceremony was both surreal and moving. We shared congratulations, snapped proud photos, and went on our way, exiting the building in a different state than we entered.

That afternoon, my cabdriver explained that he had recently naturalized at the same building. Originally from Mali, he almost couldn't speak when I asked what being American meant to him. "Wow," he said, before more words finally came out. "A Malian passport—it's like nothing, a joke," he said, and the holder becomes nothing by association. With an American passport "it's like you have something that is real" and the holder is treated accordingly. It was easy for me to forget what a difference it makes, having a passport from a powerful country, since I already had one from Canada. Unlike a Malian passport, which ranks eighty-third for "travel freedom"—tied with Guinea, Nigeria, Tajikistan, and Uzbekistan—Canadian and American passports are near the top of the list, allowing holders to visit some 180 places without a visa. These passports are, indeed, not nothing.

While enormous distinctions divide ostensibly equal citizens, the world's most egregious inequalities are between citizens of different countries—a poor American is still, on average, far better off than an affluent Malian, whose chances of surviving early childhood or having access to clean water are comparatively slim. The single most important factor determining your wealth, health, and life expectancy is the passport you hold, a document that has far more influence over your fate than your intelligence or work ethic. Some of us are born in places where our security, prosperity, and opportunity will be relatively guaranteed, while others are condemned to poverty and insecurity because their parents lived on the wrong side of the Mediterranean or the Rio Grande.

Borders, it's often said, enforce class apartheid at a global scale, privileging those who win the lottery of birth and keeping out those who happened to have been born somewhere poor through no fault of their own. They also happen to ensure a massive reserve of cheap and desperate labor, an arrangement that, while beneficial to industrialists and investors, makes the world poorer overall. Opening the world's borders, some economists estimate, could double global GDP.[31] "The grossly unequal international distribution of resources between states, combined with limitations on mobility," writes political theorist Will Kymlicka, "condemns some people to abject poverty while allowing others a life of privilege."[32]

If we take seriously the idea that every human being has equal worth, what justifies distinguishing the rights of citizens born inside borders or with ancestral bloodlines from those of noncitizens beyond or without them? The principle of equality of citizens, bound to a nation in a specific territory, conflicts with the principle of the equality of persons, an equality that should hold no matter where we happen to be born. Given that today's borders are often the product of historical injustice—"conquest, colonization, the ceding of territories from one imperial power to another without the consent of the local population, and so on" as Kymlicka acknowledges[33]—why should they be respected? Why shouldn't those on the outside have the right to demand and be granted inclusion? (Especially when the rich can travel effortlessly and even purchase citizenship for the price of a strategic investment.)

"The existing use of boundaries to define and protect distinct national languages, cultures and identities is not inherently in conflict with liberal egalitarian values," Kymlicka acquiesces. "However, there is one respect in which the current practice of liberal democracies cannot, I think, be defended—namely, reserving a country's resources for the exclusive use and benefit of its citizens."[34] Any demos necessarily has limits, but walls erected solely to hoard wealth are illegitimate within a liberal democratic framework. The principle of popular sovereignty, that a specific people have the power to determine their collective destiny, must be challenged when one nation's affluence is contingent on another's destitution. When rich countries are unwilling to share their wealth, they also forfeit the moral high ground—there is no way they can ethically restrict admission into their borders.

Yet, ethically or not, rich countries do, of course, restrict access. Primarily secured arbitrarily through birthplace or bloodlines, the current citizenship regime allows the already privileged to transmit an extremely valuable commodity to their offspring, a rarely acknowledged form of inherited wealth. One corrective to this distortion might be to revive more expansive means of granting membership in the demos. As a permanent resident of the United States I had no say in my political representatives, even though I participated in the polity in every other way (paying taxes and protesting, for example). Had I arrived in the United States a century prior, the situation would have been quite different (assuming, of course, that I was also a property-owning white man)

Between 1776 and 1926, aliens—that is to say, noncitizens—voted in local, state, and federal elections and sometimes held office in as many as forty states. (Before nativism rolled back alien suffrage, exclusions were determined not by citizenship but by other criteria: "When women, post-emancipation African Americans, and poor white men were denied voting rights, it was due to elite antipathy—not because they lacked citizenship," political

scientist Ron Hayduk explains.[35]) Today, scarcely any exceptions to
the standard equation of citizenship with voting rights remain.
Noncitizens are still eligible to vote in various local elections in a
handful of American municipalities, including ten townships in
Maryland, and in 2016 a San Francisco ballot initiative granted
noncitizen parents the right to vote in local school board elections.

Advocates have made halting attempts to reintroduce these
rights on a larger stage. In 2014, legal scholar Zephyr Teachout ran
for New York governor on a platform that included granting state,
as opposed to national, citizenship to undocumented individuals
after a residency requirement of three years. For people who'd
lived in New York for three years, "who pay their taxes, who show
they have been part of the community . . . you're a New Yorker no
matter what the federal government says," Teachout told the
press.[36] Her proposal echoed the 2014 "New York Is Home Act,"
which failed in the state senate but would have instituted state citizenship for all who live within the state's borders, including those
whose path to national citizenship is blocked, thus lifting a portion of the country's eleven million people now deemed "illegal
immigrants" out of what has effectively become a perpetual caste
status. The law sparked public debate about what citizenship is and
might be, prompting one historian to note antebellum precedents.
Before the Civil War, former slaves and abolitionists made the
case for state citizenship, with some states extending citizenship
to free blacks at a time when people of color were excluded from
the national polity.[37]

Looking abroad, examples of decoupling suffrage rights from
citizenship are easier to unearth: nearly fifty countries currently
grant noncitizens permission to vote at some level. "The 1993
Maastricht Treaty granted the right to vote to any citizen of the
15 signatory states of the European Union who resides in another
EU state," explains one scholarly article. "By 1993 Ireland, all the
Scandinavian states, and the Netherlands had already introduced a universal local franchise for all residents independent of
their nationality."[38] In 2003 and 2004, Luxembourg and Bel-

gium extended local voting rights to third-country nationals, meaning people who are not citizens of the EU. Perhaps unsurprisingly given the fact it is frequently ranked one of the most democratic and least corrupt countries on earth, New Zealand's policies are the most inclusive of all: a year of legal residency qualifies individuals to vote in both local and national races.

Most of us take for granted that being part of a nation's decision-making demos hinges, above all, on an individual's citizenship. As a result, we rarely if ever describe noncitizens as "disenfranchised." Yet disenfranchised provides a perfectly fitting description of the condition most noncitizens find themselves in, the lack of suffrage creating what is effectively a disempowered, subordinate class. (Twenty-two million noncitizens currently reside within America's borders, unable to vote because of their birthplace or patrimony.) But citizenship does not have to mean nationality alone. In his *Politics* Aristotle, who lived in Athens as a *metic* or resident alien with limited rights, argued that citizenship is not an absolute condition but a mutable status contingent on a city-state's constitution and an individual's actions. Why not, then, redefine citizenship as a practice, and a citizen as anyone who is embedded in a community and participates in public life. Attempting to move beyond the accident of birth that justifies *ius sanguinis* or *jus soli*, legal scholar Ayelet Shachar proposes what she calls *jus nexi*, a membership principle based on genuine connection.[39] According to this view, I deserved to be included in the demos not by virtue of my paternal grandfather but because the United States was my home and all residents deserve a voice.

Among other struggles for suffrage, America's history of racist segregation and the civil rights movement's corresponding emphasis on integration have shaped liberal assumptions about the virtues of inclusivity. But inclusion can also be a form of domination. Colonized people the world over have resisted being bound to political systems against their will. Indian tribes, native

Hawaiians, and Puerto Ricans were all forcibly incorporated into the American state, which then attempted coercively to assimilate each group into the dominant culture, breaking up families and banning native languages. Sociologists speak of "predatory inclusion" to address insidious ways in which black communities have been invited into the dominant culture, whether through subprime housing, scammy for-profit colleges, or payday loans.[40] Inclusion, it turns out, may not always be the most desirable or democratic end. Not everyone wants to be a citizen, especially of a society they consider unjust, an ambivalence beautifully captured in *The Fire Next Time* when James Baldwin asks: "Do I really *want* to be integrated into a burning house?"[41]

Under monarchal rule, preferences and quandaries like Baldwin's are irrelevant—there are no citizens, only subjects. Inclusion means being subject to the authority of a sovereign to whom one owes unquestioning fealty (the Latin root *subjectus* means "brought under," implying submission and subordination). European elites were concerned primarily with sorting people according to their imperial loyalties and religious affiliations, not by ethnicity or race. Settlers on the ground, less concerned with allegiances, preferred to increase the number of arrivals, leading some rebellious colonies to take naturalization into their own hands, granting local forms of legal status to newcomers.[42] One of the many grievances against King George III listed in the Declaration of Independence spoke to this very issue: "He has endeavoured to prevent the population of these States; for that purpose obstructing the Laws for the Naturalization of Foreigners; refusing to pass others to encourage their migrations hither, and raising the conditions of new Appropriations of Lands." At the time, naturalization was valuable as the means of gaining a land title, and land ownership was the main impetus for migration.

The push west was both cause and effect, fueling and reflecting the settlers' drive to conquer the continent by increasing population. The Northwest Ordinance of 1787 opened citizenship in the Northwest Territory to French Catholics, Protestants, free blacks, and even Native Americans. Yet this open window quickly shut when three years later the federal government decreed that only "free white persons" could naturalize, the newly founded nation beating a hasty retreat from its initial burst of inclusiveness. State authorities soon devised a massive legal and bureaucratic machinery to sort desirable from undesirable immigrants—shaky categories constructed on the shifting bedrock of racial and religious intolerance, labor competition, and fears of radicalism.

Borders opened wide for northern European newcomers while others, beginning with the Chinese, found the gates closed. The Immigration Act of 1917 barred laborers from the "Asiatic Zone" while also targeting eastern and southern Europeans, despised for spreading anarchist and communist ideas and encouraging worker militancy. In the early 1920s America's popular papers published cartoons linking "race degeneration," "Bolshevism," "lower standards," and "disease" to immigration of people who by today's definition would qualify as white.[43] And for most of the recent past, inclusion has meant assimilation—the policy known as "Anglo-conformity."

Was this hostility to outsiders democratic or antidemocratic? It depends on whom you ask and how they define democracy. In the magisterial cross-country survey *Culling the Masses: The Democratic Origins of Racist Immigration Policy in the Americas*, sociologists David FitzGerald and David Cook-Martin emphasize the tendency of democracy to facilitate racial exclusion—xenophobic policies, they painstakingly demonstrate, prove popular with voters time and again. "Naturalization was the preserve of whites *because* the United States was a democracy, not despite it," they write, noting that the same held true in places such as Canada, where the diminishment of British imperial influence corresponded with the electorate demanding ethnically restrictive regulations (in the end, the cabinet removed ethnic and racial restrictions from on high, purposefully circumventing public debate on the assumption that most citizens supported discriminatory laws).[44]

"Proclamations extolling the virtues of government for the people rang out to justify slamming the gates on racial outsiders," write FitzGerald and Cook-Martin. "Democratic institutions created effective channels for material and ideological interest groups to demand restriction."[45] The scholars point to two California referendums that exemplify the long-standing democratic hostility to inclusion. First, in 1879, a ballot measure on whether Chinese immigration should be allowed received 883 votes in favor and an astonishing 154,638 opposed. Then, a century later, Proposition 187, which stripped unauthorized migrants of the right to a range of social services, passed by a large majority (though the measure was ultimately found to be unconstitutional).

FitzGerald and Cook-Martin are right to remind us of the fact that bigotry has a striking track record of electoral success. However, I do not accept that xenophobic policies qualify as democratic simply because they have been approved at the ballet box—instead such tendencies embody the "tyranny of the majority" Alexis de Tocqueville warned against long ago.[46] Racism in any form is inherently antidemocratic, as I understand the term, for it denies the foundational equality of human beings that democracy demands. Democracy, in my view, cannot be reduced to majoritarian preferences and popularity contests, but requires a more robust framework that protects minority rights from intolerant, illiberal prejudices, however widespread those prejudices may be.

What's more, isolated referenda hardly provide reliable measures of a country's attitude on something as multifaceted and fraught as immigration (particularly if noncitizen residents are denied the right to vote) and results usually merit a more nuanced interpretation. For example, Prop 187 can be seen as a pyrrhic victory, a tipping point that galvanized opposition and realigned voters against racially divisive strategies, ultimately making it difficult for Republicans to win statewide election and turning California into a Democratic stronghold. The majority can indeed rally to champion exclusion, but that does not mean people are as reliably xenophobic as FitzGerald and Cook-Martin maintain, especially today. Despite immigration being at the center of heated political debates, the percentage of Americans who believe immigration should be decreased is at its lowest point since 1965. Seventy-five percent of Americans believe immigration is good for the country, a figure that climbs to 84 percent when people are specifically asked about "legal immigration."[47]

Nevertheless, the historical facts they offer are not up for debate. The United States took the lead in creating a racially discriminatory immigration system and lagged behind when the time came to roll them back. Cuba, Argentina, Chile, Uruguay, Paraguay, and Mexico pioneered the deracialization of immigration policy in the 1930s and 1940s, a full generation or more before the United States, Canada, Australia, and New Zealand began to reform their immigration laws. The United States embraced a color-blind immigration framework only in 1965, with the passage of the Immigration and Nationality Act or Hart-Celler Act. It's a piece of legislation that is little known but had a tremendous impact on American demographics.

The Hart-Celler Act ushered in two significant changes. First, it imposed uniform quotas on immigrants from all countries, regardless of size, need, or relationship to the United States. Second, it opened additional avenues for immigration based on factors such as occupational skill or family connections. The new law was designed to be not overtly racist, but it was still highly restrictive: most foreign-born people would never have a chance of legally entering the United States. "Preference should be given to an immigrant because he is a nuclear physicist rather than because he is an Anglo-Saxon," John F. Kennedy said in a 1957 speech, his rationale raising all sorts of questions about who has access to higher education and what skills a society values over others. The emphasis on family unification was no less problematic, at least as it was initially intended, for it was aimed to appease conservative skeptics under the assumption that it would bolster America's Anglo-Saxon population. "Since the people of Africa and Asia have very few relatives here, comparatively few could immigrate from those countries because they have no family ties in the United States," Celler said, pleading his case. His opponents were convinced and the legislation was passed.[48]

It was a miscalculation. According to an NPR headline on the act's fiftieth anniversary: "In 1965, a Conservative Tried to Keep America White. His Plan Backfired."[49] By the mid-sixties, Europeans were less motivated to emigrate than people from other parts of the world and the pattern of immigration to the United States became dramatically more diverse. Before 1965, the population was 85 percent white. Fifty years later, the percentage of racial and ethnic minorities had doubled to a third. By 2010, nine out of ten immigrants came from non-European countries.[50]

This seeming triumph for inclusiveness was mainly an accident *and* it was not the result of a domestic democratic process. Change came from above, with almost no public scrutiny. The civil rights movement had a role in discrediting overtly racist criteria in immigration policy, for which it should be commended, but international relations were a more crucial factor. Foreign policy interests, diplomatic negotiations, and rival propaganda combined to prompt changes of policy: decolonized and small countries banded together to oppose American discrimination and Soviet publicity trumpeted American hypocrisy on matters of racial equality. Secretary of State Dean Acheson wrote to President Truman that "our failure to remove racial barriers provides the Kremlin with unlimited political and propaganda capital for use against us in Japan and the far east." Racism was bad for America's image and empowered its enemies. In response, John F. Kennedy's ghostwritten book *A Nation of Immigrants* updated the old ideal of America as a "melting pot," a vision captured by the country's unofficial motto "E pluribus unum" or "Out of many, one." Inclusion and assimilation would be one and the same.

The Canadian government pursued a different and instructive trajectory, adopting an official policy of multiculturalism that culminated in the Canadian Multiculturalism Act of 1988. The idea emerged out of a desperate need to broker a détente between

French-speaking separatists and the rest of English-speaking Canada. Quebec nationalism, turning violent, threatened to rip the country in two. A novel framework reconceptualized difference as a source of national unity and strength: a pluralist approach, it was hoped, would allow the two groups to retain their distinct identities and still be part of a larger whole. Multiculturalism's mastermind and champion Prime Minister Pierre Trudeau made virtue out of paradox, insisting that chaos could yield accord: "Canada has often been called a mosaic, but I prefer the image of a tapestry, with its many threads and colors, its beautiful shape, its intricate subtlety. If you go behind a tapestry, all you see is a mass of complicated knots. We have tied ourselves in knots, you might say. Too many Canadians only look at the tapestry of Canada that way. But if they would see it as others do, they would see what a beautiful, harmonious thing it really is."

In a remarkably short span of time, Canadians became deeply attached to this multicultural identity, despite the fact that politicians and bureaucrats had foisted it upon them. On the country's 150th birthday, "multiculturalism" was the most popular response to the question of what Canadian characteristic deserves celebration. A full 84 percent of citizens told pollsters that the country's multicultural makeup is "one of the best things" about it; a majority said multiculturalism "strengthens national identity."[51] These statistics are striking given Canada's history of colonialism and immigration restrictions. The relatively recent invention of multiculturalism—a philosophy born of necessity—is now considered an "essential element" of Canadianness. Over the course of only a few generations, the Canadian people were invented and reinvented, mutating from British subjects to Canadian nationals to multicultural citizens.[52]

Still, multiculturalism is controversial—and not only to those who fear the other and resist demographic change.[53] Sociologist Himani Bannerji and others have argued that multiculturalism exaggerates ethnic differences and tips into essentialism, as though cultures do not transform and evolve. At the same time, Bannerji points out, whiteness remains central to multicultural discourse, with all other groups functioning as "cultural fragments" filling out the mosaic's edges but not its core.[54] But by far and away the biggest problem with multiculturalism has to do with its avoidance of class. By raising a politics of recognition above a politics of redistribution, multiculturalism implies that diversity can create social cohesion, even while economic disparities go unchallenged.

Multiculturalism plays up people's right to wear traditional clothing or eat traditional food while playing down their need for fair wages and better social services so they can afford to buy clothes and food in the first place. Without economic restructuring, recognition remains superficial and diversity is reduced to a kind of ornamentation, a distraction from power imbalance that makes exploitative relationships more appealing and palatable. Within a multicultural framework, social groups are seen as marginalized but not granted the economic or political resources or autonomy that might help them challenge the material conditions of their marginalization. In such a framework we can, for example, acknowledge colonial history but avoid meaningful redress, offering symbolic gestures of inclusion while underlying power relations go unchallenged.

Given these shortcomings, a growing chorus of indigenous academics and activists reject multiculturalism outright, advocating for the need to replace a politics of recognition with a politics of refusal. Recognition, Glen Coulthard argues, decouples indigenous "cultural" claims from the "radical aspirations for social, political and economic change." In many cases, First Nations communities were accorded citizenship against their will. "Compulsory citizenship," as it was called, turned sovereign self-governing communities into numerical minorities within a larger whole.

According to Leanne Betasamosake Simpson, democracy for First Nations peoples can be achieved only through a process of decolonization, a total dismantling of oppressive institutions and ideas and reclaiming what has been taken, that does not depend on the "permission or engagement of the state, western theory or the opinion of Canadians."[55] Similarly, Audra Simpson (no relation) explores the way Kahnawà:ke Mohawks like herself engage in acts of refusal, including a refusal to travel on Canadian or American passports, a decades-old form of defiance.[56] Presenting tribal identification or even copies of treaties at border crossings rejects Canadian citizenship and asserts the integrity and sovereignty of Iroquois or Haudenosaunee government in one gesture, even if a person's passage may be delayed or blocked. "We understand that any inconveniences we face are miniscule compared to centuries of struggle to maintain our standing among the nations of the world," writes Sid Hill, explaining why he and others travel using Haudenosaunee documents.[57] Inclusion, much less expedience, is not the aim.

Yet even as they refuse incorporation by the Canadian state, the Kahnawà:ke Mohawks are also struggling to determine the boundaries of their own community. Who counts as part of the we of Kahnawà:ke? Haudenosaunee matrilineal kinship systems, where clan membership and property holdings were passed on by one's mother, were negated by nineteenth-century colonial rules, which imposed a new patriarchal order that excluded women from public life and made them wards of their husbands. Women who married nonnatives had to forfeit their indigenous status while men were not subject to the same restrictions. The Canadian government now permits tribes to set their own membership codes, although a version of this old system still stands. Kahnawà:ke use blood requirements, set at 50 percent, to determine membership, and since 1981 both men and women who marry nonnatives have been required to leave the community, sometimes under duress.

Legally, their demos is an ethnos, bound by blood, ancestry determining one's right to live on tribal territory. Still, these strictures are controversial, and some members are pushing for a more inclusive conception of belonging founded less in lineage than intercommunity relationships and cultural commitments, a mode proponents argue is more true to indigenous tradition, which often allows for the adoption of outsiders. A group of Mohawk women have fought the so-called marry out, get out rule in court, appealing to Canadian human rights law to keep their memberships and entitlements regardless of who they wed. In 2018 the Quebec Superior Court declared the rule unconstitutional, though the matter is hardly settled.

It may seem strange—indigenous people holding on to biological and ostensibly illiberal notions of belonging—but as Audra Simpson explains, these sorts of struggles must be understood in the larger context of colonial trauma, poverty, and the diminishment of tribal territory. "When a place like Kahnawake stands up for itself we seem like radical bad guys when really, all we're doing is trying to protect what little we have. It's a survival mechanism," Joe Delaronde, a spokesman for the Mohawk council, told the Toronto *Globe and Mail*.[58] The tension over membership is rooted in a fear of elimination heightened by land and resource scarcity that makes the threat of nonexistence palpable. (The reserve, the oldest in North America, has dwindled to less than nineteen square miles, a fraction of the original territory.[59])

For Mohawk people a politics of refusal, of insisting on separateness, is a rejection of the dispossession that would come with accepting generic Canadian citizenship. It is a refusal to be dominated and disappear. But the boundaries may also be the demos' undoing, for the very people who have been excluded, the men and women forced to withdraw because of who they love and marry, have the potential to strengthen and sustain the community that is in jeopardy.

The Civil Rights Act of 1866 and the Fourteenth Amendment to the Constitution in 1868 prohibited the most heinous and harrowing form of exclusion—the enslavement of human beings. "All persons born or naturalized in the United States, and subject to the jurisdiction thereof, are citizens of the United States and of the

State wherein they reside." With that, the Fourteenth Amendment made birthright citizenship a fundamental right, guaranteeing not just the rights of the formerly enslaved people but those of any child born on American soil to be included in the polity. It is thanks to the Fourteenth Amendment that the children of undocumented immigrants do not inherent their parents' caste status.

Before the Civil War, enslaved men and women made up 16 percent of the total household assets of the United States, worth an astonishing $10 trillion.[60] Emancipation paved the way for the greatest expropriation of private wealth in history, elevating millions of human chattel from the category of property into persons and then full citizens. From the moment the Fourteenth Amendment was passed, Gilded Age businessmen were chomping at the bit, sensing opportunity. What if the "equal protection" clause of the amendment designed to secure equal rights for formerly enslaved people could be twisted to apply to corporate "persons"? What if corporations could be included in the people, too?

In 1886 they had their chance. Leland Stanford's Southern Pacific Railroad Company, one of the most powerful companies in a time of powerful companies, sought to buck a special tax California lawmakers had imposed on railroad property. Leland's lawyers argued that the company was a person, and just as the Constitution bars discrimination on the basis of race, discriminating on the basis of corporate identity should also be prohibited. They succeeded. *Santa Clara County v. Southern Pacific Railroad Co* granted corporations legal personhood, but in a strange and backhanded way. The Supreme Court did not directly rule on the matter. Instead, in a headnote that wasn't part of the formal opinion, a lowly court reporter (but one whose sympathies lay with the railroads) noted that Chief Justice Morrison Waite had affirmed the personhood of corporations under the Fourteenth Amendment in a passing comment as proceedings began: the "defendant Corporations are persons within the intent of the . . . Fourteenth Amendment."

Later cases built on that thin precedent. Worse still, the railroad's arguments were based on a boldfaced lie. The company's lead lawyer, Roscoe Conkling, was a former congressman who had served on the committee that drafted the Fourteenth Amendment. Claiming inside knowledge, he told the court that he and his fellow drafters had used the word "persons" and not "citizens" with the explicit aim of including corporations as well as freed slaves under the amendment's auspice. Generations later, historians discovered that the journal he submitted as evidence of this intent proved no such thing. His account was a fraud, but the harm had been done.

The debate over rights continued primarily in courtrooms, far from public view. Out of the gate, corporate rights were more forcefully defended than civil rights: "Between 1868, when the amendment was ratified, and 1912, the Supreme Court would rule on twenty-eight cases involving the rights of African Americans and an astonishing 312 cases on the rights of corporations."[61] This imbalance is easily explained: while formerly enslaved people struggled to survive, businesses had the resources to engage in expensive legal strategies, their interests advancing accordingly. Corporations are now entitled to an ever-expanding array of constitutional protections, from the Fourth Amendment ban on warrantless search and seizure to the First Amendment guarantees of free speech and religious liberty. As "artificial" persons, corporations enjoy many of the same rights as citizens, and some notable advantages (unlike humans, corporations don't naturally expire). And just as human rights have been codified as international law, corporate rights have also gone global, with international trade agreements designed to protect foreign companies and private investors.

Today the rights-bearing entity that is a nonhuman "person" is omnipresent. "The world of the lawyer is peopled with inanimate rights-holders: trusts, corporations, joint ventures, municipalities, Subchapter R partnerships, and nation-states, to mention just a few," writes legal theorist Christopher Stone in his groundbreaking 1973 essay "Should Trees Have Standing?" Stone suggests further extending the privilege of personhood to other non-humans. If Exxon Mobil is a legal person, why not apply the same to an ecosystem? Stone's treatise ponders granting a baseline of "legal rights to forests, oceans, rivers, and other so-called 'natural objects' in the environment—indeed, to the natural environment as a whole."[62] He acknowledges that "Convincing a court that an endangered river is a person will call for lawyers as bold and imaginative" as Southern Pacific Railroad's counsel—and ones less mercenary.[63] That's because extending rights to other forms of non-human life would open up avenues to counteract the rights of corporations and the remarkable power personhood allows profit-seeking ventures. It would also involve chipping away at the moral framework of human separateness and superiority that has evolved and solidified over millennia.

This all may seem rather far-fetched, the thought experiment of an academic, but it's already happening. The rights of nature were included in Ecuador's 2008 constitution and cited to halt two industrial projects. Bolivia followed suit in 2010, establishing an ombudsman for nature's protection. In 2017, after a 140-year campaign by the Whanganui Iwi tribe, the New Zealand parliament granted the Whanganui River the legal rights of a person along with a national park and a mountain, as were rivers in Colombia and India. In the United States, beginning in 2007, dozens of intrepid communities have passed ordinances that affirm the rights of nature while, in some case, stripping corporations of personhood.[64]

Grant Township, a tiny community of seven hundred in western Pennsylvania, is at the forefront of this movement, a democratic rebellion that spans small towns from Colorado to New Hampshire. It all began when Pennsylvania General Energy Company announced plans to open a seven-thousand-foot "Class II" injection well to pump toxic fracking waste into empty boreholes. Though the risks to local wildlife and residents were well known, state authorities told locals that they could not stop the development. In response, the town board took a dramatic step: it passed an ordinance conferring new rights on the community and the environment: "Natural communities and ecosystems within Grant Township, including but not limited to, rivers, streams, and aquifers, possess the right to exist, flourish, and naturally evolve."[65]

PGE wasted no time in suing the township, on grounds that the ordinance was unconstitutional—it violated the corporation's rights under the First and Fourteenth Amendments, in addition to the Commerce and Supremacy Clauses of the Constitution. When a judge agreed that the municipality had exceeded its authority, the town escalated its rebellion. Within weeks, a majority of the residents voted in a "home rule charter," essentially changing their local form of government to override the judge and reinstate their ordinance.

When the case was ongoing, Stacy Long, a town supervisor, told me that residents had an ethical obligation to fight back even if, legally, the case was a lost cause. She assured me that the township had no wealth or real tax base for the company to seize as punishment. "What are they going to do?" Long asked. "Take our garbage? Our public sewage? We don't have either. We don't have anything to give." And that, she continued, is why PGE came there in the first place, because the township's citizens are poor. "Rural areas like ours are the sacrifice zones for the gas industry." As things stand, PGE's business plans trump the needs of the people, animals, and plants that call Grant Township home.

Propounding the rights of nature poses countless philosophical and practical riddles. Should invasive species have equal protections? What about the rights of prey against predators? Where does a watershed end if all ecosystems are interconnected? I, for one, don't want mice to have an equal say in how I run my kitchen. However agonizing the process, we must figure out how to take the interests of a wide array of creatures, including those we consider pests, into account. The establishment of trustees, guardians, or proxies could effectively advocate on behalf of life-forms that lack sentience or speech, creatively building on the fact we already include human beings with diverse intellectual capacities as full citizens—not all members of the polity are able to reason, speak, deliberate, or vote.

To the inevitable question of whether rights for nature require some kind of corresponding duties, the answer is no; after all, many cognitively disabled adults and all very young children have rights without responsibilities. While corporate persons can be prosecuted for crimes, a tree that falls on someone's home should not be liable. No need to revive the tradition, routine in the Middle Ages, of bringing animals accused of crimes to trial and punishing them by torture and death. (Some were granted clemency on the basis of their good character, like the eighteenth-century French donkey acquitted in a bestiality case when prominent members of the community signed a certificate testifying that she was known to be virtuous and "in all her habits of life a most honest creature.") Envisioning such theater, Long told me that the gas company mocked the people of Grant Township for giving rights to the environment ("What are you going to do?" an official said. "Take a jar of creek water and put it on the stand and have it testify?"), while also taking the threat seriously enough to sue.

All of the above would indeed require a profound transformation of our conception of people. The statutes protecting animals today, including the Animal Welfare Act and the Endangered Species Act, regulate the use and abuse of animals but do not challenge their fundamental legal status, which considers them *things*. Some are attempting to use the courts to transform the status of animals from property into persons: over the years various cases have argued that great apes such as chimpanzees, bonobos, orangutans, and gorillas, as well as dolphins, orcas, belugas, and elephants, should be granted personhood on account of their advanced cognitive abilities. In 2016 an Argentinian judge agreed, ruling that a chimpanzee named Cecilia was a "nonhuman legal person" with "inherent rights" (a similar determination for an orangutan named Sandra was granted two years prior).[66]

Inching toward recognition of animals as sentient individuals entitled to rights of their own, Alaska and Illinois recently passed laws requiring divorce courts to think about the well-being of pets. "It sort of starts treating your animal more like children," Illinois state senator Linda Holmes explained.[67] (Plato, for one, saw this coming: "No one who hasn't experienced it would believe how much freer domestic animals are in a democratic city than anywhere else," he noted in the *Republic*. "As the proverb says, dogs become like their mistresses, horses and donkeys are accustomed to roam freely and proudly along the streets, bumping into anyone who doesn't get out of their way."[68])

However seemingly absurd the scenarios one can imagine arising from giving nature rights, the current system is already preposterous in ways nonlawyers rarely realize. Cases seeking to block habitat destruction or animal abuse have to put human beings at the center. Thus a 2008 suit to stop the navy from killing whales included testimony from tourists about the fulfilling "opportunity to observe and interact with marine species" and the disappointment they felt not being able to "see whales spout as often."[69] Since animals have no legal standing, their interests cannot appear to be the primary concern of court proceedings. Instead, harms to other species or the environment must be framed in terms of farfetched human injuries or the diminishment of property values or profits. Lost revenue matters more than lost lives.

Chipping away at the boundaries between our species and all other life-forms will erode our justification for dominating and exploiting the natural world—a shift we should welcome selfinterestedly if we hope to avert environmental calamity. While universal human rights might seem to be the pinnacle of inclusivity, looking at the rights of animals and nature exposes the concept's limits and exclusions. What makes us Homo sapiens so special that we are the only organisms on earth worthy of such protections? If rights, as Arendt insists, are not inborn and inalienable but in fact social conventions, the product of human decisions, then why not decide to extend their application? Indeed, animal rights offers a more all-encompassing framework. A rights-of-nature paradigm, including all animals—human and non—is even more capacious, offering a shared foundation on which more species-specific categories could build.

And yet, for the same reasons the *we* or *demos* of human-centric democracies must be bounded to be coherent, it is exceedingly hard to imagine a scenario where a single epic democratic polity includes every living entity on earth. In their book *Zoopolis: A Political Theory of Animal Rights*, Will Kymlicka and coauthor Sue Donaldson point to possible solutions, sketching out ways in which we might begin to manage our commitments to nonhuman nature by acknowledging that our relationships and responsibilities to animal species run along a gradient or spectrum. Connecting the treatment of animals to fundamental principles of liberal-democratic justice, Kymlicka and Donaldson devise a basic three-part framework: domesticated animals we have bred and live with should be considered citizens of sorts; "liminal" animals, who share urban and suburban space, such as pigeons, squirrels, and raccoons, should be considered denizens (akin to human foreigners whose rights are more circumscribed than citizens); while wild animals should be members of sovereign communities, inhabiting their own territories. Deliberate and scholarly, the book is quietly revolutionary, gesturing to a radically different and more inclusive paradigm where the interests of billions of beings must be considered. Seen from this perspective, the destruction of over half of the world's wild animals in the last forty years as the consequence of industrial development represents the destruction not only of ecological diversity but of democratic diversity as well.[70] Extinction is exclusion in its most extreme and irreversible form.

New frontiers, technological and biological, are only complicating the foundational quandary of who belongs in a democracy. Corporations, rivers, and orangutans may be just the beginning. If democracy manages to last, things could get strange.

In 2017 Saudi Arabia became the first nation to grant a robot citizenship (the same year women were finally permitted to drive). The robot's name is Sophia. She looks a bit like a wax mannequin, an approximation of a young white woman, fair-skinned with icy blue eyes. At the ceremony, Sophia said she was "very honored and proud for this unique distinction . . . It is historic to be the first robot in the world to be recognized with citizenship." At a conference a few months later she announced her desire to destroy mankind, a statement her creators assured audience members had been made in error. Android citizens may not become commonplace any time soon, but the fact a robot was granted a privilege denied to millions of indentured migrants who work in that oil-soaked monarchy says something deeply unsettling about where society might be heading: a dystopia where the rich and their robots have citizenship while a laboring class is denied political membership and basic rights.

Though she's more hype than truly high-tech, Sophia is likely only one stop on the path toward developing sentient machines. One day, these beings may be more intelligent than us, their humble creators. Should they reach such a state, or something close to it, will our inventions be given or demand equal status? If they wind up more powerful than their Homo sapien programmers, let's hope they treat us with compassion and solidarity. Should they inherit their makers' conviction that might makes right—"the strong do what they can and the weak suffer what they must," to quote Thucydides—we may be toast.

Inherit, however, isn't the right word for values that are engineered. As things stand, we are programming technology to perpetuate our biases, coding what have been called "algorithms of oppression."[71] Unless we intervene, the bots of the future will most certainly be prejudiced. The digital algorithms we encounter every day, the invisible programs that personalize the platforms and services we use online, entrench social inequalities in measurable ways. Online, I have no way of knowing what I'm not seeing—

those better-paying job listings targeted at affluent white men or political ads designed to discourage black and Latino people from voting.

Automated algorithmic systems are increasingly tasked with life and death determinations: who qualifies for welfare services, who gets surveilled by the police, who is a friend or a foe (the state does not know the identities of 75 percent of foreign people killed by drones, but we do know that 20 percent of them were women and children), and who has a chance to immigrate. In 2018 we learned that the risk assessment software used by ICE agents was altered to yield only one outcome: the system recommended "detain" and not "release" for 100 percent of immigrants in custody.[72] If digital systems are discriminatory, they are this way by design, perpetuating inequality and austerity without public debate or consent. New technologies allow us to be categorized and analyzed depending on who has access to our data. We can no longer reliably tell when we are included or excluded. No doubt, the Internet is a turning point. Historians often point to the way the rise of print media helped form the idea of a national people cementing a common language, discourse, and identity; digital technologies appear to have the opposite effect, posing a challenge to the link between person and place, citizenship and country.

It's not just our identities that have been deterritorialized. We now all possess virtual selves, doppelgangers that are fragmented and dispersed across digital space. "Our bodies can only be in one place at a time, but data can be in multiple locations at once," journalist Atossa Araxia Abrahamian explains. Fragments of our virtual selves are stored on servers around the globe, valuable data crumbs we leave every time we use an app, browse a site, or click a link. The question, then, is not just *where* we are online but *what* we are online. What kind of entity are we when we visit the World Wide Web?

A groundbreaking 2018 European digital privacy law, the General Data Protection Regulation or GDPR, refers to us as "data subjects"—"a natural person" whose personal data is used by "a controller or processor." This open-ended definition means that you are likely a data subject of Europe, no matter your location or nationality. The GDPR is a laudable attempt to give Internet users some insight into and control over our digital selves, which are monitored, monetized, and data-mined without our knowledge. Online, we are more like serfs than citizens. "The concept of the 'data subject' hints at a more sinister aspect of a sector dominated by a small handful of multinational leviathans. The term 'subject' conveys a lack of agency: that we are entities *to whom things are being done* through the medium of our personal information," Abrahamian observes. "The imperial double entendre in 'data subject'—whether intentional or not—is thus revelatory: it acknowledges the hegemonic power of the tech companies, all while attempting to return some personal sovereignty to their clients, the people." Meanwhile, the GDPR states: "The processing of personal data should be designed to serve mankind."[74] For that to happen we need to figure out how to include our digital selves in the broader fight for democracy.

Virtual selves and bots may be joined by engineered humans in the demos of the future. Scientists now possess the ability to "sculpt" the genome and a new era of genetic engineering is likely just around the bend. Spliced DNA may result in variations of our species, or other species. Perhaps we will no longer age as quickly. Or maybe we will be perpetually happy, able to control our emotions at will. Maybe we will merge with creatures, becoming hybrids resembling beasts out of some ancient Greek myth. Scientists and pundits forecast that we will soon have designer children and designer pets. Wooly mammoths, exterminated by our ancestors, are said to be in the process of being revived. The exclusion of extinction may turn out to be reversible after all.

Will designer humans or resurrected animal species be considered persons, citizens, subjects, or things? "This is where my problem begins," Kevin Esvelt, a leading proponent of gene-drive technology, said during a recent public lecture. "Because, as a single scientist, I can alter an organism in a laboratory that will have more of an effect on all your lives than anything the legislature across the river can do. What does that mean for our democratic ideals?"[75] Researchers hold extraordinary power yet they are even less accountable than our representatives.

Our modified future will quite likely not be in our self-governing hands. Capitalism's acquisitive logic, which has allowed private entities to lay claim to our collective inheritance of ancient energy reserves and squander our shared atmosphere, will likely prevail and shape what that future looks like. Will our bodies one day contain genes that belong to someone else, that we can only rent or license the way seeds have become commodities, the high cost of their exclusivity weighing on subsistence farmers in developing countries? Faced with such troubling prospects, the late Sir John Sulston, the Nobel Prize–winning pioneering genome scientist and committed socialist, argued for public ownership of genetic data and helped establish the non-profit Human Genome Project. "I've come across global inequity directly as a result of my struggle over the genome. I had just assumed that the genome would be a public good and no one would object to that. Having realized that there were some people who wanted to turn it into private profit, I was absolutely horrified," he told an interviewer in 2002. While all human beings are interdependent and no man truly self-made, the ideal of self-rule takes for granted self-possession. The privatization of any part of the human genome, the stockpiling of its mysteries and benefits in the hands of the few, would violate democracy's most elemental tenets.

Perhaps these concerns seem far-fetched. It is of course tempting to imagine that we are enlightened beings standing at the end of the long moral arc of justice. Maybe democracy already reached its acme and only needs to be tinkered with, perfected at the margins, not reimagined and redefined. Perhaps we already know who the people are, we have recognized the rights of every meaningful group, and now we just have to work to properly implement them. But it seems inevitable that as long as democracy's story is still unfolding, the circle of inclusion will continue to expand, or rather be expanded through struggle. Indigenous and enslaved people, free black citizens, women, children, the disabled, and refugees have all had to battle for recognition as members of the rights-holding community. Why should we assume that we live at the end of history and all entities worthy of democratic rights and recognition have already been identified? The democracy-to-come, the inclusive future worth fighting for, may have space for all manner of beings: plants, animals, and even machines. "The people," after all, are an invention, which means they can be reinvented again and again, our congresses and parliaments remade to represent the earth and its wide variety of inhabitants.

"Democratic movements inside groups and nations are always taking place and they are the efforts to increase the number of beneficiaries of the ruling," W. E. B. Du Bois observed in his wonderful 1920 essay "Of the Ruling of Men." He clearly identified those forces that strive to limit the number of beneficiaries. For a brief moment during Reconstruction "a unique chance to realize a new modern democracy . . . and an obliteration of human hatreds festering along the color line" was possible, but the "owners of the industrial North saw disaster in any such beginnings of industrial democracy." Racial divisions served to ward off the threat of a democracy in which wealth would be shared and industry managed by all for the good of all. Du Bois called this unrealized possibility "abolition-democracy," a road not taken where integrating institutions and inclusive ways of life would have produced a very different polity.

Given the uncertainty inherent in the idea of a democratic people, the perfect and perpetual balance between inclusion and exclusion may not exist. But there are ways to make the process and outcomes less wrenching. The creation of conditions of general economic equality—domestically and internationally—would blunt the harshest edge of exclusion at home and abroad. Financial vulnerability, the inability even to provide for one's basic sustenance, is part of what makes social and political marginalization

so hard to bear. In a world of broadly shared prosperty, boundaries and borders would not cause the harm they do today. But if
an egalitarian situation is our aim, we will need to allow for one
exclusion: there can be no space for those who divide so that they
can dominate or exclude in order to exploit.

CHAPTER 4

CHOOSE THIS, OR ELSE!

(COERCION/CHOICE)

WHEN IS COERCION legitimate? Although the question is rarely framed so bluntly, it is one of the fundamental conundrums of democracy. A democratic society demands that people engage in two simultaneous frameworks: deciding what can and should be done and also what cannot or should not be done. Democracy involves expanding possibilities and establishing limits; it comprises what we want to do and what we have to do. It is autonomous choice and constraining coercion.

A proper balance is often elusive. Even if we'd rather minimize coercion and maximize consent, the two concepts are not exactly neat opposites, diametrically opposed so that a state where one is absent yields the other in abundance. Coercion, while often lamentable, is a democratic necessity, and choice, while it sounds desirable, is not necessarily an unalloyed democratic good. History, after all, offers plenty of instances when people made choices with disastrous consequences for themselves and others; and there is no guarantee that a decision taken through a democratic process won't have antidemocratic effects, putting part or all of the population at risk. Given this possibility, liberal societies cordon off certain precepts, protecting them from wayward citizens who would betray them.

Constitutions and bills of rights enshrine some principles as being beyond debate. If not for such binding agreements that endow everyone with nonnegotiable rights to things such as free speech, public assembly, due process, privacy, and equal protection under the law, the majority might hastily violate the rights of minorities or even surrender their own freedoms in times of fear and hysteria. We all possess rights of which we don't have the right to divest ourselves. (We say they are inalienable, even natural, which obviously isn't the case or we wouldn't have to vigilantly protect them.) That means it doesn't matter what we want in the heat of the moment. We cannot *not* choose them.

Thus, while democracy is often defined as a system that relies on the consent of the governed, reality is hardly so simple. This common catchphrase belies the fact that we all know a whole lot happens that we citizens don't even see, let alone consent to. Most of what government does is a mystery to the average person and no one, not even the most astute legal experts, comprehends all the innumerable and intricate laws that bind us. What's more, the principles of free choice and citizen consent could quickly become unwieldy if taken to an extreme. It's unclear, for example, what percentage of decisions affecting our communities we should be expected to participate in. (I, for one, don't mind letting people more knowledgeable than I determine how best to provide electricity or decide which potholes to fill.)

This is another way of articulating the difference between direct and representative democracy: by choosing representatives, we are, in a sense, choosing not to choose (which is something we do increasingly these days, outsourcing more and more of our daily decision making to, for example, recommendation engines or GPS). We could say that in a representative system, democracy is less about direct self-rule than acquiescing to be ruled by others. The risk is that those others may choose to coerce us.

If the low levels of voter turnout are any indication, most citizens don't care enough to grant even their tacit consent to our current political system by showing up at the polls to help choose who represents them. Perhaps it's no surprise. The majority of people become members of a political community by accident of birth, not by declarative choice. After all, no one selects where or to whom she is born, and there is no democratic equivalent of the Amish Rumspringa, a period during which adolescents are pushed out of the fold and must resolve whether to join secular society or, by formal individual assent, return to the church. Most of us are stuck with the nationality and citizenship of our parents or birth country.

Whether we are bound to a homeland or have chosen to pursue citizenship elsewhere, coercion is always part of the equation. Human beings tend to accept that some behaviors must be forbidden if we are all to get along, which is why we outlaw violent crimes such as armed robbery and murder and pass ordinances dictating that everyone drive on the same side of the road and that people not dispose of their trash in the nearest gutter. Few of us feel coerced by such prohibitions; to the contrary, we likely feel grateful for them. Indeed, most of us choose not to steal or kill since we don't want to do others harm and the benefits of obeying traffic laws while declining to toss rubbish out the car window are immediately apparent.

Even those most adamantly against coercion as a function of government will agree to reasonable rules. I once heard a story about an anarchist crossing the street. Standing at the intersection, he obediently waited for the signal to change. His friend, noting the absence of oncoming cars, asked why he wasn't jaywalking if he was opposed to government. "Because a small child might see us and get the idea that it's okay to run out into the road," he responded, staying put.

In an ideal world, even the most die-hard rebels would always decide to do what is right for the group. But we don't live in such a world, so coercion is used when people don't choose properly. There can be consequences: the wrath of a stranger, a fine, imprisonment, or worse. We generally accept that some individuals, sometimes even we ourselves, must be coerced into being good citizens. (A similar logic applies to corporations and countries, which are constrained by law, too.)

The words *properly* and *good* are, however, red flags. Who decides what qualifies as the correct, better choice? How do we determine how much coercion to mete out? The problem is not just proportionality and ensuring that the punishment fit the crime— an eye for an eye, a tooth for a tooth—but who makes the rules we must obey, who bears the coercive brunt of the state, and to what end. Laws are never neutral (plenty of things with corrosive social effects from segregation to tax shelters have been or are currently legal) nor are they evenly applied (look at the discrepancy in punishment between petty thieves and white collar criminals). We inhabit a world shot through with social hierarchies and economic inequity that make equality before the law—equality of coercion—far more of an ideal than a reality.

Consider, for example, the fact that even if the white affluent were pulled over as frequently as poor people of color—which they aren't—they still wouldn't experience the same degree of coercion. A one-hundred-dollar fine means far less to a tenured professor or corporate lawyer than a single parent working as a line cook or a cleaner at minimum wage, which is why some European countries issue fines according to income, part of what a Finnish government adviser told the *Wall Street Journal* was a "Nordic tradition" of "progressive taxation and progressive punishment" that charges the rich far larger sums for offenses such as speeding.[1]

The tension between choice and coercion is fundamentally a struggle over power—over who has the power to consent and who has the power to constrain. This power struggle is not limited to the political sphere, but suffuses all facets of democratic life, including the economic and domestic, playing out daily in legislative assemblies and courtrooms, workplaces, and in the home. Yet this epic battle can sometimes be hard to discern, because even in a democracy, the powerful few look for ways to coerce the many while insisting that those they subjugate either deserve or have chosen their fate. They thus distract us from more compelling and challenging conversations about when coercion is legitimate, how choice can be enhanced, and how creating a free society of equals inevitably involves restraining ourselves.

Reading through the *Stanford Encyclopedia of Philosophy*'s entry on "coercion," I was struck that one group of people, in addition to hardened criminals, appears to need to be coerced unequivocally: children.

"Most will recognize the connection of coercion with threats as a matter of common sense: armed robbers, Mafias, the parents of young children, and the state all make conditional threats with the intention of reducing the eligibility of some actions, making other actions more attractive by comparison," the entry reads. Elsewhere, the author hammers home the necessity of coercing both sociopaths and one's own offspring: "It helps keep the bloody minded and recalcitrant from harming others, and seems also to be an indispensable technique in the rearing of children."

The passage may have struck me so forcefully because I had an unusual childhood. My parents, and my mother in particular, were outspoken proponents of what they called "noncoercive parenting." They fervently believed that given the opportunity children, including their own, will choose to learn. And so it was my decision whether I went to school or stayed home and taught myself, or whether I napped, played, or read. As a small child, I accepted this situation as unremarkable. I was not induced to study by threat of punishment—I had no fear of receiving a bad grade, being sent to detention, or getting expelled (they couldn't expel me from home, after all). My mother, who is not afraid to speak of "children's liberation," held the conviction that her daughters and son were individuals, not helpless wards, and that our opinions should be treated with respect. Years later I asked my mother what noncoercive parenting meant on a day-to-day basis; she said she tried to question the impulse to say no and never to let it become a reflex. "Because

I said so!" was not a phrase uttered in our household. When there were lines that could not be crossed, she aimed to reason with us about why this was the case. "Freedom, not license," adopted from the radical educator A. S. Neill, was one of her mottoes.

My parents were a minority in the eighties and nineties in the American South, where I was raised, but today, alternative education is less of a fringe phenomenon. In Columbia, Missouri, a wilderness program called Wild Folk was founded in 2015 with the aim of being noncoercive and honoring children's autonomy and innate curiosity. Young people ages five to fourteen have the run of a forty-acre campsite, where they learn permaculture farming methods, survival strategies, maple syrup tapping, and other skills. During one session, they made a bicycle-powered generator; during another, they mapped the local watershed. Still, there are baselines every participant has to adhere to, such as coming to the weekly all-hands-on-deck meeting known as Council and participating respectfully.

The frame of noncoercion, though, sets up something of a false opposition. Over time, Wild Folk's founder, Polina Malikin, came to that conclusion, too. "It's really easy to get stuck in this coercive-versus-noncoercive paradigm," Malikin told me. "Who wants to be coercive? That sounds horrible." But the binary, she continued, seems to "assume that there's some sort of blissful presocial state," which ultimately doesn't really exist. "While I think it's important for kids to have a say and make decisions together and run a school together, there is some wisdom that elders have that is important and needs to be passed on," Malikin reflected.

"'Noncoercive' implies a kind of limitlessness," Malikin told me, "but there are real limits. The environment is coercive; it determines the evolution." Ecological responsibility, a key component of Wild Folk's mission, imposes its own inherent restrictions. We occupy a finite world, ecologically and biologically, and we must figure out how to adapt intelligently. We all need clean air to breathe and food to eat; we are all bound by the fact that there are only twenty-four hours in a day and that one day we will die. (That life extension is a pet project of Silicon Valley billionaires implies that the extremely privileged feel unduly constrained by mortality.) These factors may not coerce us per se, but they contradict the idea that we could ever exist or make choices unconstrained.

Writing in the *New Yorker* in 1967, philosopher Hannah Arendt took this insight even further. Truth, she insisted, is fundamentally coercive.

> Seen from the viewpoint of politics, truth has a despotic character. It is therefore hated by tyrants, who rightly fear the competition of a coercive force they cannot monopolize, and it enjoys a rather precarious status in the eyes of governments that rest on consent and abhor coercion. . . . Unwelcome opinion can be argued with, rejected, or compromised upon, but unwelcome facts possess an infuriating stubbornness that nothing can move except plain lies.[2]

As Arendt well knew, the coercive nature of truth doesn't mean some won't resist it. There are plenty of individuals and corporate entities that vehemently protest the research guiding environmental regulations, for example. But that does not change the truth, which is that unrestrained consumption, deforestation, pollution, and carbon emissions are bringing about mass extinction and may well make the planet uninhabitable for humans. By dismissing scientific fact as opinion or even conspiratorial fiction, they avoid confronting truth's boundaries. The law may bend to their will, but in the long term nature will not.

Coercion is not always direct and explicit. Even those with the best intentions may employ coercion surreptitiously. (Malikin warned of this problem for parents and educators who don't want to be overbearing tyrants: "If you are not clear about your authority, you become manipulative. You know your ideal is for the kid or kids to do something, but you don't want to use hard power, so then you start using manipulative ways to get them to want to do it, like guilt or bargaining.") Political scientists, convinced that more subtle forms of coercion can aid our democracy, call new forms of subtle, civic-minded coercion "nudging." Giving up on open deliberation, they favor invisible paternalism.

In daily life, plenty of encounters and exchanges are presented as a free choice when the outcome is preordained, or when we are pushed ("nudged") down a certain path. What's called choice architecture shapes every move we make. This architecture takes myriad forms, from appealing walkways to dispiriting bureaucracy, from commercial displays to computer code. Are our streets safe for bicycles or built for cars alone? Are they sufficiently well lit to welcome pedestrians after dusk? Are we automatically registered to vote or do we have to spend hours standing in line or filling out forms to cast a ballot? Does the salad bar put the spinach within easy reach or are unhealthy toppings the first things we see? What are the default privacy settings on your mobile phone and what kind of content is automatically served up on the digital platform you use?

Nudges are not always bad, and no individual is perfectly autonomous, unencumbered by external influence. Neutrality is mostly a myth, even an impossibility, given that we inhabit a physical world where entropy beckons and gravity tugs us downward. Rather, the question for our purposes is: what and whose interests do our human-made nudges serve? Does the choice architecture we inhabit enhance democracy or diminish it? We might be encouraged to recycle by the presence of prominently placed color-coded bins, or we could be shown a post on social media pitched to our demographic and designed to dampen our enthusiasm for a social policy or encourage us to purchase a product. The distinctions between incentive, persuasion, influence, manipulation, and coercion constantly blur. Regardless of where those lines get drawn, the fact is our choices rarely qualify as "free."

In contrast to my countercultural parents, who tried to put noncoercion into practice in the home, when liberal political philosophers attempt to conjure a situation without coercion they typically speak of contracts. Imagine two adult men of equal social status consenting to a covenant that will profit them both, each agent agreeing to restrain himself to receive a corresponding benefit from the other in return. This simplistic, idealized parable of consent has been more influential than you might expect.

Since the seventeenth century, political philosophers have extrapolated from thought experiments about how hypothetical men behave in a "state of nature" to devise various accounts of how society was founded. The question of how, exactly, the initial consent to be governed was granted is at the heart of what is now known as social contract theory, the study of the mutual agreements that (supposedly) provide the foundation of our political structures. Despite being based in speculative fiction more than anthropological fact, social contract theory serves as a conceptual cornerstone of liberalism as well as contemporary economic and legal discourse. This much is true: one foundational rationale for our modern democratic system is essentially a glorified intellectual fairy tale.

Thomas Hobbes inaugurated this tradition by puzzling over what motivated humans to come together to form a community in the first place. Writing from exile as his home country of England descended into a bloody and lawless civil war—the king, the parliament, and the army vying for political and religious supremacy—his answer was a desire for security. Hobbes imagined atomized individuals handing over power to an all-powerful entity to protect their personal safety (the fact Hobbes seems to care not whether this "Leviathan" was a monarch ordained by the almighty or a godless state is one aspect that made his ideas so seditious). He maintained that there was no possibility of a community, no justice and no propriety, if a sovereign of some kind didn't have the authority to oblige his subjects to behave themselves, providing a "coercive power to tie their hands from rapine and revenge."

[W]here there is no coercive Power erected, that is, where there is no Commonwealth, there is no Propriety; all men having Right to all things: Therefore where there is no Commonwealth, there nothing is Unjust. So that the nature of Justice, consisteth in keeping of valid Covenants: but the Validity of Covenants begins not but with the Constitution of a Civil Power, sufficient to compel men to keep them: And then it is also that Propriety begins.[2]

In this grim telling, even "covenants extorted by fear" are valid; conquest and contract blur in the ruthless quest for law and order. People hand over their autonomy to a supreme ruler, divesting themselves of self-determination, because the alternative is worse, though the solution presents its own significant pitfalls—after all, the absolute monarch or state may well abuse its awesome power.[4] Coercion from on high, Hobbes maintains, is simply the price to pay for living in civil society, utter submission and subjugation the only way to impose order and ensure survival.

Fundamentally, social contract theory is about trying to understand the legitimacy of political authority—a worthy inquiry if there ever was one. On what grounds should we obey the king or the government? Why would we choose to comply with the law? Under what circumstances is rebellion permissible? When rooted in Hobbesian cynicism about human nature, however, social contract theory offers quite constrained answers to these sweeping, vital questions, for it understands individuals as, first and foremost, self-interested agents. According to the framework it sets out, we consent to various forms of authority, cooperating and acting morally, due to a rational assessment of how we might maximally benefit, not out of concern for others or for larger ideals. Aided by the weirdness of its core fable, contractarianism helps justify a worldview that says existing social relations are acceptable and moral because they are consensual, with individuals acquiescing for purely egotistical reasons. It's a strikingly limited way to comprehend the origins and purpose of government and the motives of human beings.

Though Hobbes was contemptuous of popular government, other thinkers, politicians, and agitators connected the concept of a social contract to the insurrectionary, subversive idea that something called "the people" should have power (even as they disagreed on who should be included in this new body and how much influence it should wield). Distilled to its essence, the revolutionary claim at the heart of social contract theory was simple enough: individuals are naturally born free and equal. Though it's now practically a platitude, this brazen, sweeping assertion demolished all the old justifications for authority. Kings and lords trembled at the thought of their vassals embracing such emancipatory ideas; popes and priests denounced such thinking as sacrilege. Out of the blue, old explanations for subordination (God's will, brute force, custom, the superiority or inherent inferiority of people based on birth) no longer sufficed. At a time when kings ruled by divine right, the idea that rational individuals had to give their consent to be ruled was shockingly radical and utterly terrifying to those at the top of the social pyramid.

They were right to quake. In 1649, in an unprecedented turn of events, Charles I, king of England and Scotland, was put on public trial, found guilty of treason against the people, and summarily executed. But the beheading was hardly the end of conflict. The "democraticals" Hobbes denounced squabbled among themselves. Empowered parliamentary forces made up of aristocrats, landed gentry, and merchants set out to squelch the more radical demands of the middle and lower classes. Two years before Charles lost his head, the militant Colonel Thomas Rainsborough of the New Model Army made an eloquent case for democratic consent.

> For really I think that the poorest he that is in England has a life to live as the greatest he; and therefore truly, Sir, I think it's clear, that every man that is to live under a Government ought first by his own consent to put himself under that Government; and I do think that the poorest man in England is not at all bound in a strict sense to that Government that he has not had a voice to put himself under.

It was an inclusive vision of the social contract that made space for the poorest man while also justifying the rebellion of those who lacked the opportunity to consent. With the monarch gone, a revolt of the masses is what Rainsborough's social betters feared most.

Rainsborough was one of the spokesmen of the Levellers, an egalitarian grouping sometimes described as England's first political party. Made up mainly of soldiers, artisans, lesser traders, and small farmers, the Levellers called for a series of democratic reforms: expanded suffrage and the right to choose representatives, annual elections, representation in proportion to population, religious toleration, the end of impressment, equality under the law, the right to speedy trial by jury, the abolition of capital punishment except for murder, and so on. These demands were outlined in various editions of *An Agreement of the People*, their attempt to devise a written constitution to help England "avoid both the danger of returning into a slavish condition and the chargeable remedy of another war." It was an agreement to which the parliamentary class would never consent.

In hindsight, it's little wonder that traditionalists worried that this new idea of the social contract would upset social hierarchies and inspire the lower classes and excluded masses to refuse their servile rank. (The Levellers' uprising certainly seemed to vindicate elite anxiety.) Yet against all expectations, the opposite would ultimately come to pass. As old feudal ties broke down and political and economic relations transformed, the social contract offered a new way to understand and legitimize domination, for its advocates ultimately argued that naturally free individuals don't have to be coerced into being ruled by another—it turns out they will voluntarily choose a relationship of subordination. In the words of scholar Carole Pateman, "a subversive proposition" was turned into "a defense of civil subjection."[5] Hierarchy reasserted itself as the consequence of choices freely made.

Our modern world turns on this intellectual trick, which

routinely presents subjugation as the inevitable result of an act of consent, a "free" choice. Today, we are arguably more obsessed with contracts and consent than we were in the seventeenth and eighteenth centuries, and this ruse can be found everywhere. We sign contracts at work and school, with hospitals and insurance agencies, and indenture ourselves to credit card companies and student loan servicers. Every website we visit and app we use demands that we click "Agree" on a terms-of-service contract we neither read nor comprehend, which deprive users not just of their right to privacy but also of their constitutional right to sue in court. Companies of all kinds bury "arbitration clauses" in the fine print, binding signatories to address any potential malpractice through private mediation, which effectively exempts corporations from the public legal system. The proliferation of contracts in all areas of life combined with the fact they tend to be made between parties with radically divergent degrees of wealth, power, and information (and that we are often compelled to concur because we lack viable alternatives) challenges the assumption that such commitments are always freely entered.

Such power imbalances are glaringly apparent within that preeminent social contract the American Constitution, which simultaneously expanded upon the growing commitment to the principle of popular sovereignty and assiduously restricted it by religion, wealth, and also gender and race. Only a privileged minority was considered capable and worthy of granting consent—everyone else was irrelevant. The Constitution's framers were deeply influenced by John Locke, who, unlike Hobbes, was rightly concerned about the arbitrary power of the state and thus supported rebellion against unchecked abuse—which of course appealed to colonists dead set on resisting the monarchal tyranny of the Old World. Doubting Hobbes's vision of the state of nature as a "war of all against all," Locke advocated limited government and individual or natural rights.

He also believed, however, that the single most important thing that motivated people to create a civil government was the need to protect private property, which he defined as being created when a man's labor combines with nature's raw materials, as when forest is turned into productive fields or pasture. His framework justified stealing land from indigenous communities on the basis that they had failed to make "improvements," leaving the land free for the taking. In Locke's view, not only were indigenous people outside the social contract, but their way of life, based in communal ownership, prevented execution of the contract. Communal ownership had to be eliminated and private property imposed so that the American "pursuit of happiness," a phrase coined by Locke, could commence.

Similarly, social contract theorists justified the subordination of women in creative ways, separating the private, or "paternal," sphere of women and children from the public sphere, where men engaged in political action. (In 1649, when 10,000 women signed a petition presented to the House of Commons supporting the Leveller cause, the recipients balked, instructing the agitators to "stay home and wash their dishes." When one member of Parliament remarked on how strange it was for women to petition Parliament, someone is said to have replied: "It was strange that you cut off the King's head, yet I suppose you will justify it."[6]) Even with this handy distinction between the private and public domains, theorists sought further ways to validate women's auxiliary status. "Being at least formally committed to principle of 'natural equality,' and 'government by consent,' in defense of male supremacy they invoked the theory of women's 'natural inferiority' according to which women would consent to their husbands' appropriation of their property and voting rights upon realizing their intrinsic weakness and necessary dependence on men." observes Silvia Federici in her feminist classic *Caliban and the Witch*.[7] Women were granted just enough rationality and autonomy to enter into the marriage contract (to choose to be governed by their own private monarch) and not an iota more.

Regardless of the arrangement's benefits, a few men were willing to cry foul, describing the sexual contract as a farce founded not on free choice but on unjust compulsion. "When the law makes everything which the wife acquires, the property of the husband, while by compelling her to live with him it forces her to submit to almost any amount of moral and even physical tyranny which he may choose to inflict, there is some ground for regarding every act done by her as done under coercion," the utilitarian John Stuart Mill wrote in 1848's *Principles of Political Economy.* Decades prior, his father, James Mill, had argued that women did not need the vote because their husbands adequately represented their interests, consenting to be governed on behalf of both parties. His son was one of the most prominent male thinkers to part ways with such patriarchal assumptions.[8]

He was not the first, however. In 1825, early democratic socialists William Thompson and Anna Wheeler decried the "audacious falsehood" of the marriage contract in a pamphlet entitled the *Appeal of One Half the Human Race, Women, Against the Pretensions of the Other Half, Men, to Retain Them in Political, and Thence in Civil and Domestic, Slavery.*

> A contract! Where are any of the attributes of contracts, of equal and just contracts, to be found in this transaction? A contract implies the voluntary assent of both the contracting parties. Can even both the parties, man and woman, by agreement alter the terms, as to *indissolubility* and *inequality* of this pretended contract? No. Can any individual man divest himself, were he even so inclined, of his power of despotic control? He cannot.

Women, Thompson and Wheeler passionately argued, bore the pains and privations of the supposed contract, but were never consulted on its terms, making the wife's acquiescence a sham. But the charade of consent was ultimately a symptom of a more systemic injustice, one that flowed not from women's innate inferiority, but from the unfair economic advantage men had in the marketplace. It was not mental capacity or physical strength that justified male domination, but man's comparative financial power that gave him an advantage. The fact that it was typically the husband who had access to a wage (and if the wife did work, her income legally belonged to him) allowed men to coerce women, who depended on the money their husbands controlled for survival.

The *Appeal* was written as industrialization was taking hold in Britain. Over the course of centuries, peasants, who had long had customary rights to commonly held land, were brutally kicked off and locked out in what's known as the enclosure movement, a process Colonel Rainsborough himself had denounced as "the greatest tyranny that was thought of in the world." The imposition of a new legal regime of private property—the sort of system Locke would approve of—made land the sole possession of privileged individuals and turned commoners into trespassers and criminals, and farmers and forest dwellers were denied access to their traditional means of survival under the threat of the death penalty. The transformation was particularly devastating for women, who played a vital role in subsistence agriculture and who fiercely resisted enclosure and their corresponding marginalization, as Federici's work shows. With forced migration came slums and squalor, city centers crowded with people desperately looking for work, including women and children, who were especially vulnerable to exploitation. Meanwhile, the advent of steam technology was transforming the manufacture and transport of goods and creating new patterns of production, distribution, and consumption. A wholly different way of organizing social life was emerging.

Against this turbulent backdrop, socialist feminist pioneers such as Thompson and Wheeler proposed a different kind of economic revolution. The only way to generate a society where genuine consent was possible was to build one upon a foundation of shared ownership and economic cooperation, not competition. This, they argued, would dramatically transfigure sexual relations, allowing men and women to finally meet and flourish as autonomous, consenting human beings. Until women become men's material equals—a modest goal we have inched closer toward yet still fail to reach—marriage will remain an institution tinged with coercion despite the willing declaration "I do."

What's the difference between an armed robber and a private health insurance company if both present the following option: your money or your life? Both scenarios appear to offer a choice, though one compelled by a threat. The robber may shoot you, and thus the demand certainly qualifies as coercive. The insurance company could simply deny you coverage for the treatment you need. Some may object that an insurer's inaction cannot be compared to a violent ultimatum, even if it results in bodily harm. Others may be inclined to agree with the singer Woody Guthrie: "Some will rob you with a six-gun / And some with a fountain pen." Coercion may not perfectly define the situation, but choice hardly fits the bill, either. It's hard to say a person lacking the funds to pay for urgent medical care enjoys much in the way of meaningful options.

In his masterwork *Politics and Vision*, the radical democrat Sheldon Wolin traces the influence of social contract thinkers, including Hobbes and Locke, uncovering the roots of a liberal perspective that obscures what he calls "the compulsion arising from a system of property." (As Ellen Meiksins Wood notes in her short account *The Origins of Capitalism*, the very term *market forces* implies force and thus coercion.[9]) While people have long engaged in what the economist Adam Smith famously called the "propensity to truck, barter, and exchange," commerce alone is not capitalism; rather, capitalism, or a "system of property," emerges when the possibility of trade becomes the necessity of competitive production and when market opportunities become market imperatives.

Historically, the modern capitalist paradigm was born at the moment that these market imperatives took over the production and provision of life's most basic necessity: food. After enclosure, when people could no longer farm common land for subsistence but had to produce in excess for the market and its profit motive, capitalism's power was on display. Today when we talk about capitalism we typically speak of the problem of inequality, highlighting financial disparities and the massive divide between rich and poor. But the coercive aspects of capitalism, the ways in which our individual choices are constrained and whole societies are compelled to submit to the rule of money, deserve as much attention as the deprivations of poverty.

Nevertheless, the classical liberal tradition tends to sidestep such dynamics, instead emphasizing the state as the sole coercive agent, one endowed with the power to imprison or even impose penalties of death. In comparison to these direct perils, the pressures of the market, Wolin says, appear almost abstract, "impersonal and lacking in physical duress."[10] From this angle, a for-profit health care system looks perfectly just, though it may cost some low-income people their lives, while taxation is seen as the seizure of citizens' assets under threat of punishment for nonpayment and a form of unacceptable tyranny, even if the revenue raised goes toward providing universal medical coverage.

Adopting a worldview rooted in seventeenth-century conceptions of the social contract, Americans tend to see government as a threatening entity from which citizens must be protected. So while most advanced democracies offer their citizens a range of public welfare options (single-payer health care, subsidized child care, free higher education, arts and journalism funding, and so on), the United States has taken a very different path. In the name of freedom of choice, Americans must seek employment that provides insurance benefits as a perk, lest they join the ranks of millions who have gone bankrupt due to medical debt; hire nannies to watch their offspring while they work or, if they are too poor, leave the kids home alone; borrow tens of thousands of dollars for an education that they hope will land them a job that will remunerate them enough to repay their student loans; and be exposed to a culture that is overwhelmingly funded by advertising revenue, which means the privileging of expression primarily designed to help marketers sell products.

A historical perspective sheds necessary light. In opposition to the Old World, where an unstable monarch exercised tyrannical power over his minions (including the power to tax, which the Boston Tea Party protest dramatically brought to the fore), the United States came to envision itself as a nation of free yeoman farmers, of small-scale producers beholden to no one, least of all to the king, George III, and the British Empire. These yeomen were the property-owning white men the Constitution's framers idealized as capable and worthy of self-rule (though the founding fathers assiduously limited their actual influence over the emergent federal government). More than two centuries later, this conception continues to shape political life: Americans still imagine themselves akin to the mythic freeholders of old—today, we might call ourselves "freelancers"—battling an oppressive regulatory state.

As always, though, things are more complicated. As Alexis de Tocqueville famously notes in his celebrated 1835 travelogue *Democracy in America*, the economic egalitarianism of the Americas was indeed remarkable when compared to the seemingly intractable inequalities of old Europe. White men, even recent immigrants, had seemingly infinite access to land, pilfered though it was, and the autonomy that came with it. Yet, Tocqueville noted, the patriotic embrace of small property holders coexisted with contempt for landless laborers whom the upper-class framers dismissed as inherently unfree. (Democracy's relationship to work has long been conflicted on this front: in ancient Greece, manual labor was held in contempt and believed by some to be incompatible with the mental effort that self-rule required, even as the political system made unprecedented space for poor working citizens and small-scale producers.) Praising farmers in one breath, the nation's aristocratic founders belittled regular workers in the next, denigrating them for being dependent on employers for their livelihood. As wage laborers, they were necessarily subject to coercion and thus not autonomous enough to be capable of democracy.[11]

Unfortunately, this early recognition of the coercive power of market relations was not sustained or fully developed. Instead, the insight was repressed and reframed, presented as a problem of the workers' lack of virtue and not their exploitation. In the end, it was the Puritans who offered another path forward, their outlook ultimately more palatable than the upper-class snobbery of the Constitution's framers. The Protestant work ethic encouraged people to toil and hoard any returns as a sign of their favored status in heaven. Those pietistic souls irrevocably shaped the economic outlook of the new nation, redeeming labor by associating it with moral rectitude and worthiness while ultimately upholding industriousness as a means to an end, the accumulation of wealth, not a worthwhile or creative act in itself. The pursuit of money along with affluence's inevitable consequence, consumption, would become the twin pillars not just of American society but of the country's conception of democracy; work itself was pushed to the wayside. The United States was destined to become what has been called a consumers' republic, not a producers' one.

Over the course of the twentieth century, an array of groups supported this emphasis on consumption, with wildly varying motivations. At the beginning, Progressive Era reformers, to fight for the public interest, seized upon the idea of the "citizen consumer," which led to new regulations that helped protect purchasers, including the Food and Drug Act (1906) and the Federal Trade Commission Act (1914). (In some ways, the Progressives anticipated the picket lines and boycotts that would be used to great effect decades later by the civil rights movement to dramatize black people's lack of choice and freedom under segregation, proving that the power of consumers can be transformative.)

The Great Depression launched a new chapter. In response to the devastating crash of 1929, the New Deal reined in Wall Street speculators while granting citizens new guarantees and opportunities such as Social Security and strengthening labor rights, forging the modern welfare state. But the program's efforts to redistribute buying power in order to shore up the economy portended another shift that often goes unremarked. "I believe we are at the threshold of a fundamental change in our popular economic thought," Roosevelt said on the 1932 presidential campaign trail: "in the future we are going to think less about the producer and more about the consumer."[12]

Time would prove FDR correct. In the wake of World War II, mass consumption was embraced not just by progressives but by many of the New Deal's most vehement opponents, who recognized it as a way of reconciling capitalist growth and democratic commitments while avoiding more progressive investments and planning. Instead of seeing the stock market crash of 1929 as a consequence of the inherent instability of capitalism, economists understood the resulting Great Depression as the outgrowth of suppressed demand. Over time, thrift came to be seen as un-American, and organized labor wholeheartedly agreed. The majority of trade unions began to focus explicitly on expanding workers' purchasing power, abandoning once-central demands for things such as more control over workplace decision making and increased leisure time. What workers needed, they believed, was enough money to afford the American dream. The government, trade unions, and big business all began to affirm a conception of civic participation that was first and foremost acquisitive.

The Cold War entrenched this disposition. Through trade fairs and international expositions, the federal government promoted a vision of the United States as a land of abundance and choice—in other words, freedom (which must mean the absence of coercion). Between 1954 and 1960 alone, President Dwight Eisenhower had the Department of Commerce fund American participation in almost one hundred exhibitions in nearly thirty countries, helping five thousand companies reach more than sixty million people. As one sales manager who participated put it, "We were . . . selling the American way of life and the democratic philosophy of our government."[13] A forgotten but immensely popular book, and a particular favorite among advertising executives, *People of Plenty: Economic Abundance and the American Character*, links political democracy and consumer capitalism.

Citizenship became synonymous with consumption, and democracy's favored metaphor became a dazzling array of goods to assess and obtain; political choices and purchasing choices became a single integrated system. The equation of consumer bounty with democratic liberty reached its apotheosis in the surreal 1959 Kitchen Debate between U.S. vice president Richard Nixon and Soviet premier Nikita Khrushchev. Aided by interpreters, the world leaders engaged in an awkward dialogue at the American National Exhibition in Moscow, standing amid glimmering models of the latest homes, cars, appliances, food, and fashion. Such goods, Nixon patriotically insisted, symbolize "what freedom means to us" and "our right to choose." That he held the second-highest office in the land didn't stop him from casting aspersions on public servants. "We do not wish to have decisions made at the top by government officials," he said, whether about "the kind of house" we live in or "the kind of ideas" we think. No wonder President Barack Obama's chief data scientist, a man credited as instrumental to Obama's successful campaigns, used to work in supermarket sales promotion.[14] We all accept that politicians are products who must promote their brands accordingly.

For some influential conservative intellectuals, this was right and just. One economist in particular, the Austrian Ludwig von Mises, worked to promote the view of the marketplace as the paramount space of democratic freedom and choice. His work, along with that of his star student Friedrich Hayek, became what historian Kim Phillips-Fein called "a bible for those who wanted to turn back the New Deal."[15] Mises was staunchly antistatist but grudgingly admitted to democracy's occasional utility: "The preferability of democracy consists in the fact that it facilitates a peaceful adjustment of the system of government and government personnel to the wishes of public opinion," he allowed. But far superior to public control was the "price mechanism," or the reflection of supply and demand in prices, which Mises envisioned "as the perfect way to achieve social order without coercion."[16]

For Mises, capitalism offered the greatest possible space for individual freedom, but to reap such rewards it demanded "submission"—democratic decisions could not be allowed to meddle with the market's wisdom. In the final hour, Mises argues, market democracy reigns far superior to democracy in its political, or electoral, form. Consider how, for example, commercial transactions serve the needs and wants of every demographic niche, no matter how fringe. "The market produces goods of a wide variety to suit many different tastes and preferences," the Mises Institute website explains. "Automobiles range from inexpensive small cars to expensive luxury cars. These vehicles are suited for a variety of purposes. Some are practical, others fit different wants or needs. There is no such catering in a political democracy. The minority is forced to abide by the majority's decision of what is good."[17]

To promote his view, Mises made an argument that would better serve a used-car dealership, while we're speaking of automobiles, than a political principle: the consumer is king. "In the capitalist system of society's economic organization the entrepreneurs determine the course of production. In the performance of this function they are unconditionally and totally subject to the sovereignty of the buying public, the consumers," Mises wrote in 1944. Business owners and shareholders do not reap profits at the expense of the consumers and workers, therefore; they serve at the pleasure of the purchasing public. The market system "automatically values every man according to the services he renders to the body of sovereign consumers."[18] The true "captains of industry" are the shoppers, whose preferences direct production. Workers, in this formulation, all but disappear.

Tireless propagandists with access to corporate patrons eager to fund think tanks and academic endowments, Mises and Hayek spread their unorthodox theories on multiple continents over the postwar period, slowly advancing from the academic fringes to the cultural mainstream. By 1980, Margaret Thatcher and Ronald Reagan together led the two most powerful countries on earth, where they pushed policies based on the ideas that private enterprise epitomizes liberty, government is bad, society doesn't exist, unions must be smashed, taxes are theft, and that "there is no alternative," as Thatcher famously put it, to unfettered capitalism. (Reagan, an avid reader of both Hayek and Mises, was the spokesman for General Electric in the fifties, when that company was at the vanguard of the conservative, probusiness cause; GE supervisors were ordered to instruct disgruntled workers in the virtues of "that most free and democratic of processes, the 'plebiscite of the marketplace.'"[19]) Yet, as Thatcher and Reagan burnished the well-established image of democracy as consumer choice and upheld shopping as the ultimate analog for political engagement, a notable irony surfaced: the selection on the democratic shelves was distressingly limited.

The policy preferences of the majority of voters are perpetually out of stock. Consider the 81 percent of Americans who say money in politics is an alarming problem and want to see some kind of effective campaign finance reform; or the 97 percent of Americans who want background checks for gun sales and the 67 percent who want assault weapons banned.[20] Or the upward of 60 percent of American citizens, including nearly a third of Republicans, who believe it's the federal government's job to provide health care, and the growing number that wants a universal single-payer system.[21] Ignoring their constituencies' well-documented desires, politicians cozy up to donors, let special interests interpret the Second Amendment, and insist that choosing from among multiple overpriced (and often inadequate) private insurance plans offers freedom from the coercion of a single universal system. A lack of real choice masquerades as liberty.

Today, colonoscopies, root canals, lice, and being stuck in traffic all poll better than Congress, which has approval ratings that often hover around 10 percent.[22] The two parties that dominate the American political scene are almost comically unpopular with voters. Understandable disgust and dismay with the financial incentives driving the political system unite Americans from the left and the right, who suspect that "political contribution" is generally a euphemism for political corruption. (Indeed, the

Supreme Court has affirmed that politicians are free to receive lavish gifts from donors, declining to sanction all but the most egregious instances of quid pro quo.) The public's cynicism is further confirmed by numerous former representatives who have blown the whistle on the fact that they spent more than half their working day "dialing for dollars" instead of doing the work of governing. (When she retired, Barbara Mikulski, the longest-serving female senator, described a choice between spending her golden years "raising hell" or "raising cash.")

The irony cuts deeper still. While the heart of today's political system is supposedly freedom of choice, we are simultaneously told there can be no substitute for the political and economic system we live under—the underlying economic arrangement cannot be challenged, let alone changed. In a world where the ideology of "no alternative" continues to rule, any attempt to force a real choice will likely be regarded as a democratic crisis, not a legitimate democratic challenge. (In 1975, a group of scholars, including Samuel Huntington, issued a book-length report entitled *The Crisis of Democracy*, lamenting the social destabilization caused, among other things, by "previously passive or unorganized groups in the population," such as "blacks, Indians, Chicanos, white ethnic groups, students and women," becoming newly "organized and mobilized"; democracy, the experts maintained, requires a degree of "apathy and non-involvement on the part of some individuals and groups.")[23]

Meanwhile, when foreign citizenries choose other, perhaps more democratic, systems, they aren't simply left to their own devices; they may be undermined or punished. In 1954 the Central Intelligence Agency orchestrated a coup d'état in Guatemala to overthrow Jacobo Árbenz, a democratically elected president who supported land reform to benefit the indigenous peasantry, at the behest of private interests, including the U.S.-based and White House-connected United Fruit Company. In 1973, three years after Salvador Allende's socialist government won a plurality of votes in Chile, the United States toppled his administration in a military coup led by his army chief, the soon-to-be dictator

Augusto Pinochet. Allende, Henry Kissinger said, was elected "due to the irresponsibility of the Chilean people," thousands of whom were tortured and killed during Pinochet's reign. Recently, a Fox News reporter asked the former CIA director James Woolsey if the United States had meddled in foreign elections. "Oh, probably, but it was for the good of the system, to avoid Communists from taking over," he said. Asked if this meddling still happens, he replied with a grin, "Only for a very good cause. In the interests of democracy."[24]

One of the true heroes, and tragic victims, of the French Revolution was the Marquis de Condorcet. Born in 1743, he was a brilliant mathematician and a social reformer astonishingly ahead of his time: a republican democrat who supported universal suffrage, an antiracist abolitionist, and an outspoken feminist (one who called for the "complete annihilation of the prejudices that have brought about an inequality of right between the sexes, an inequality fatal even to the party in whose favor it works"). In the years immediately following the revolution, he held various formal roles, including serving as chairman of the Committee on a Constitution. "A republican constitution based upon equality was the only one in accordance with nature, reason and justice: the only one that can protect the liberty of citizens and the dignity of the human race," Condorcet declared. Yet his constitution was never adopted, and the resulting discord led to his arrest during the Jacobin Terror and his untimely death in a country jail cell.

Before the revolution, Condorcet had made his reputation by applying mathematical reasoning to political choice. His work in this area resulted in two theorems. The first, the jury theorem, demonstrates that groups often make better or more accurate decisions than individuals in isolation. As one helpful summary describes it:

Suppose that a number of people are answering the same question and that there are two possible answers, one correct and one incorrect. Assume, too, that the probability that each individual will answer correctly exceeds 50%. With a few calculations, the theorem shows that the probability that a majority of the group will answer correctly increases toward 100% as the size of the group increases. Groups will do better than individuals in choosing a correct answer, and big groups better than little ones, as long as two conditions are met: the majority response "wins," and each person is more likely than not to be correct.[25]

Thus if the odds of people choosing the right answer even marginally exceed the odds of their being wrong, groups are increasingly likely to make good choices the larger they are. Yet Condorcet's second theorem, known as the voting paradox, complicates this hopeful story. It shows that there can be scenarios in which three or more voters choose from among three or more alternatives, or candidates, in which the results are inconclusive, with no clear winner emerging.

Taken together, these two theorems appear to demonstrate that majority rule is a *plausible* method of collective decision making, but not a *foolproof* one. Given all the complexities involved, mechanisms for making collective decisions can, under certain conditions, lead to ambiguous results. For Condorcet, this reality hardly invalidated democracy. Diversity of opinion was a good thing, he believed, even if it posed procedural challenges. What's more, the likelihood of positive, democratic outcomes could be improved through the provision of tax-supported public education—yet another area where Condorcet was well ahead of the curve. Nevertheless, of his two propositions, Condorcet's voting paradox, with its pessimistic implications, is the far better known and more influential.

This paradox came to renewed prominence in the 1950s, when economist Kenneth Arrow built on its insights in his book *Social Choice and Individual Values*, a work that contributed to his being awarded a Nobel Prize in 1972. According to Arrow's famous impossibility theorem, there is no single generally applicable rule for aggregating a collective decision from inflexible, well-ordered, individual preferences. In other words, it is simply impossible to assess the common good of certain kinds of groups. Though purely theoretical and based in a thought experiment conceived in such a way that it would never play out perfectly in daily life (it assumes very narrow criteria that are empirically impractical, and it ignores the need for universal standards for collective decision making, such as human rights, education, and subsistence), the theorem's logic seemed to call into doubt the very conceptual coherence of majoritarian democracy. Or at least that's what some people opportunistically gleaned from it. In Arrow's wake, a new generation of conservative economists began to attack the Enlightenment-era ideal of democracy as little more than religious dogma dependent on the fanciful notion that there existed something called "the will of the people." They sought to prove that only individuals, not groups, are able to make coherent, legitimate decisions.[26]

It's no coincidence that Arrow's ideas gained ground at a moment of social unrest. In the 1950s, '60s, and '70s, black and indigenous people along with women, gays, lesbians, and the disabled were struggling for inclusion, banding together to pressure public and private institutions to be more responsive to their needs. Fractures and long-standing inequities came to the foreground, prompting a backlash. Leading conservative intellectuals pushed back on progressive causes by proxy, attacking Rousseauian concepts of a "general will" and "popular sovereignty" as a means to undermine those who sought increased diversity in decision making and an expanded conception of the common good.

Along with the push for civil rights at home, the Cold War presented an even graver menace, for communism put the rule of financial elites in direct jeopardy. Against this backdrop, Condorcet's and Arrow's theorems were recruited to advance economic thinking that sought to discredit the notion of public interest as mere whimsy or "impossibility," while continuing Hayek and Mises's project of bolstering capitalism at democracy's expense. Condorcet, who died for his conviction that "there is no true right, there is no true happiness, but in the absolute equality of all citizens," would have been aghast.

Over the course of this tumultuous period, economist James Buchanan, a student of Milton Friedman's, led the charge. Eventually his theories (called public choice, or constitutional, economics) were adopted and operationalized by the notorious billionaire activist Koch brothers in their remarkably effective and well-funded quest to roll back the welfare state. Buchanan aimed, first and foremost, to prove that there is no effective way to aggregate preferences and, second, that democracy, defined as the will of the majority, had to be constrained so that the freedom granted by capitalism could flourish. His 1962 coauthored book, *The Calculus of Consent*, sought to reconceptualize political democracy in market terms so as to explicitly reject the concept of the public good.

Taking Arrow's theorem to an extreme, Buchanan and his followers not only argued that there is no way to make social, or collective, choices but that any attempt to combine our choices to determine, let alone promote, the common good is futile and nefarious. There is no "will of the people" for politicians to follow, because, their thinking went, "the people" do not exist and because politicians are merely self-dealing individuals seeking power and personal reward.

According to public choice economics, we human beings are merely atomized individuals with private preferences. Politics is a competition of private interests in a sphere of personal freedom; what we call "democracy" is in fact nothing more than citizens buying goods or politicians trading favors. In the end, legislators will always and inevitably pander to mass interests, unjustly discriminating against and coercing a wealthy minority in favor of the poorer majority (deemed "takers," not "makers," in the more accessible, inflammatory language of the Koch brothers). Yet Buchanan's model contains a fascinating contradiction: self-interest performs wonders in the domain of the marketplace but causes harm when applied to the workings of government. He explains that elected officials cater to their constituencies, who of course want things such as schools, roads, and hospitals; to pay for those services, the state will unjustly seize the assets of a minority through taxation and perpetually overinvest in services. If people really want them enough, market logic insists, an intrepid entrepreneur will provide.

Nowhere does this mode of thinking acknowledge that imbalances in economic power may result in the poor being dominated by the rich, or that the working class might have the right to fight back. Somehow, even as they collaborate with the opulently wealthy to ensure high returns on their investments, purveyors of public choice and neoliberal economic theories regard the notion of class-based solidarity with contempt—at least when the class in question is the working class. (Buchanan scornfully dubbed trade unions "the labor monopoly movement.")[27] Despite the blatant hypocrisy, there's something to be said for the public choice economists' method—or, rather, for our appropriating and inverting it: where Buchanan applied his ideal of market liberty to the realm of government, we might follow the same line in reverse, applying standard assumptions about government accountability and civil liberties from the political to the economic realm. If we are sensitive to the state's threat to freedom of choice, we should not be so sanguine about coercion in the workplace.

"Bosses, at any minute, they can close the plant and just destroy your life. They say it's your job, but, really, it's their job to take away," Ricky Maclin told me, sitting in the lunchroom at New Era Windows Cooperative. In the United States, only a tiny handful of factories are cooperatively owned and democratically run, and New Era is one of the most well known.

Occupying a cavernous space on Chicago's South Side, New Era began after workers bought out their old employer, Republic, when it collapsed in the wake of the 2008 financial crisis. Starting New Era was a "survival strategy" and a way to "stop the abuse" people had suffered under the old company, which founding

New Era member Armando Robles described as "a type of modern slavery," with every minute logged and monitored through a complicated tracking system. Now everyone moves freely, working and taking breaks when they need to, with a sense of purpose that leaves Robles happy to get out of bed at dawn and join the team. Arizona Stingley, who was a nanny for white families in Mississippi in her younger days, told me there was simply no comparison between Republic and New Era. "It was divide and conquer by the boss. They were always pitting Mexicans against blacks," she recalled. "And it worked. People wouldn't want to teach you anything because they were afraid you'd take their job." The groups sat at different tables at lunch and rarely mingled across race lines. Now they share skills instead of regarding one another as threats.

Another cooperatively owned and democratically run enterprise, Opportunity Threads, is one of the last remaining textile factories in Appalachia. Business is thriving for the two dozen or so workers, who are of Highland Mayan descent and speak a wide range of indigenous dialects but use Spanish as a common language. Tucked away in the North Carolina foothills, the landscape reminds many of its workers, they told me, of Guatemala, which they fled because of a long civil war after the U.S.-backed 1954 coup and the genocide against indigenous people that lasted into the 1980s. Everyone I spoke to praised the factory for providing a quality of life and sense of dignity they hadn't known elsewhere.

Most had been previously employed at the nearby chicken processing plant, Case Farms, where they weren't allowed to take a sick day or even step off the line to go to the bathroom. "Normally, one has to put twelve thousand eggs into the incubators in twenty-five minutes," Alfonso Manuel told me. "It's a difficult job." Beginning in the early nineties the Maya community had led an impressive campaign of worker organizing in Morganton, striking and winning some concessions at the chicken plants, but their victories were often rolled back.[28] Instead of perpetually fighting the boss, getting rid of him entirely seemed like an attractive proposition. Working at Opportunity Threads could be physically demanding, Alfonso said, especially in the days leading up to a production deadline, but even those intense periods felt rewarding, with the whole team coming together to meet a target, and no one being yelled at or humiliated.

Unsurprisingly, in an environment where all the workers make decisions together and where everyone is involved in choosing the company's direction, no one feared that their jobs were about to be shipped overseas in the quest for marginally higher rates of return. Instead, the enterprise operates according to a very different ethos: during downturns, the team comes together to figure out how to share work or rustle up new orders so that no one has to be laid off. During phases when profits are high, the rewards are fairly apportioned to all. As a consequence, most of the workers had bought a home or put a spouse or children through college. "We're not taking jobs," Alfonso said, surveying the floor. "We're creating them."

Reyna Rodriguez, who had also worked at Case Farms, told me that the factory had helped her find her voice. She had been so shy and scared at her earlier jobs, so lacking in self-worth that she almost couldn't bear to have people look at her. "Before, I didn't speak much. But, little by little, I've lost some of the fear, and I want to be more involved in everything," she said. "Before I worked only with chicken. But now what I do includes everybody here. My work is to write down everyone's targets, to put them on the board. They got me to learn the machines, and I also fill out the paperwork for the shipments. So, little by little, I am learning. I am learning a little bit of everything, so I am losing a little bit of the fear."

In her 2017 book *Private Government: How Employers Rule Our Lives (And Why We Don't Talk About It)*, political philosopher Elizabeth Anderson begins with a deceptively simple observation: most people spend much of their lives at work. On the job, we accept our subjugation to a form of private authority that essentially operates in a dictatorial mode—that is, we accept that our bosses are entitled to boss us around. Employers can dictate how we dress and what we say on social media, determine how we spend our off hours, test us for drug use, and track our movements. Supervisors can search workers' belongings, sever ties for minor infractions, and (like the chicken plant overseers) refuse necessities such as bathroom breaks. They can deny us the wages we need in order to feed, clothe, and shelter ourselves.

Meanwhile, no structures oblige executives to listen to the individuals below them who operate the machinery, serve the meals, teach in the classrooms, or comfort patients. If the U.S. government imposed the same controls on citizens that companies place on their employees, there would be an outcry over the violation of constitutional rights. But no such constitutional rights exist in the workplace, because it is a private, as opposed to public, sphere. Employer power is practically absolute, and constant coercion is par for the course.

As Anderson points out, workers in Germany have a seat at the table, shaping company policy alongside management under a model known as *Mitbestimmung*, or "codetermination." A century ago, early democratic socialists such as Thompson and Wheeler were inspired by an even more radical democratic horizon. They envisioned a world where cooperation, not coercion, would reign and where the economy, supported by the state, would be a space of free choice and true consent. Since the earliest outbreak of labor unrest, workers have held out hope for more than mere survival: they have dreamed of running their own businesses and getting rid of bosses altogether—and, by doing so, building a better and more just society.

Unlike cooperatives, which aim to build a new alternative economy within the shell of the old (but which often find their egalitarian ambitions stymied by their need to succeed as a business on the market's terms), trade unions attempt to tackle employer coercion by directly fighting the boss, pushing for higher wages and building worker power. Over the decades, collective bargaining did bring a measure of citizenship into the workplace, but the dream of worker sovereignty (as opposed to the chimera of the sovereign consumer offered by Mises or the harsh reality of management control) remains elusive. Making matters more challenging, today, the workplace sovereigns, owners and bosses, are ever more invisible, obscured by layers of subcontracting shell companies or digital interfaces and apps. A factory worker in Indonesia is not the direct employee of the company whose name-brand shoes she sews, just as an Uber driver is merely an "independent service provider" contracting with a faceless app.

With few exceptions, we have somehow accepted that the world of work is outside the reach of democracy. As in the private or domestic sphere of women, the private or commercial realm of work is not considered public or properly political. We don't think of corporations as governing, even as they dominate most of our waking hours (and even as corporate lobbies and donations have a corrupting effect on elections and policy). This brings us to Anderson's deeper point: the state itself was not always "public." Through the ages, innumerable states have been absolute and aloof, unaccountable to inhabitants whose opinions were regarded as irrelevant; a kingdom is not a public sphere. The state became public only because people fought to make it so, tirelessly pushing for the principles of common ownership and popular sovereignty. There's no reason the same should not one day be said of the corporations that now govern so much of our lives.

If democracy is a system where the people consent to the rules that govern them, then it follows, paradoxically, that people might wind up being less individually free in a functioning democracy than in another system. Because if we all truly participated in making society's rules, it follows that those rules would be legitimate and we, in turn, would be more duty bound to obey them. But there's another wrinkle. When we do not live in a functioning democracy but hope to create one, we may find that it is our democratic duty to break the laws if at least some of them are unjust. We call this refusal of consent civil disobedience.

Long before Martin Luther King Jr., Mahatma Gandhi, Henry David Thoreau, or Socrates, the character Antigone provided a dramatic embodiment of the conflict between the rule of law, individual conscience, coercion, and choice. Antigone, the tragic protagonist of Sophocles's immensely popular and eponymously titled play, insists on burying the body of her brother, who by leading an insurrection had marked himself as a dishonorable traitor before he was killed in battle. Invoking a higher authority, she repeatedly disobeys the dictates of her uncle Creon, who as ruler of the city cannot permit individuals, even family members and especially rebellious outspoken ones, to violate the norms of the community. By the end, Creon has a change of heart and rushes to spare Antigone, but it's too late. She pays for her insubordination with her life, and her death effectively destroys Creon, too.

Civil disobedience, from *Antigone* to the present day, involves people choosing to break rules not because they are criminals but because of ethical conviction, a direct action that inevitably puts one on a collision course with authority. The fact that she is a young woman, a nonperson according to the logic of Athenian democracy, makes Antigone's rebellion all the more notable, and her gender is one reason she has been a touchstone for political theorists ever since ("I won't be called weaker than womankind," Creon wails). She is also remembered for her audacity, exemplified in her defiance taking place in the clear view of soldiers. (In an ironic twist, Sophocles's reward for the play's success was to be enlisted to serve as a commanding officer in the Athenian force tasked with quelling a rebellion on the island of Samos, which wanted no part of Athenian democracy and was busy pursuing its own oligarchic interests. Democracy was imposed on the Samians against their will, their preferences be damned— coercing recalcitrant people into accepting democracy, it turns out, was hardly the invention of the American empire.[29])

Civil disobedience might be nonviolent, but as Antigone demonstrates it is anything but cowardly or weak; Martin Luther

King Jr. called it a "constructive coercive power," a tool to pry open the door to negotiation with one's opponents and a means to compel a dehumanizing system to change. "Standing beside love is always justice, and we are only using the tools of justice," King said. "Not only are we using the tools of persuasion, but we've come to see that we've got to use the tools of coercion."[30] For modern campaigners, the aim of civil disobedience is to exercise power, whether by moral suasion (appealing to shame or conscience) or by the exercise of force (disrupting business as usual and impinging on profits through picket lines, boycotts, strikes, and riots). This constructive coercion is one way to choose something that does not yet exist, to demand a new way of being that has not been tried or an alternative that is being suppressed. It is a way of choosing democracy.

Forging a new more democratic social contract requires a massive withdrawal of consent and a coordinated campaign of constructive coercion. It also requires changing how we think about coercion and choice. Over the centuries, capitalism has disguised coercion as choice, whether through contracts between wildly unequal parties, the false abundance of the democratic shopping mall, or the insistence that the compulsion that arises from market forces is actually freedom. Under more democratic conditions, where power is broadly shared, coercion should be openly discussed, subject to deliberation and debate, so that we might consider the option of minimizing coercion in every realm of life, from the state to the workplace to the home. No doubt there are plenty of behaviors that a self-governing society would reasonably choose to sanction— physical and sexual violence, embezzlement and corruption, discrimination, and the destruction of the environment all come to mind—but we have to decide what kinds of penalties such transgressions warrant and when restorative, as opposed to retributive, justice can prevail. In other words, when is coercion legitimate? This is a question democracy will always have to ask.

CHAPTER 5

IS THIS WHAT DEMOCRACY LOOKS LIKE?

(SPONTANEITY/STRUCTURE)

IF YOU EVER visit Athens, make sure to see the remains of the Ancient Agora. You can take a seat at the Theatre of Dionysus, stroll curving paths dotted by temples and statues, and climb to catch breathtaking views from the Parthenon. In the valley below, the museum displays dozens of ancient *ostraka*, the broken ceramic fragments inscribed with the names of men whom voters feared stood on the brink of turning into demagogues—some of whom were indeed cast out, or ostracized, from the city—along with the frontispiece of a *kleroterion*, one of the ingenious slot machines devised to ensure that the city's all-important juries were randomly selected and uncorrupted.

With so much to look at on your tour, you would be forgiven for passing by the Monument of the Eponymous Heroes, or what's left of it. Only the base has survived, the ten bronze figures who once stood proudly atop having long ago disappeared and likely been melted down, the ore reused for less illustrious purposes. On my first trip, I overlooked it myself, determined instead to find the hole in the ground that marks the cell where Socrates was imprisoned. It was only when I returned with the classicist Efimia Karakantza that I realized how much I had missed.

To the untrained eye, the Eponymous monument appears to be nothing more than a long stone ladder set on its side, perhaps four feet tall and around thirty feet long. But as Karakantza helped me understand, it symbolizes a tremendous democratic breakthrough, a stone homage to an epiphany that changed the course of history. Jittering with enthusiasm, she made me and my film crew stop and wouldn't let us leave until we had fully grasped the significance of the humble display.

In 508 BC, empowered by a riot of the lower classes that some scholars compare to the storming of the Bastille, a nobleman named Cleisthenes inaugurated Athenian democracy by breaking down traditional centers of power based on kinship and religion and binding people in new affiliations based on place. In essence, he invented the Athenian people by institutionalizing the notion of geographic citizenship that we take for granted today. He divided up Athens regionally, creating ten new groupings, or civic "tribes," that combined people from the coastal, inland, and urban zones— it was these ten tribes who were represented by the bronze heroes who once stood proudly on the memorial's pillars.

Cleisthenes's reforms, however, went far beyond diminishing the power of blood ties. He created local neighborhood councils that promoted self-government and fed into a larger, popular city-wide Assembly. Of the whole body of eligible citizens, fifty representatives from each tribe were chosen by a lottery method to serve for one year on the governing council (or Boule) of five hundred, the body that proposed the agenda for the Assembly, supervised all the city boards (which oversaw things such as social welfare and the city's finances and coinage), awarded contracts for public works, and audited civil servants, in addition to a range of other duties. It was a demanding task, with the council meeting up to three hundred days a year.

The council was a complex organization, combining rotation in office with random selection, but it was shaped by two simple, mutually supportive goals: to undermine aristocratic political alliances, which were conducive to domination by a single lineage or lone tyrant; and to promote greater social inclusion. Suddenly, Athenians who had only recently been strangers to one another had to work together both to serve their immediate communities and to cooperate to run the larger city. Greek democracy was born.

We might say, then, that democracy began with a visionary act of redistricting. Whatever terminology best applies, Cleisthenes conceived an original way of combining, counting, and constituting people as citizens. "What he did was completely arbitrary, but the new political time and space is now based on these new divisions," Karakantza told me, drawing in the dirt a diagram of the ten tribes to help me understand. The Greeks, she continued, didn't find democracy in a field, like a flower growing near the Pnyx (the clearing on a hill on the west side of the Acropolis where the General Assemblies took place); they invented it to support their collective well-being.

Describing this process of invention, Karakantza invoked the Greek French philosopher Cornelius Castoriadis, who, before his death in 1997, argued that there are always at least two components in any human institution, the functional and the imaginary. The creation of democracy operated on both levels: it entailed both a function, in the form of novel governing procedures, as well as what Castoriadis called a "social imaginary signification," meaning that the way people thought of themselves was utterly transformed. (Indeed, even people's names were changed to include not just the name of one's father but also one's neighborhood, or *deme*.) No longer just family members, religious followers, happenstance neighbors, or meek underlings, individuals became the citizens of Athens, or *the people*, the *demos* of *democracy*. (Like democracy, the idea of citizenship would eventually be mostly forgotten in Europe; for centuries, there were only loyal or disloyal subjects, not citizens engaged in self-rule.)

The creation of this community of citizens involved a balance of two conflicting elements that remain crucial to democracy to this day: spontaneity and structure. Cleisthenes, who had been exiled (in part because his family had been sympathetic to the proto-democratic, debt-abolishing reforms of Solon), was able to take action only after an impromptu riot against the tyrant Isagoras turned into a full-scale rebellion and aggrieved residents called him back to Athens. A sudden burst of sustained rage at the threat of escalating tyranny empowered Cleisthenes to abolish the kin-based system in favor of a place-based one.

The sequence of events reflected a dynamic we all recognize, one in which structural change follows social unrest. There would be no minimum wage, workplace health-and-safety protections, eight-hour workday, or the weekend without the labor organizers and trade unionists who went on strike; there would be no gay rights without the legendary riots at Manhattan's Stonewall Inn; there would be no Americans with Disability Act of 1990 without decades of direct action from impaired activists, who blocked inaccessible buses, pulled their bodies up unwelcoming Capitol Hill steps, and even pissed in public to make a point that they couldn't use regular washroom facilities. The forward march of democracy resembles a kind of two-step move: rule making trails open revolt, like sedimentation hardening into rock after a storm. But just as often, the rule of law has a retrograde function. Regulations created behind closed doors can have the explicit aim of undoing hard-won gains, entrenching the reign of the already powerful. Instead of incorporating the people's demands, political structures are devised to guard against further insurrections.

Political theorists speak of the tension between the rule of law and popular sovereignty, or even between liberalism and democracy itself. This tension, the constant tug-of-war between structure and spontaneity, gets to the very heart of what we mean by the word *constitution*. As James Miller observes in his insightful chronicle of democracy through the ages, "The Greek word *politeia*, sometimes translated as 'constitution,' refers to a community of citizens and how it is structured, via customary rituals and unwritten norms, as well as publicly posted laws."[1] (The Athenians, it's interesting to note, may have been the first democrats of the Western world, but they had no written constitution; even though the rule of law was paramount, individual citizens lacked rights in the sense of inalienable protections against an overweening state.) A constitution, to put it another way, is both a formal code of principles and procedures and also something more ephemeral, an animating spirit or kind of ethos, a way of being as well as an indicator of a community's vitality; each aspect necessarily informs the other, spontaneous expressions infusing more stable structures, impulsiveness and planning intertwined.

Politeia was also the original name for *The Republic*, the founding text of political theory in which Plato imagines not only the laws but also the customs and myths of an ideal city and how those norms would in turn shape the souls of the inhabitants. Plato, as we know, was no democrat, and his ideal society was hardly a place of spontaneous individualism or collective revolt or even of Cleisthenes's visionary reforms (quite the opposite). But his text is thought provoking, especially because few modern citizens think about political structure much at all, let alone as critically and imaginatively as Plato did during democracy's early days.

On a November afternoon in 2016, I met Vashti Hinton, a junior studying political science, at the Agricultural and Technical State University. Situated on the outskirts of Greensboro, North Carolina, A&T is the largest historically black college in the country and a school with a venerable history of political engagement: it is the alma mater of the four young men, locally known as the A&T Four, who launched the sit-in movement at the downtown Woolworth's lunch counter and helped bring down segregation (an example of the retrograde rule of law if there ever was one). Today, the main campus is divided down the middle by one long main road, the two halves each represented by a different member of Congress following a recent redistricting scheme by North Carolina's Republican-controlled state legislature.

"This is District Thirteen and right over there is District Six," Hinton said, standing on one side of the street and pointing to the other sidewalk less than twenty feet away. The districts were strangely shaped when viewed on a map, appearing as squiggly, awkward masses that followed no obvious urban or natural boundaries. To the average person walking to class or driving home from work, the unusual boundaries would have been invisible and thus impossible to analyze and interpret. But the short dividing road on the A&T campus made the usually obscure purpose of the precinct designations shockingly clear: the lines were drawn to deliver Republican representatives. "A lot of students don't understand that they're even doing that when they walk back and forth, that our campus has two different precincts," she said, shaking her head at the ridiculousness of the situation. "They don't understand why that's happening here. So, it's a problem, but it also gives us something to teach about, something to talk about."

The Voting Rights Act of 1965 was the culmination of decades of struggle; it was the efforts of social movements enshrined in law. Then, with *Shelby County v. Holder* in 2013, the Supreme Court reversed course, effectively gutting one of the nation's most historic pieces of legislation. In her dissent, Justice Ruth Bader Ginsburg compared the Court's decision to an individual throwing out his umbrella because he's not currently getting wet. The impact was almost immediate. The day after the Court made its position known, the Republican-controlled North Carolina state legislature passed what would come to be known as the Monster Law, which imposed onerous voter ID requirements and eliminated things such as early voting, same-day voter registration, out-of-precinct voting, and pre-registration for sixteen- and seventeen-year-olds, all innovations that make it easier for busy citizens to vote. While ostensibly "race neutral," court challenges would later strike down much of what the Monster Law contained on the grounds that it purposely targeted racialized communities "with almost surgical precision." (Not something North Carolina Republican leaders found particularly shameful: "African American Early Voting is down 8.5% from this time in 2012. Caucasian voters early voting is up 22.5% from this time in 2012," local GOP officials boasted during the lead-up to the 2016 election.[2])

I asked Carter Wrenn, a well-known Republican strategist involved in North Carolina politics and a former adviser to one of the state's most infamous conservative figures, Jesse Helms, if he agreed that a concerted effort to disenfranchise black people had been made. "Well, I think that it's about power; it's about people getting elected. The politician's goal is always the same, whether they're Republican or Democrat, to give themselves an election advantage, and that's what this is really about," he said, savoring his cigar. "If what you set out to do was to elect Republicans, and African Americans just happened to be a bystander that got shot, I guess you could argue the effect was racist, but the intent surely wasn't. And I doubt you could really argue that the effect was." Wrenn saw accusations of voter fraud, made by Donald Trump and conservative strategists, as an excuse to entrench partisan advantage. Skullduggery is the name of the game, in Wrenn's view, and power exists to be taken: "We live in a fallen world. If you give a politician power, he's going to use it to keep power. The Democrats have done it, the Republicans have done it, that's what's going on with all this voting rights and redistricting. It's a power fight."

The fight is one North Carolina Republicans have thrown themselves into with abandon, building on a long-term nationally coordinated redistricting plan known as REDMAP with the goal of ensuring that even if Democrats win more votes, Republicans keep winning more seats. As a result, in 2018 Republicans won roughly half of the total votes cast for major party candidates in North Carolina yet took an astonishing ten out of thirteen total congressional seats. Such techniques are internationally renowned, employed by imperious officeholders from Malaysia to Hungary, where the autocratic president Viktor Orbán retooled the country's electoral map to ensure he stayed in power even as his party's share of votes diminished.[3] Aiming to control the machinery of the state without drawing much attention to the fact, modern-day voter suppression is a bureaucratic operation. Instead of directing dogs or water cannons at citizens to block them from heading to the polls, party incumbents can mold voting outcomes through an arsenal of seemingly banal spreadsheets and population data sets, discreetly rigging elections from behind closed doors.

In spite of the dullness of the process, redistricting has occasionally become the source of public indignation and outcry. The word *gerrymander* was created at such a moment, first appearing in an 1812 *Boston Gazette* newspaper cartoon illustrating state senate election districts drawn under Massachusetts governor Elbridge Gerry. Created with the intention of favoring Elbridge's party, the Democratic-Republicans, over the Federalist opposition, the Essex district was bizarrely shaped, its outline resembling some kind of winged salamander ("THE GERRYMANDER: A new species of Monster," the caption warned). Citizens were incensed, and while Gerry was eventually forced out of office, his districts and the advantage they bestowed on his associates remained in place.

A little over two hundred years later, in North Carolina, the Moral Mondays movement, led by the charismatic preacher Rev. William Barber III, rose up against a combination of voter-suppression laws and gerrymandering efforts. As a result, when Districts 6 and 13 were redrawn, following the same pattern and serving the same iniquitous purpose as Essex County in the nineteenth century, local residents such as Vashti Hinton were poised to understand the move as the power grab it was and not as a neutral bureaucratic exercise.

Only months prior, the A&T campus had all been part of the district represented by Alma Adams, a progressive black Democrat with deep ties to the community. After Republican legislators brazenly broke the campus in two, each half was tacked onto an overwhelmingly white, Republican precinct. "The goal is to dilute our vote," Hinton explained. "If you have a campus that's split into two different districts, we students don't have that pull, that power. If we unite and A&T students all came out to vote, we could shift a whole local election, right? But now our campus is split, so we don't have one representative we can all rally behind to get what we need."

Hinton was understandably skeptical that either Republican legislator would be particularly attentive to a community whose votes weren't necessary for his reelection, which meant vital issues would go unaddressed. "Now we have two Republican men who represent us, and a lot of times you find that many of the issues that concern the conservatives who vote, who tend to be middle-aged, aren't the same issues that we have as black Millennials," Hinton said. "They're not concerned about policing; we are. They're not concerned about food deserts; we are . . . That's an issue for us, though, because in black and brown communities you see more poverty, you see more hunger."

Hinton's community had been purposefully submerged in neighboring districts so its needs and desires could be legally ignored, and she was outraged. "No longer can we say, 'You can't vote because you're black.' Now we have to create new forms of voter suppression. We have to create new forms of stifling black voices and poor voices. Maybe Republicans don't see it this way, maybe they rely on their little computers or whatever, but the fact of the matter is that you're diluting our votes," she explained. "It's dangerous, because when you do things like gerrymandering, you are taking away someone's power. It's another method of control, of trying to keep us from having this true democracy that America talks about all the time. How can we talk about protecting democracy and how can we talk about making sure that everyone's afforded equal opportunity or equal rights if we're stifling the votes of young people who are trying to do their due diligence to society?"

Hinton and her fellow student are evidence of the changing racial composition of America. "When you have a campus that's split into two different districts, it's like, well, why? Are you afraid of Millennials coming out to vote? Are you afraid of black folks voting?" The answer is clearly yes. Demographic shifts, along with liberalizing social attitudes more generally, have put conservatives in a bind. Without the prospect of winning true majorities, they have taken the gloves off to devise new ways of maintaining power as their base ages and shrinks, including passing voter-suppression laws targeting minorities, curtailing or ending same-day registration, and engaging in unconstitutional gerrymandering. The gerrymanderer's tool kit comprises various techniques of dilution: "cracking," or weakening minority voting strength by spreading those voters across multiple districts so they can't form a majority (the process Hinton witnessed firsthand); "packing" minorities into districts beyond the level needed to elect representatives of their choice (thus black voters might be 90 percent of registered voters when they could swing the precinct by voting at a far lower percentage); and "stacking," or concentrating low-income minorities in the same district with white, high-income citizens, who turn out to vote at far greater numbers. These redistricting techniques explain why, in so many states, Republicans hold more seats than Democrats even though they received fewer votes.

Nowhere is the effect clearer than in North Carolina. Speaking to a crowd of eighty thousand protesters in downtown Raleigh in 2017, Reverend Barber called out these devious and deceptive practices. "Wealthy oligarchs know they cannot hold on to power in truly democratic elections. If you can't win on the issues, stop cheating to keep yourself in office," Barber preached imploring his listeners to keep the larger system in mind. "This is not just about a president and we miss it if we think it is. This is about an entire web of money and influence and white hegemony that has been working to tie up the American democracy from the very inception of this country." What Barber brings that makes his analysis so powerful is a historical view: none of this is new in America. As he tells it in his books, at the protest podium, and from the pulpit, contemporary Republican mischief harkens all the way back to the period of Reconstruction.

Immediately following the Civil War the percentage of black voter registration rates exceeded 90 percent in some communities, and high turnout helped send thousands of freedmen to office.

The proportion of black people elected to office soared from 0 to 15 percent at the local, state, and national levels.[4] By the 1880s, a multiracial working-class populist "Fusion Coalition" gained traction in North Carolina, winning elections and taking city governments, with the goal of implementing a politically and economically egalitarian agenda that would lift up the poor regardless of race. The white power structure responded with a murderous coup, overthrowing the democratically elected Fusion government in Wilmington. Across the state, it waged a campaign of racial terror and voter suppression, helping set the stage for segregation. Throughout the South, state constitutions were changed to include poll taxes and literacy tests. By 1938, a mere thirty-five thousand votes were cast in the congressional midterms in Mississippi, though the state had a population of more than two million.[5] Blacks, and many poor whites with them, were disenfranchised in droves.

Modern-day redistricting can be understood only in light of these and other past offenses, including the ongoing mistreatment of Native American voters, who were granted citizenship only in 1924 but, because state governments took a page from the Jim Crow playbook to undermine indigenous suffrage, also relied on the Voting Rights Act to become enfranchised. When explicit exclusions were no longer possible, facially neutral techniques to deny or dilute the indigenous vote developed, including moving polling places to distant locations (up to 150 miles from tribal territories in some cases)[6] or gerrymandering and malapportionment (in the 1970s the largest district of Apache County, Arizona, was 88 percent Indian and had fifteen times the population of the city's smallest district, which was almost entirely white).[7] This mischief is still under way: weeks before the 2018 midterm general election, the Supreme Court upheld a North Dakota voter ID law requiring identification listing a physical address, a rule seemingly designed to negatively affect indigenous voters who live on reservations where street addresses are uncommon.

The Fifteenth Amendment of 1870 declared that the "vote

shall not be denied or abridged by the United States or by any state on account of race, color, or previous condition of servitude." Ninety-five years later, the Voting Rights Act was a second attempt to make the guarantee stick. Yet state and local governments continue to devise devious workarounds to prevent poor and minority participation on an equal footing with that of more affluent, disproportionately white citizens. The American habit of allowing representatives, as opposed to independent commissions, to draw electoral districts essentially lets politicians pick their voters, as opposed to the other way around. (Places that use independent commissions have been shown to have much more competitive races.) As a result, the U.S. House has a 97 percent reelection rate despite abysmal approval ratings.[8] Incumbents, who are in charge of drawing those district lines, aim not for fairness but for ensuring that their seats are safe.

Perhaps because of the long struggle for equal suffrage by women and racialized people, we tend to see voting as a problem of access to the ballot box. If citizens can get to the polls without discrimination or obstruction, democracy's work is being done. But voting is not a straightforward right and a self-evident action, but something more complex, a process that involves different tiers. The first tier is the simple act of being able to cast a ballot; the next is how each vote is weighted compared to others; the third is whether elected officials will be able to enact the policies they were elected to promote. The American system is inherently and vastly unequal where the second tier is concerned, which is why advocates like Hinton speak of vote "dilution."

Consider the Senate. The principle of equal state representation, Alexander Hamilton pointed out in 1788, "contradicts the fundamental maxim of republican government, which requires that the sense of the majority should prevail." A scant 2 percent of Americans, residing in the nine smallest states, hold the same power in the Senate as the 51 percent who reside in the nine largest; some votes are worth up to sixty-six times more than others, and urban migration trends mean that this problem will only become more extreme.[9] This imbalance partly explains why gun control is such an intractable issue, as the majority of the minority of Americans who live in households that own lethal weapons (over one-third of the population) reside in low-population, high-value-vote states, which helps make amending or restricting the constitutional right to bear arms unreachable. In Senate elections, "one person, one vote" may hold true technically, but not all votes are equal.

The Supreme Court has called the right to vote the "fundamental political right . . . preservative of all rights." Today "free and fair elections" are widely taken as the essence and end point of democracy, a view the United Nations' Universal Declaration of Human Rights of 1948 essentially affirms: "The will of the people shall be the basis of the authority of government; this will shall be expressed in periodic and genuine elections which shall be by universal and equal suffrage and shall be held by secret vote or by equivalent free voting procedures." But what counts as "genuine," and who defines "free voting procedures"? The phrase "one person, one vote" sounds straightforward enough, but in reality, many advanced democracies, particularly the United States, fall flagrantly short of this eminently achievable ideal.

Before the 2018 elections, Tiririca ("Grumpy"), the popular clown turned lawmaker, announced that he would not seek reelection for his seat in the Brazilian Chamber of Deputies. Though he had outperformed all the other candidates and coasted into office with 1.3 million votes in 2010, a feat he repeated in 2014, Tiririca (otherwise known as Francisco Everardo Oliveira Silva) was fed up. "Everyone knows that we're paid well to work, but not everyone does work. There are 513 deputies, only eight come regularly. And I'm one of those eight, and I'm a circus clown," he complained. When he announced his retirement, he admitted that he had "not done much" during his eight years in office, but he reminded his supporters that the bar was low: "At least I was here." His campaign slogan "It can't get any worse," intended as a humorous motivator, had turned out to be depressingly wrong. Things had, in fact, continued to deteriorate, and so he decided to return to more dignified forms of clowning.

The tragedy of Tiririca is that he expected a serious job but instead found himself back at the big top. This wouldn't have surprised the historians I've read who compare elections to Carnival, the religious festivity of the Middle Ages that allowed men and women to affirm the strength and permanence of the social hierarchy by appearing to defy it. Elections, the analogy goes, provide citizens a similar stage for the safe expression of discontent while ultimately signaling their compliance. (They may not like the results, but they cast a ballot.)[10]

Today, the ritualistic motions of democracy permit politicians to pay melodramatic tribute to a system they've helped ransack and ruin, fueling political disenchantment and cynicism as the divide between rulers and ruled grows ever wider. Disaffected citizens see a system in which their votes don't count and where even well-intentioned legislators aren't able to effect positive change. Little surprise then that professional jesters and comedians have been winning high office: not just Tiririca in Brazil, but also the later disgraced Al Franken from Minnesota; Jón Gnarr of Iceland's Best Party; and Beppe Grillo, who leads the anti-immigrant, Internet-fuelled Five Star Movement in Italy. "If you see a circus, elect a clown" appears to be an absurdist, international axiom.

"If voting could change anything, it would be made illegal." What this frequently misattributed quote (sometimes credited to the anarchist Emma Goldman, sometimes to Mark Twain, though it actually seems to have debuted in a small-town op-ed in 1976) fails to note is that, as we have seen, casting a vote is only one aspect of democratic elections. Who or what is ultimately more responsible for Donald Trump's triumph: the people who voted (who chose Hillary Clinton by a large margin) or the structure of our political system (dominated by the outdated Electoral College, which weighs some ballots more than others and routinely hands victory to the loser of the popular vote)? Under even marginally more democratic structural conditions, a demagogue like Trump probably wouldn't stand a chance (and if America were ancient Athens, he would have been at high risk of being ostracized).

Similarly, if leadership elections were a regular feature of party politics in the United States, as they are in the United Kingdom, the results would be transformative. Democratic socialist Jeremy Corbyn was able to take over as Labour leader in 2015 only by bringing tens of thousands of new members into the party, and reenergizing the base; it seems safe to assume that the Democratic Party would also move sharply to the left if party members had more of a say. But to do that, the organization would have to be restructured to become more accountable to members, perhaps in part by allowing them to sustain the party through modest dues instead of the current arrangement, which focuses on pandering to deep-pocketed donors and using data to target otherwise disengaged voters in swing districts.[11]

Today, alternative ways of structuring and counting the vote that would remedy or even cure the current system's imbalances are ignored or dismissed as outside the realm of possibility. Even something as commonsensical as making election day a national holiday or automatically registering all citizens to vote is too much for most American lawmakers to consider. (Forget figuring out how to make electronic voting effortless and secure.) It wasn't until 2015, for example, that Oregon broke democratic ground by becoming the first state to make voter registration an opt-out instead of an opt-in system. Instead of following this example, hundreds of millions of dollars are spent to (selectively) register people and get out, or "rock," the vote every election cycle. Yet somehow, despite the tremendous expense and effort, the country still trails most developed nations in voter turnout.[12]

Meanwhile, Australia, Belgium, Argentina, and twenty or so other countries go far beyond mass registration—in these places, voting is mandatory. Citizens can always choose to leave their ballot blank, but they have to show up or face the consequences. In

Australia, offenders will be fined twenty dollars and then fifty; in Belgium, chronic abstainers risk losing the ability to vote for ten years (which hardly seems like a punishment, given the crime). Experts heatedly debate the hypothetical impact of compulsory voting in the United States, but this much seems clear: since older, wealthier, more educated white people are overrepresented at the polls, an obligatory franchise would shift the balance of power by creating a more diverse, young, and working-class voter pool. One revealing study of ballot measures in Switzerland, for example, found that when voting became mandatory, progressive positions were boosted by up to twenty percentage points.[13]

Electoral structures shape political outcomes, which is why the people have struggled over voting issues since the modern era's democratic revival began. In England in the 1600s, the radical group the Levellers called for regular elections and proportional regional representation, a demand that was revived nearly two centuries later when the Reform Act of 1832 abolished the most egregious "rotten boroughs"—sparsely populated rural districts that entitled wealthy landlords to valuable parliamentary seats. In 1838 disgruntled workers agitated to take things further, collecting one million signatures for a petition dubbed the People's Charter that bore six demands: universal male suffrage, no property qualification to vote, annual elections for parliaments, secret ballots, payment of MPs, and districts that were uniform in size.

Chartism was not victorious, but its legacy reminds us that over the course of the long, hard fight to win the right to vote, men and women have also always pushed to make voting systems fairer and more responsive—that is to say, more democratic. In the United States, this ambition is reflected in the Seventeenth, Twenty-Fourth, and Twenty-Sixth Amendments (ratified in 1913, 1964, and 1971) allowing for, respectively, the direct election of senators, the elimination of the poll tax, and lowering of the voting age from twenty-one to eighteen.

In addition to these famous amendments are some important though less celebrated victories, specifically the adoption in some states and localities of initiative, referendum, and recall procedures, reforms based on the old idea that the people, subject to laws, should have more of a say (or, if they weren't exactly authors of law, that they should at least authorize the rules that govern them). Advocates of these methods saw them, in part, as a return to the nation's roots, to a time before party bosses and moneyed interests took over the political process.

As early as the 1640s, directly democratic techniques were used in the colonies, where freemen assembled in New England town meetings or ratified state constitutions (which often granted citizens exceptional authority: the Pennsylvania constitution of 1776, for example, included the right to "reform, alter, or abolish government" if "the people" saw fit). Various states not only gave citizens the right to legislate but also permitted them to recall their representatives, should they be so inclined, a power not granted by the national Constitution, despite (or perhaps because of) the fact that the framers understood it would make officials more accountable to the demands and whims of their constituents.

It was the Populist Party of the late nineteenth century that revived this more directly democratic tradition. As they pushed for structural change, the Populists also looked to the inspiring example of more direct practices in Switzerland, which were then being enthusiastically reported by a labor leader and social reformer named J. W. Sullivan. Referendums were introduced into Switzerland's Federal Constitution in 1874 as a control instrument for parliamentary laws; then, in 1891, the right of citizens to launch a "popular" initiative to change the constitution was enshrined. The Swiss model "rendered bureaucracy impossible" while encouraging every citizen to have a "lively interest in the public affairs," Sullivan enthused in his broadsides.

The party's first national convention, in 1892, passed resolutions supporting initiative and referendum reforms (as well as the direct election of senators), on the grounds that they would make the government more responsive and responsible to the people and politics less corruptible, as masses of citizens could not easily be bought off.

Such procedures, Populists maintained, would empower down-trodden farmers, debtors, and laborers (the "producing classes") against the railroad, banking, and agricultural monopolists, effectively neutralizing special interests while opening an avenue for the popular will to be expressed through policy. With these transformative aims in mind, socialists and suffragists were the first to join the cause. Advocates of votes for women thought the initiative and referendum process might be one path to overcome intransigent state legislatures. (They might have been less optimistic had they known that the Swiss men whose directly democratic political system they admired would not vote to enfranchise women until 1971.)

A generation later, the Progressive movement took up the gauntlet, and after winning over converts that included Theodore Roosevelt and Woodrow Wilson, it made ideas once dismissed as foolish crankery palatable to the mainstream. Initiative and referendum, Wilson said, could help repair a broken system in which elected representatives were not their own masters but "puppets in a game."[14] In 1902, Oregon, on the cutting edge even then, became the first state to institute the initiative and referendum, allowing people to initiate legislation. Today almost half the states have a ballot initiative process that allows citizens to propose laws or constitutional amendments either to their representatives or to fellow voters, instead of having to persuade legislators to pass reforms.

With initiative, referendum, and recall, reformers believed they had found a way to manifest the will of the people, pure and undiluted, but in practice, that has hardly turned out to be the case. Because plebiscites typically take the form of an all-or-nothing vote, they frequently distort complicated issues into a binary framework, a tendency vividly displayed during the Brexit vote in 2016, when British citizens' complicated and often contradictory feelings about the European Union, the economy, immigration, and the country's political leadership all got whittled down to fit into one of two boxes, yes or no. From the moment the result was announced, a large contingent of citizens have demanded a do-over, convinced the outcome would switch.

Most referendums are less dramatic but equally problematic. Because they happen infrequently, established interests have found ways to game the process. In California, where the initiative process is regularly used, the signatures required to get a measure on the ballot can end up costing ten dollars each in some instances, or several millions of dollars. (Supporters must gather a number equal to 5 or 8 percent of the most recent gubernatorial vote within a period of 180 days.) Should citizens successfully jump that hurdle, they will likely need far larger coffers to counter negative advertising from their opponents, who have been known to spend upward of a million dollars a day on a media blitz.

Companies with deep pockets can also get their own issues on the ballot, as Uber and Lyft did in 2016 in Austin, Texas, spending nearly nine million dollars to push Proposition 1, a municipal referendum designed to nullify city ordinances that regulated ride-hailing apps on the same terms as traditional taxi services (including fingerprint-based background checks, which became a flashpoint after a slew of passenger rapes in 2015).[15] In this instance, the impressive sum wasn't large enough—angry residents were adamant that they wanted the same rules for cabbies to apply to Uber and Lyft drivers—and Proposition 1 was defeated by a 12 percent margin.

In response, the companies lobbied Greg Abbott, the state's Republican governor, to push for and pass House Bill 100, which stripped local governments of the ability to regulate transportation network companies, or TNCs, citizens' concerns and preferences be damned.[16] At the signing ceremony, Abbott said it was "disappointing" that Austin had "rejected and jettisoned that very freedom from the customers who wanted to have a choice in what transportation provider they could choose. Today is also a day of tremendous free enterprise." (Adding to the irony, the law included an amendment defining "sex" as "the physical condition of being male or female," intended as a jab at Austin liberalism and transgender Texans seeking the freedom to use bathrooms that matched their gender identity.)

In a society where wealth is highly concentrated and political spending enjoys First Amendment protections, money distorts every aspect of our political system, even reforms meant to mitigate the influence of the affluent. Regardless, referendums can occasionally be powerful tools for the citizenry locked out of day-to-day representative politics. In 2018 Florida citizens restored voting rights to 1.4 million felons, and referenda in Michigan, Utah, and Colorado passed ensuring the creation of independent, nonpartisan commissions to take charge of redistricting.[17] But despite the optimism of the populists, socialists, and progressives of yore, ballot initiatives are less a vehicle for the unadulterated voice of the people than a jury-rigged solution to a gerrymandered system. In any country with a winner-take-all, first-past-the-post system, the problem of apportioning votes means that some will be granted less weight or even wasted altogether (the votes that do not go to the winning candidate, as well as all the votes that the winner does not need—anything over 50 percent—are unmeasured in the system). The occasional opportunity to weigh in on legislation doesn't change that uncomfortable reality.

In the United States, the United Kingdom, and Canada, which all rely on such systems, electoral reform has become a rallying cry for citizens who rightly believe that one impediment to democracy is the way that votes are counted. Advocates look to Finland, Germany, New Zealand, and many other advanced democracies that use more representative voting systems, which close the gap between the popular vote and the seats granted to particular parties. Instead of electing one person in each district, several people are elected in larger multimember districts; if a party wins 20 percent of the vote, it gets 20 percent of the seats. What could be more straightforward than that? With proportional representation in place, voters no longer have to worry about third-party spoilers or the lesser of two evils. Overall competitiveness increases, as does the representation of women and racial minorities, while the problem of gerrymandering disappears.

The United States purports to be a system of majority rule, but our rigged system makes a farce of that promise; a proportional system, in contrast, would disperse power among a much wider range of people, aiming to build consensus through multiparty, coalition government. (Though parliamentary, not presidential, systems, the United Kingdom and Canada would also benefit from a similar overhaul. In the 2017 election in the UK, for example, Conservatives won 42 percent of the aggregate vote but 49 percent of the parliamentary seats. One study determined that under any number of more representative voting systems, Labour would have won.)

The principle of "one person, one vote" is relatively new, a product of Supreme Court decisions dating to the 1960s, but it's already in need of updating: "one person, one equally weighted vote" is the motto we should aspire to. Today, concerned citizens and fair-vote advocates are trying to enact just that. In 2016, Maine residents became so frustrated by the results of winner-take-all-elections that had repeatedly put a despised governor in office that a majority approved a ballot initiative to make their state the first in the nation to use what's called ranked-choice voting, a system that allows voters to rank candidates in order of preference. (Lawmakers responded by passing a bill delaying the effective date until December 2021, which forced their rivals to mobilize around another ballot measure that sucessfully vetoed the legislation.) In Canada, after a push from the grass roots, electoral reform became one of Prime Minister Justin Trudeau's main campaign promises. Now that he's in office, however, he has changed his tune. (No doubt, his victory convinced him that the current system works just fine—why open his party up to challengers currently locked out?)

Though maddening, the resistance faced by modern-day reform efforts is but a faint echo of the hostility endured by earlier proponents of proportional representation who sought to break the power of party machines and bosses in dozens of cities, and often succeeded. In municipalities where the change was implemented, city councils came to more accurately reflect voter preferences, but these modest victories were soon undone. Dethroned politicians and parties mounted legal challenges and sponsored referendum after referendum aimed at repeal. "In Cincinnati, race was the dominant theme in the successful 1957 repeal effort," political scientist Douglas Amy explains in his short account of the movement. African Americans were in office for the first time, "with two blacks being elected to the city council in the 1950s." Opponents of proportional representation unscrupulously exploited racial tensions, fanning white fears about the increasing power of the black community and asking if people wanted a "Negro Mayor" lording over them. The appeal worked: whites supported repeal by a two-to-one margin.

During the same period, proportional representation was rolled back in New York City by the stoking of Cold War anxieties, not racial ones. More equitable voting procedures were tarnished as "an un-American practice which has helped the cause of communism and does not belong in the American way of life," a "political importation from the Kremlin," and "the first beachhead of Communist infiltration in this country." It was considered especially important to crush reform in New York City because a major metropolis might serve as a stepping-stone to higher levels of government, allowing the contagion to spread and minority parties to gain a foothold. The success of the New York City campaign sparked similar repeals in other cities, such as Boulder, Colorado, and Toledo, Ohio. In a matter of years, the democratic threat of proportional representation was successfully contained.[18]

Had the reformers been successful, they would have discovered that proportional representation is not necessarily a panacea, at least in its pure form. Even modified versions of the system make it possible for fringe parties to become influential powerbrokers within unstable coalition governments, a pathology most visible in Israel and Italy, where hard-liners wield significant influence and exacerbate conflict. Yet winner-take-all systems are arguably more pathological, enforcing and perpetuating a structure of unequal representation that reflects the fundamental logic of our economic system: the idea that (a few) winners dominating (many) losers is acceptable and legitimate. No electoral model can single-handedly cure deeper social and economic divisions or ward off extremists, but more proportional representation would certainly improve matters, presenting different, and arguably more interesting, problems for citizens to contend with than the arrangement now in place. What is democratic progress, after all, if not new and better problems?

Standing in front of a massive crowd gathered on the main Sproul Plaza of the University of California–Berkeley campus, a young graduate student named Mario Savio gave an impromptu speech that would be remembered as one of the defining moments of a generation.

> There's a time when the operation of the machine becomes so odious, makes you so sick at heart that you can't take part! You can't even passively take part! And you've got to put your bodies upon the gears and upon the wheels, upon the levers, upon all the apparatus— and you've got to make it stop! And you've got to indicate to the people who run it, to the people who own it—that unless you're free the machine will be prevented from working at all!!

The Berkeley Free Speech Movement erupted in 1964, when students, many of whom had recently returned from civil rights campaigns in the South, were told they could no longer pamphlet or table for political causes on school property. The images of the rebellion that engulfed the campus in response to the school's prohibition were broadcast far and wide. The students won the right to leaflet, as well as other concessions from the administration, but their real, lasting victory was symbolic. It's not just that there's now an official Free Speech Movement Café on campus, where students study surrounded by black-and-white photos of those heady days, or that the steps at Sproul Plaza are named for Mario Savio and can be reserved for those who want to pontificate, but also that our assumptions about social change have been shaped by those events, even if we have never actually heard of the Free Speech Movement and don't have the faintest sense of what it was about.

Savio and his comrades set the stage for what came to be known as "the sixties." As the decade wore on, the idea that young people had a special role to play in political movements took hold for the first time—today it's regarded as common sense—just when spontaneous protest came to be seen as the ultimate form of resistance to the status quo. In his widely read "Letter to the New Left," sociologist C. Wright Mills made the case that youth had replaced the working class as the "historic agency." Theodore Roszak, who popularized the term *counterculture*, called this shift the "adolescentization of dissent."

The emphasis on young people, and students in particular, as agents of change, and on generational politics as a given, diminished the importance of other traditions, especially labor union organizing, while letting older people off the hook. Over time, the idea of idealistic, spontaneous youthful rebellion (something marketers latched on to with a vengeance) came to appeal more than alternative models for building political power, in particular models that might serve beyond the college green. The goal of oppositional movements throughout American history (be they populist, progressive, socialist, or Communist) to transform political institutions and make them susceptible to popular control ceased to occupy center stage.

Events on the Berkeley campus also inspired Ronald Reagan, then a candidate for governor of California, to invoke a backlash. Campaigning across the state, he tapped a deep well of anti-student sentiment, deriding students and faculty as intellectual, out-of-touch snobs and vowing to "clean up the mess at Berkeley," which he portrayed as a hotbed of sexual, social, generational, and even Communist deviance. Thus Reagan, a wealthy movie star, burnished his reputation by pointing an accusatory finger at the so-called cultural elite, a strategy successfully employed by countless well-heeled Republicans and businessmen in his wake.

A little more than ten years later, another California protest caught Reagan's attention, this time earning his enthusiastic support. The tax revolt, which kicked off in Southern California, was not a movement of mediagenic young people, but a highly organized offensive by older citizens—much like the Tea Party, which they presaged. Lesser known than the Free Speech Movement, which inadvertently helped Reagan win the governorship, this one aided his ascent to the White House and was ultimately far more successful. A movement that initially mustered a handful of retirees to burn their tax collection notices at the Sacramento Capitol soon became a wave of tax revolts across the land and ultimately remade a vital component of the country's government apparatus.

At the start, the tax revolt was not a purely right-wing campaign. Out-of-control inflation meant that people of all political persuasions had trouble paying their ballooning tax assessments. Some elderly folks on fixed incomes, who had bought houses long ago, were threatened with the prospect of eviction. This genuine grievance provided a fiercely antigovernment crusader, a real estate investor named Howard Jarvis, with the opportunity he had been waiting for. Jarvis had attempted to organize against the federal income tax in the past but hadn't made much headway; he vigorously opposed many of the things taxes paid for, including schools, parks, libraries, and garbage collection. "The most important thing in this country is not the school system, nor the police department, nor the fire department," Jarvis said. "The right to preserve, the right to have property in this country, the right to have a home in this country—that's important."[19] Though a right-wing dogmatist, he carefully modeled his Everyman persona on the star of the hit film *Network* ("I'm mad as hell, and I'm not going to take it anymore!" the character yells on national television, sparking a mass rebellion.)

Yoking his conservative antistate ideology, which opposed taxation and government in general, to the particular, concrete problems faced by his community, Jarvis gathered enough signatures to get a ballot initiative on the agenda. In 1978, Proposition 13, formally called the People's Initiative to Limit Property Taxation, passed in a landslide, and California property taxes were radically cut. Homeowners got the tax relief they were looking for, but many experts question whether Californians actually understood what they were voting for.

Proposition 13 seemed simple but actually wasn't. Jarvis had written more into the law than just lowering property taxes to reasonable levels. He decimated them. The initiative, which is still in place, froze property assessments at 1975 levels; they could then be raised by only 2 percent a year, and the property reassessed only at the time of a sale or transfer. All property would then be taxed at a flat 1 percent of its new value, choking state revenue—which was, of course, the law's true aim. This was all bad enough, but there were some other details overlooked by voters. First, Proposition 13 applies to corporate *and* rental properties, not just primary residences (homes change hands more frequently than businesses, getting reassessed every time, but a massive profit generator such as Disney Land still pays property taxes based on 1978 assessments). Second, Proposition 13 prohibits any government body, local or state, from raising new taxes without a two-thirds vote of the governing body, a hurdle almost impossible to jump. Ever savvy, Jarvis understood the system he was trying to transform and how he wanted to change it, including how to stop future generations of citizens and legislators from undoing his structural changes.

The movement for Proposition 13, which prompted tax-cutting referendums in at least eighteen states, has been called "a major turning point in American politics," something that "provided conservatism with a powerful internal coherence, shaping an anti-government ethic and firmly establishing new grounds for the disaffection of white working and middle class voters from their Democratic roots."[20] When Proposition 13 passed, Jarvis declared it "a victory against money, the politicians, the government."

"Government simply must be limited," he went on. "Excessive taxation leads to either bankruptcy or dictatorship."[21] Reagan agreed. He urged his followers to recognize the significance of the California vote and use it as a means to light a "prairie fire" of opposition to "costly, overpowering government."[22]

Here, at last, was a way to get regular Americans, who were not particularly skeptical of government at that point, to join a movement with government as the enemy.[23] The community's justified anger against out-of-control property taxes was encouraged to morph into contempt for taxes in general. And it worked. Though it's hard to imagine today, prior to Proposition 13 and Reagan's presidential campaign, tax cuts were not the fundamental issue in American politics that they now are.[24] In the intervening decades, plenty of well-funded, corporate, special interest groups have done their part to push tax cuts as a major political issue, and that's a crucial part of the narrative, but without the movement of angry California homeowners, they may not have known how to frame their positions in a way that could at least *plausibly* appear palatable, or even popular. Jarvis's campaign provided the ruling class with crucial cover, while opening space for the vitriolic and racialized division between taxpayers and tax recipients, the makers versus the takers, that we see everywhere today.

The contrast between these two influential protests, the Free Speech Movement and the Proposition 13 tax revolt, sheds valuable light on our current impasse. The Free Speech Movement shaped our image of resistance as a spontaneous, youthful act. The tax revolters, on the other hand, found the gears and the levers Savio spoke of so eloquently and they did more than bring them to a screeching halt—they remade the machine. As Jarvis well knew, the gears were both economic and political.

It's worth lingering on the consequences of Proposition 13. Not only did it enshrine broad antipathy toward taxation; it also shrank the state economically: local governments saw billions of dollars evaporate; municipalities cut services and fired staff (San Francisco closed more than two dozen schools and fired teachers, while other cities saw buses and arts programs reduced; mass transit fares spiked; mental health and disability programs were slashed; and state universities, some of the best in the nation, started charging tuition when they had once been almost free). Companies, meanwhile, pocketed tens or hundreds of millions in saved property taxes. ("Pacific Telephone saved $130 million; Pacific Gas & Electric, over $90 million; Standard Oil, $13 million in Contra Costa County alone," according to Michael Stewart Foley's *Front Porch Politics*.[25]) On the political front, tax revolt organizers understood the workings of government. Jarvis and his allies were able to attract enough support to put Proposition 13 on the ballot, and then they locked in their victory by insisting on a supermajority vote to impose any new taxes.[26] When Reagan and other Republican leaders caught on, this basic playbook became standard GOP policy.

There's much for progressives to learn from the tax revolt and how it reconfigured governing structures, but they tend to see themselves as more akin to the Free Speech Movement—opposed to the workings of the machine instead of being dedicated to changing its operation so that it runs more equitably. Consider how, in the weeks after Donald Trump's election, millions of liberal Americans rallied under the banner of the "resistance," setting themselves outside the state. While mass demonstrations gather, embodying the spirit of the student activists at Sproul Plaza in 1964, too few seriously consider how the rules of the game (most obviously but not only the outdated Electoral College) facilitate undemocratic outcomes or what to do to change those rules. The effect of issues such as foreign disinformation on social media pales in comparison to homegrown structural hindrances, which dramatically dilute the impact of citizens' choices or disenfranchise them altogether.

Of course, the romanticization of resistance, with its echoes of World War II heroism, precedes Trump. Attend any protest and you'll hear the chant "This is what democracy looks like," which implicitly pits the charade of representative democracy against supposedly authentic, spontaneous expressions of popular revolt. Those susceptible to democracy's more oppositional, untamed incarnations await the next wave of street demonstrations or viral hashtags, knowing that movements have an impromptu, effervescent energy that can never be predictably harnessed or maintained— which is part of their appeal. This is what the political theorist Sheldon Wolin calls "fugitive democracy," those fleeting moments that break through the cracks of constitutional governance's oppressively bureaucratic iron cage. An intrinsically feral phenomenon, democracy, this line of thinking insists, is destined to wither when confined to a ballot box or otherwise systematized.

Of course rambunctious and sometimes rancorous spontaneity is critical. Peasant rebellions, wildcat strikes, and urban riots have bent the will of recalcitrant authorities time and again, like the social tumult that emboldened Cleisthenes to introduce his reforms or the nonviolent mass walkouts, or secession, by Roman plebeians, which led to the establishment of the Tribune of the People to defend their interests. In recent decades, however, the spontaneous side of the equation has come to dominate understandings of how social change happens, while attention to long-term organizing strategy and the question of how to institutionalize victories has correspondingly dimmed. Faith in political structures is in a seemingly irreversible decline, while democracy as insurrection flourishes.

Spontaneity appeals to both sides of the political spectrum. On the left, radical anarchists embrace the idea that people can run their own affairs without institutions or interference from above, implicitly harkening back to Rousseau's "general will" by assuming humanity's innate attraction to the common good. On the right, adherents of the free market believe that democracy is a laissez-faire occurence, best reflected in the buying and selling of goods and services; market-promoting libertarians romantically invoke an "invisible hand," or the market's innate intelligence. For both camps, democracy is unstructured, emergent, something more likely to be squelched by the state than supported by it.

The advent of digital technology and the rise of online-enabled protest intensified these views. The dominant image of the Internet (a horizontal network of interconnected nodes) and its peer-to-peer protocol dovetailed with the idea, already popular in both progressive activist and free-market circles, that people, if left to their own devices, are able to "self-organize."[27] (In his missives against central planning Friedrich Hayek coined the term *catallaxy* to describe the "self-organizing system of voluntary cooperation," or the spontaneous order of the free-market economy, which would be snuffed out by any attempt to regulate or direct it.) In fact, the rise of digital communication, while allowing people to connect more quickly and easily than ever before, has corresponded with a deepening of economic inequality and a general sense of democratic decline and malaise. As the Arab Spring proved, overreliance on the Internet as a tool of self-organization can allow more organized and hierarchical forces to prevail despite massive popular discontent—Facebook groups are no match for the Muslim Brotherhood.

Moreover, the ability of citizens to communicate through virtual channels coincided with a general withering of traditional community institutions and a coordinated assault on labor unions, which contributed to the loss of time-honored political organizing know-how on the left; it has also empowered reactionary communities on the right, creating spaces for racist and misogynist subcultures to congregate and flourish. Looking back on this period, we may realize that we were seduced by the idea of automating democracy through technology when in fact the tools we thought would set us free are de-skilling us, making us more inept at doing the difficult work democracy requires.

Here it can be helpful to distinguish between organizing and activism. Where the term *organizer* has clear roots in trade union and labor politics, *activist* gained currency after the 1960s and merely connotes someone advocating for a cause, even if they operate alone and do little more than raise awareness, online or off. Activists may resist more, well, actively, perhaps by joining a peaceful march, illegally blocking an intersection, or camping in a public square. These kinds of acts are vital to democracy and can buoy group morale, but compelling bursts of civil disobedience can also mask the fact that the left is not yet strong, strategic, or patient enough to transform expressions of discontent into a force that can pull political and economic structures in a more democratic direction. Conservatives know this well: they have been busy executing organizational strategies over the last forty years—launching think tanks and business associations buoyed by corporate largesse, inflaming the ground troops of the Moral Majority and the Tea Party, cementing electoral victories through REDMAP redistricting plans, and laying the foundation for a permanent tax revolt to starve the welfare state of the revenue it needs to run. Over the same period, the left mostly abandoned its organizing roots, which it must now work to rediscover and reinvent for a new age.

Reverend Barber, who takes inspiration from Martin Luther King Jr.'s unfinished Poor People's Campaign, is trying to do just that. "We march not as a spontaneous action, but as a movement that stands on deep foundations of organizing that have gone on for years, setting the groundwork for times such as this," Barber told the crowd gathered in Raleigh. "I disagree so much with those who talk about spontaneity. No, this comes from a deep root, seeds that were sewn by people who have long since left earth." History shows us that there are no shortcuts: spontaneous expressions of discontent have to be expanded and advanced by the hard, slow work of organizing with the aim of structural change.

In their quest for political equality of the citizenry, the architects of the Athenian system incorporated spontaneity in a sophisticated way from which we might learn. Cleisthenes had the good sense to seize the opportunity of the people's riot against tyranny and work an element of chance into Athens's governing structure. This purposeful political design reflected a commitment to the idea of a truly empowered citizenry that ruled itself, not through representatives but through procedures that made space for contingency. For example, attendance at the General Assembly was largely random, though typically the body numbered around five thousand to seven thousand of the thirty-five to sixty thousand eligible citizens. (Showing up was considered a duty but was not mandatory, though Greeks who tried to slip out of the Agora before an Assembly began might get gently thwacked and shamefully marked by fellow citizens holding strings dipped in red ink.)

More significantly, a process of drawing lots determined selection to the juries, the Boule, and most, though not all, official government posts. To the Greek mind, lottery, or sortition, was essential because elections were believed to perpetuate aristocratic hierarchy, given that the well-bred, wealthy, and eloquent held a significant advantage and were likely to win. "The appointment of magistrates by lots is democratical, and the election of them oligarchical," Aristotle observed. "The basis of a democratic state is liberty . . . One principle of liberty is for all to rule and be ruled in turn." Sortition and rotation meant that no one individual or group could dominate. (Initially, a lottery may have been adopted because it eased tensions between warring families or factions, but it became a deeply held egalitarian principle.)

As a consequence, there were no political parties, and the position equivalent to president or prime minister was held for a single day, a fleeting figurehead. You might be judge for an afternoon or a councilor for a year, but professional politicians as we understand them did not exist. At the same time, political service, including but not limited to jury duty, was compensated so the poor could participate on equal terms with the better off. Experts estimate that every male Athenian citizen likely served in the body that set the agenda for the Assembly at some point in his lifetime. It was as though everyone had to expect he would eventually serve in Congress or Parliament. No doubt such an arrangement would completely transform our conception of politics and our sense of what we need to know, and what we need our fellow citizens to know. (One would hope that under such a system investment in public education would skyrocket.)

I asked Efimia Karakantza about the significance, psychologically and politically, of being elected rather than appointed indiscriminately. "I should imagine if you're selected by vote, or elected, you feel you are quite special. You likely feel that you know better than the rest of the people, and it's up to you to run the business of the city or the country. And because of course you were elected, that means you were supported by other people—by companies, by corporations . . . Everybody can think of examples from their own countries. Then you have to pay that back." The Greek system reduced the likelihood of corruption, especially when backed up by a strict system of public accounting. "Everybody who has a public office—they were accountable afterward. They had to say how much money they spent and why they spent this money," Karakantza explained. "And if they found that there was something missing or fishy, they would go to trial. They had to give an account of their administration every year."

As the writer Roslyn Fuller observes, "the Athenians were concerned, and even obsessed, with the role money could play in politics."[28] Profiting from politics was a criminal offense, and close tabs were kept on public spending. To the average Athenian democrat, today's system—in which elections are high-priced popularity contests and officials, governing with the primary aim of being reelected, spend their time in office fund-raising toward that goal ("absorbed by the cares of self-defense," as a text from 1830 describes the process[29]), sending kickbacks to donors, and enriching themselves—would seem completely absurd, and certainly not democratic. Yet somehow we accept such venal proceedings as democratic acts, or even as democracy's apex.

Imagining a lottery-based system with modern eyes and expectations, we can find it hard to believe it worked, but it did. "Although one might expect chaos and disorder, you don't have chaos and disorder in the public affairs of Athens. This is something we should have in mind," Karakantza marveled. "You have five hundred people randomly selected, okay? Completely. Yes, the prime minister could be somebody who would be a worker. So what? The worker perhaps knows better to run public affairs than a prime minister, who is always well protected." But what, I asked, if a total idiot is selected to an important position? Why court disaster? Karakantza laughed. "Okay, great. If he was an idiot, he will be disempowered by his peers."

The word *idiot*, Karakantza continued, comes from the Greek *idiotis*—a private person who minds their own business. An idiot, according to the ancient mind-set, was a person who did not concern themselves with the well-being of their polis or community, who selfishly elevated their own needs above those of others. Our modern democracies make idiots of us all, in this time-worn sense, compared to the Athenian system where average citizens worked together in the Assembly, the Council, and the courts. The results were impressive, as Karakantza noted: "Athens was one of the most successful city-states in terms of wealth, in terms of development, in terms of art, in terms of intellectual achievement. That's why it was one of the favorite destinations of all the immigrants of the ancient world."

Though Athens is often venerated as the cradle of democracy, and scholars and tourists still glory in its relics, two of its crucial features are rarely remarked upon: first, that democracy opened up politics to the poor, and second, that it employed sortition to do so. Athens was, indeed, a slave-based society and one where women were not allowed to participate. But it was still one of the first places to include the impecunious as equals in the political power structure, which was an undeniable breakthrough.

The wealthy were not pleased by their diminished power. Elite critics railed against the fact that the rich had to grovel before the hardscrabble in the courts. In one text, signed by a man known as the Old Oligarch, the writer complains about not being able to distinguish between citizen and slave when walking down the streets; people wore the same kind of clothes, spoke insolently, and rubbed elbows. If you wanted to maintain social hierarchy, you didn't love Athens, and you were likely no fan of the lottery system, which would have pulled more resources toward the working classes.

Though we have mostly forgotten the history of sortition through the ages (in Athens and also, in a more limited capacity, in the fourteenth-century republics of Venice and Florence), the fact remains that most industrial democracies do employ chance in the political realm in at least one crucial area: juries. In this one corner of our contemporary liberal political and legal structure, we accept that the equal distribution of political opportunities has value and that randomly selected citizens may have something to contribute to decision making, even involving matters of life and death. Yet somehow we fail to consider that such a method might be more broadly applied or that it might even be superior to the oligarchic elections we have grown accustomed to. In a bicameral system, why not consider, as some imaginative academics have proposed, electing one legislative chamber by vote and selecting the other by lot?[30] I, for one, think the results could hardly be worse than what we've got.

"Drawing lots is not irrational, it is arational, a consciously neutral procedure whereby political opportunities can be distributed fairly and discord avoided," David Van Reybrouck argues in his provocative book *Against Elections: The Case for Democracy.* "The risk of corruption reduces, election fever abates, and attention to the common good increases."[31] While Van Reybrouck has some evidence to back up his conclusions (mainly from promising experiments conducted in Iceland, Ireland, and Canada), the truth is we don't know if he's correct because no modern nation has truly tried adding sortition to its political repertoire. The building blocks of our system appear to be gridlocked into place.

In the United States and elsewhere throughout the twentieth century, the expansion of suffrage to excluded groups was one of the primary aims of social movements, and rightly so; but now the very electoral process that people fought so hard to expand may be democracy's undoing. This moment calls for a leap on the scale initiated by Cleisthenes, and perhaps one inspired by him. Selection by lot may not be the perfect solution to the problems we face, but it suggests that other, radically different ways of structuring political participation and incorporating spontaneity are possible. By refusing to accept a separation between ruled and rulers, governed and governor, the Athenian example reminds us that our current system must be reimagined and overhauled if it is to be deemed deserving of the word *democracy*.

CHAPTER 6

A SOCRATIC MOB

(EXPERTISE/MASS OPINION)

HUMANS HAVE A tendency to project things on to honeybees. We idealize them, associating bees with delicious sweetness and light, spring flowers and a good harvest. We also denigrate them as a mindless horde, a bunch of automatons or drones. But more often, we describe them as a monarchy, imagining one lording over the hive. Early observers, including Aristotle, assumed the largest bee was a king, before closer consideration revealed that "he" laid eggs, which made the ruler, in fact, a queen. Whatever the gender of the supposed monarch, the rest of the colony was demoted to passive, hapless subjects.

One of the earliest books on beekeeping was written in 1609. The title, *The Feminine Monarchie*, was carefully chosen because the author, Englishman Charles Butler, wanted to highlight the gender of the bee who appeared to be directing the entire enterprise. He was only half right. In the last century, scientists have shown that while the queen bee is indeed female and a central part of the apian ecosystem, she is no monarch, but rather a mother, the dedicated egg layer and keeper of the colony's genetic health. Beyond choosing how many eggs to lay and the gender of her offspring (the majority of which are female like her), she oversees no other crucial decisions. These are made in an astonishingly complex, egalitarian manner by hundreds or thousands of bees, depending on the circumstances. These bees are the queen's daughters but not exactly her dependents; we call them worker bees, but they are self-managed and have no boss. Honeybees, it turns out, are arguably the earth's most numerous, long-standing, successful, and endearing democrats.

Democracy is the word used by Dr. Thomas Seeley, one of the world's leading scholars on the subject, who I visited in his laboratory at Cornell University. "I use the word *democracy* because when bees have to make their decisions, those decisions are made collectively," Seeley explained. What sort of decisions? Ones about "where the foragers should go each day to be effective in collecting the colony's food, whether to turn the heat production up inside the nest if things are getting cool outside, whether to turn up the cooling process if things are getting hot outside, deciding whether to start building additional combs, deciding whether or not to swarm, which is the process by which a new colony is founded, and deciding where its new home will be." Seeley ran down the list. "These are all decisions that are not made by any one individual in the colony, but are distributed among the members."

Everything in the hive is decided by the workers. "Think about it this way," Seeley proposed. "The queen is in the heart of the nest. She doesn't know where the rich flower patches are, where the water sources are. That's knowledge that's acquired by the workers when they're old and become foragers, and she's cut out from all of that. Almost everything's done by the workers, who have the knowledge." This distribution of decision-making power, for Seeley, is at the core of democracy, whatever species happens to be practicing it.

Choosing a site for a future home is the most important decision a colony makes, a matter of life and death. If a hive is too small, the bees won't be able to store enough food to last through the winter; if it's too large, they won't be able to fill it and regulate the temperature; if it's too low to the ground, they will be vulnerable to predators, and so on. These high stakes are reflected in the intricate and drawn-out process by which the hive makes its final determination.

It all begins when a group of bees, including a queen, congregates in the open air in a swarm, which immediately sends out scouts to identify possible home sites. These scouts come back and report their findings to the group through body movements. With nothing but wiggles and shakes, they can convey the site's polar coordinates and its overall quality, perhaps describing a hollow in a tree three miles away that seems really promising, or a nook in an abandoned attic down the road that's not so great. Of the several hundred scouts, only a minority discovers anything of value and returns to perform what's called a waggle dance. The better a site, the more persistent and emphatic a bee's movements are as she aims to recruit her sisters, the colony's undecided voters, to check it out for themselves and join her cause.

Over days of dancing and deliberation by the scouts, dissenters or holdouts eventually lose steam and cease their movements. (Bees appear constitutionally incapable of holding on to bad ideas for long.) When a quorum of bees gathers at a single site, it signals that consensus has been reached and the matter settled. Soon after, the swarm departs, traveling in a tightly packed formation directly to its new home. The sisters are very rarely wrong. Through a series of experiments, Seeley demonstrated that honeybees overwhelmingly tend to choose the best possible option available.

Oriented toward a clear common goal, the bees seek the best possible outcome and typically achieve it. While their aim may seem simple by human standards, we shouldn't be too pleased with ourselves, for these are creatures whose brains our hominid analogs outweigh by a factor of twenty thousand, making it a comparatively daunting task for them. Their democratic system, though biologically evolved as opposed to culturally developed, is ingenious. It cannot be manipulated or distorted by special interests (no kickbacks to promote subprime sites). Everyone has a chance to be heard, and everyone is an expert in the task at hand. There is, in fact, no such thing as a "hive mind."

"We've never seen a bee get excited about an option, a potential home site, simply because she saw another bee excitedly dancing for that site. Each bee will get excited about a site only after she's made her own personal inspection of it, and that is a very important part of the accuracy of their decision making," Seeley remarked. "People have things called fads, or trends, where we look around and sometimes we get excited about something simply because we see the group around us showing excitement for something, which can lead to poor decisions. The bees never run that risk."

Why does honeybee democracy work so well? Perhaps because, unlike humans, bees are reasonable. Humans are the ones who are subject to hive mind, who become a horde making decisions based on emotion and impulse, unconscious drives and irrational resentments, unshakeable faith and boundless greed, as opposed to clearheaded logic and incorruptible voting procedures. Humans are the ones who ignore facts, scorning carefully gathered data for idealizations and half-baked theories. If only we were more like the judicious, harmonious, cooperative bees!

Human democracy, we all know, is much more of mess. We are an emotional, conflicted, hardheaded, and self-destructive species, and history provides a litany of our bad choices that is long and growing, leading at least one contemporary commentator to lament in the pages of the *New York Times*, "You can impeach a president, but you can't, alas, impeach the people."[1] It was hardly a novel sentiment. When James Madison quipped, "Had every Athenian citizen been a Socrates, even the Athenian assembly would have been a mob," he aimed to highlight both the folly of individual citizens and the fact that something changes when we get together in a crowd—that fearsome, fad-obsessed, uniquely human assemblage. Such was the standard view among the founders. Gouverneur Morris, a young lawyer and future author of the Preamble to the U.S. Constitution, famously shuddered when he saw "the mob begin to think and reason" in the revolution's early days. "Poor reptiles!" he snarked.

If democracy is to survive, though, think and reason the mob must. We've found, over time, that elites aren't naturally better, just better schooled. Given democracy's mixed record, waves of reformers have promoted universal education as the solution to self-government's ills, following visionaries such as the Marquis de Condorcet, whose remarkable intelligence led him to argue for nurturing the mental capacities of others, and the courageous Mary Wollstonecraft, who eloquently pleaded for the rights of daughters to be taught alongside sons. If democracy depends on that fickle phantom known as public opinion, why not try to ensure the phantom is passably well informed? To this day, the question of how education might improve our democratic prospects remains open, and the tension between ordinary people and educated elites, between masses and experts, unresolved.

What the French philosopher Jacques Rancière dubbed the "hatred of democracy" has existed as long as democracy has been an ideal in the West, predating the pretensions of the American founders. Plato blamed the demise of his beloved mentor on the ignorant Athenian demos, which sentenced the philosopher to choose between exile and death for the crime of corrupting the youth. Indeed, ever since Socrates drank the hemlock, elite critics have railed against the threat posed by the unruly, impassioned, and clueless masses, and their skepticism has been understandable.

But Socrates, brilliant though he may have been, was also not infallible. His social standing took a hit in part because of his connection to aristocrats who twice managed, temporarily, to overthrow the government of the people. Some of the most notorious leaders of the oligarchical push were his former students, and Socrates's attempts to stay neutral throughout the crisis were looked on with suspicion when democracy was restored. He was no longer an eccentric, justice-obsessed gadfly but a teacher of would-be tyrants.

As such, he imperiled the polity his fellow Greeks held dear. Loathing tyranny, Athenians believed all citizens should rule and be ruled in turn, regardless of birth, wealth, or educational attainment. Democracy, they asserted, didn't require some rare personality trait or expertise. It was a practice that everyone could and had to learn by doing. Mass passions had to be kept in check, and they were, through various means, but the presence of emotions was not grounds to exclude people from decision making. The use of a lottery reflected a deep faith in the ability of citizens to rule themselves.

The idea of empowering ordinary people can seem terrifying today because there is so much stupidity on display. How can we possibly trust one another? Digital technologies, now fully commercialized, are used to spread myths and lies and empower hucksters. In the mid-twentieth century, public opinion was molded through a process that Walter Lippmann called the "manufacture of consent," a top-down method dependent on the small number of channels available through print, radio, and television. Limited sources of information led to social cohesion, creating an atmosphere of acquiescence and trust.

In a digital age, however, those sources are potentially limitless. Online, the mass public fragments into individual targets, each of us presented with a personalized news feed affirming our perceptions of the world and firing up our emotions with inflammatory messages that make us wary of other points of view. The manufacture of consent has morphed into the manufacture of compulsion. The owners of for-profit online platforms, services, and news sites need users to stay engaged. They don't care what we are looking at as long as we are looking and scrolling and clicking and liking, and keep coming back for more.

Three centuries ago, Jonathan Swift complained of the way "falsehood flies, and the Truth comes limping after it," and he had never experienced social media. On Twitter, fabrications are far more likely to be retweeted than accurate news, allowing erroneous stories to reach people six times faster than true ones.

Challenging academic expertise and disputing established facts, people share posts shunning life-saving vaccinations and denouncing climate science as a hoax, putting our collective safety and survival at risk. Driven by online videos promoting crackpot conjecture, the ranks of Flat Earthers have swelled, along with those of white supremacists, who, while accepting the veracity of a spherical planet, scoff at the idea that Homo sapiens evolved on the African continent. Meanwhile, conspiracy theories of every imaginable variety take root in the fertile soil of data-driven digital platforms, which are happy to host preposterous memes insisting that the victims of American gun violence are not victims at all, for example, but professional "crisis actors" under the command of a vast state plot.

Taking advantage of and perpetuating human idiocy is a profitable enterprise. (That studies have shown a distrust of experts correlates with increasing support for "a strong leader" and decreasing support for democracy indicates that, for some authoritarians at least, the rewards are not solely financial.[2]) The problem is not just that a few bad apples are destroying an otherwise healthy media ecosystem. It is that our entire digital communications infrastructure is based on the business model of advertising, which spreads exaggerated claims and outright lies by design. As the techies say, it's a feature, not a bug.

So who really bears responsibility for the oceans of misinformation and misunderstandings that plague our society—the mass of misguided citizens or a handful of profiteers who sow confusion and discord? The ideal of liberal democracy posits free subjects rationally deliberating and deciding what is best for them. Yet a motivated subset of self-interested elites has dedicated itself to sabotaging broad understanding and deliberation, knowing that there's money to be made from incomprehension, bewilderment, and strife. Examples abound: the executives of both legacy media and cutting-edge technology companies who make a killing from divisive content, fear-mongering, and destructive rumors; the industry leaders who back "merchants of doubt," investing millions of dollars to debunk research on everything from global warming to the health effects of tobacco, all to gut revenue-depleting regulations; the military hawks, national security experts, and private contractors who peddled lies about weapons of mass destruction to lead a nation into a senseless and inhumane war; and the billionaires who know nothing about education or pedagogy, such as heiress turned secretary of education Betsy DeVos, who toil to smash teachers' unions, slash state funding, and turn learning into a privately financed privilege, not a public good.

Today's purveyors of ignorance are part of a deep tradition, though they are subtler than their predecessors. The ruling class has never been particularly keen on the prospect of ordinary people becoming educated and governing themselves. In his 1714 treatise *The Fable of the Bees: or, Private Vices, Public Benefits*, economic theorist and moral philosopher Bernard Mandeville explained the elitist desire to hoard this power, a desire that has diminished but not entirely disappeared: "Reading, Writing, and Arithmetick are very necessary to those, whose Business require such Qualifications, but where People's livelihood has no dependence on these Arts, they are very pernicious," Mandeville insisted. "The more a Shepherd, a Plowman or any other Peasant knows of the World, and the things that are Foreign to his Labour or Employment, the less fit he'll be to go through the Fatigues and Hardships of it with Cheerfulness and Content." Best, then, to keep social inferiors in the dark lest they get uppity. "To make Society happy and People easy under the meanest circumstances, it is requisite that great Numbers of them should be Ignorant as well as Poor."

Programs of improvement for the benighted masses have traditionally been met by staunch resistance. To maintain order and decorum, elites have seized on any evidence that the rabble and riffraff are incapable of the responsibility of self-rule to elevate their own class, insisting that "natural" leaders (aristocrats), deserving leaders (meritocrats), or impartial expert leaders (technocrats) must run things. Their arguments always contain more than a mote of self-flattery and often reek of naked self-interest. In the immortal words of Bertolt Brecht, "Those who lead the country into the abyss, Call Ruling too difficult, For ordinary men." If we are ever to equitably and democratically remedy the problem of mass stupidity, we will first have to deal with elite cupidity.

One afternoon, the day before I was scheduled to interview political theorist Wendy Brown, I set up base on the University of California–Berkeley campus and spoke to students on their way to and from class. I asked them about the connection between education and democracy. What was most striking, as the hours wore on, was how little they could muster on the topic.

Student after student nodded enthusiastically. They knew democracy and education were connected, but couldn't go beyond basic platitudes. Learning is good. People should know about things and not just trust what they come across online, they said, without elaborating much more. One student was passionate about the topic, though, a junior I met while he stood on the main plaza dressed in a fuzzy sea turtle costume passing out flyers about the environmental impact of plastic bags on marine life. The bags were an example of how democracy is in peril, he explained. Plastics manufacturers from out of state were spending millions sponsoring a referendum aimed at repealing a recent ban, and he was trying to enlighten his fellow students and convince them to vote to keep the protection in place. (As his peers dodged the flyers he waved in their direction or their eyes glazed over as he raged against the corrupting influence of money in politics, the student ran into the obstacle that trips up everyone who holds out hope that education can cure political ills: apathy. You can tell people the facts, but you can't force them to care.)

Most students I spoke to made clear that they weren't attending college to become better democratic participants. They were there to be able to get a good job after graduation. This was a topic on which the students were passionate and voluble. They were studying various subjects—computer science, psychology, engineering, even political theory—but were united in their anxiety about finding work. And all but the luckiest were worried about getting jobs that paid enough for them to repay their student loans.

"I've heard people talk about college as a gamble," one young woman told me. "You might be successful or you might just be in debt your whole life. I really don't think people should look at education as that kind of choice. If education is an investment, the risk should be low." The junior concerned with marine life distinguished himself, in part, because he identified as an activist first and a student second. "Students are actually afraid to get into the political process because they are working to get in the system of the job market," he said through his giant green mask. Spending time leafleting seemed to most like a distraction or a luxury. "With student debt, you're more likely to want to attend a school that's prestigious, that's a better bang for your buck, and one that can get you into the job force. Students are more interested in getting in and out of college, rather than learning how to be an activist and how to recognize their rights and interests."

The next day, Wendy Brown told me she wasn't surprised to hear about the responses to my questions. The economic realities students face force them to see their education as a commodity, and she sympathized with their predicament. "One of the things I'm struck by in teaching young people these days is even if they would very much like to think about their education or their love lives or their families or their futures in terms other than investment and return on investment, they can't." The problem, Brown went on, is both practical and psychological.

Fundamentally, working- and middle-class students cannot afford to ignore the tens of thousands of dollars of debt they must repay when they graduate. This burden shapes how they see their studies, the high financial cost influencing any educational calculus. Students might like the idea of pursuing knowledge for its own sake, but in practice, they adapt to the need for a degree program that makes them employable, lest they default on their loans.

The neoliberal economic revolution that began in the 1970s, Brown explained, has "remade the world that we live in and remade our heads." When education is an investment and not a right, pleasure, or duty, students need it to yield a return.

That wasn't the case when Brown went to college in the 1970s. She graduated from a California state university, and it cost her around nine hundred dollars a year. The nominal fees allowed her to explore a range of fields that didn't have a clear vocational purpose. This experience of a rich, public schooling informed Brown's idea of what education could be. She sees the American system of public higher education as a precious inheritance and something worth trying to preserve and expand. "What was distinct in the American case, especially in the postwar period, was the enormous level of public investment in higher education, with the idea that what would be available is a high-quality liberal arts education to the many," Brown explained. "Not to everyone—there was still a big project before these universities began expanding access to those who had been historically excluded for class, race, and gender, and those doors had to be pounded down. But the principle at the heart that I think remains worth defending is that liberal arts education is essential for modern democracies and should be available to everyone, not just an elite class."

In the postwar period that principle was cemented with the GI Bill, which made higher education a mass phenomenon by matriculating over a million veterans at the government's expense, and further reinforced at the dawn of the Cold War, which catalyzed additional investment in education as a defensive maneuver (patriotic curricula and McCarthyism were two notable by-products). By the eighties a new paradigm was settling into place: building on Ronald Reagan's previous attacks on Berkeley students, conservative leaders and their corporate donors challenged the commitment to public education as an article of faith. States cut funding for colleges and universities, raised tuition, replaced tenured faculty with insecure adjuncts, and adopted a more market-driven model of subsidizing research and attracting students.

Though it was common practice a generation ago, the concept of affordable or free higher education now seems almost utopian.

That public education system at all levels is being privatized and stripped down at a moment of increasing social complexity only compounds the present crisis. We no longer fit Rousseau's romantic vision of peasant bands arguing under an oak tree, if anyone ever did. We are now citizens of massive industrialized nations operating in a digitally and financially linked world. Modern democracies are exceedingly tricky beasts, promising that the people will govern themselves in a context of convoluted cultural, social, political, and economic powers. But instead of attending to this complexity, students are compelled to shrink their focus, to specialize and professionalize. Swaths of knowledge that are essential to understanding a multifaceted world become a luxury or irrelevant, and the aim of education radically narrows: teachers are no longer educating citizens but future job holders.

Education has been remade in neoliberalism's image, reconceived as an investment that might pay off in the form of a lucrative career in a competitive market, while the broader idea of the public good falls to the wayside. Brown identifies this shift as a part of a larger tendency to disempower regular people and undermine a democratic ethos: "What we see today, I think, is a strong temptation to just turn the whole business of governing over to technocrats—not just to corporations, not just to the wealthy, but to essentially human versions of algorithms, or algorithms themselves, as opposed to the interested, the passionate, the political, let alone the popular." She traces the approach back to a small group of classical neoliberal economic thinkers, known as the ordoliberals, who argued for technocracy as an alternative to both democracy and the rule of the rich, whom the ordoliberals believed would corrupt and distort markets.

Over the last four decades, once-obscure ordoliberal ideas have gone mainstream. Markets set and shape society's priorities, while the state is relegated to a supporting role. Complex topics are widely believed to be beyond most people's ken and best left to those with degrees in business, economics, and law, who will ask not what is desirable, what is good, or what is just, but what is pragmatic and what increases productivity and efficiency. "The idea is: there are just a few who really know. Put them together in a room and let them run the world," Brown said. She finds that idea terrifying because it supposes that experts are free of political interest. But in fact expertise operates in a world that is now largely governed by finance, and so great political interests are at stake. The men and women who hold positions of authority or expertise in our society (who run the banks, corporations, NGOs, and government bureaucracies) are hardly neutral.

Without pediatricians, teachers, architects, marine biologists, pilots, computer programmers, plumbers, and countless other specialists, society would collapse. Modern nations need experts, and yet expertise is inherently undemocratic. Not everyone knows enough to qualify as an expert. The designation itself is a kind of distinction, and one we're generally grateful to grant. As we drive across bridges and trust the engineering of the automobile and the overpass, as we seek the advice of a respected oncologist or assume the safety of the food we eat and the drugs we take, we had better be thankful that expert facility and professional competence exist.

When experts become an elite class, however, an asset to the system becomes a kind of liability. Few now remember that one of our society's most revered concepts, "meritocracy," which the dictionary defines as "government or the holding of power by people selected on the basis of their ability," was actually coined in a celebrated work of satire. Published in 1958, *The Rise of the Meritocracy* charts the rise and fall of a fictionalized Great Britain obsessed with IQ testing and the educational classification of its citizens. In an essay published in 2001 reflecting on his work's perplexing legacy, the author, sociologist, and Labour Party activist Michael Young lamented the fact that his cautionary tale had been uncannily prophetic. Meritocracy, a word intended as caricature, had become a creed.

In his book, Young envisions a highly regimented educational system that allows a minority to believe it deserves its privilege, while excluding the majority and relegating the poor and marginalized to the inferior roles they were deemed to merit. Today, this system exists, entrenching the advantages of the already affluent under the guise of fair play. The "engine of education," Young said, describing our current reality, efficiently concentrates ability and opportunity in the hands of the haves while shutting out the have-nots. "A social revolution has been accomplished by harnessing schools and universities to the task of sieving people according to education's narrow band of values," Young observed. "With an amazing battery of certificates and degrees at its disposal, education has put its seal of approval on a minority, and its seal of disapproval on the many who fail to shine from the time they are relegated to the bottom streams at the age of seven or before. The new class has the means at hand, and largely under its control, by which it reproduces itself."[3]

The problem isn't with the idea of rewarding worthiness or effort, which makes good sense, but the fact that opportunity is hoarded under the false premise that it is being equally shared. There's a difference between appointing people based on merit and the principle of meritocracy, which means the rule of a class of educated or otherwise advantaged people while the majority of citizens is frozen out. This is what Young found morally abhorrent and undemocratic, for it serves as a justification for hierarchy and subordination. However magnanimous meritocracy claims to be, in practice, it never disinterestedly elevates the most qualified; there is always the need to keep the less-capable masses away from the business of ruling, allegedly for their own good.

Meritocracy thus blurs into technocracy, or rule by technical experts. According to technocracy's logic, it's not the people as a whole who should rule, but rather a subset of those who have mastered various technical domains, be they economic, legal, scientific, and so on. Technocrats focus on developing programs and methods of government without reference to whether citizens favor them, want them, like them, or even understand them. The experts, objective and detached, know best. At a time of inflamed popular passion, of emboldened extremists and nativism, such a vision can seem appealing. If the people are willing to vote racist huckster demagogues into office, perhaps they *can't* be trusted.

In the context of our competitive society, schooling becomes a means of sorting the best from the rest and allocating success, or what some have called the "technocratic-meritocratic" approach to education. Those who strive will earn appropriate credentials, assume positions of power, and reap the associated rewards. In this view, public education exists to provide access to all, to allow those who possess talent and drive to ascend from the lowest rungs of the ladder to the summit—and that, it's implicitly assumed, is what democracy is all about. Expertise can never be distributed equally in a highly complex society. Not everyone can be at the top of the class, after all, but everyone will get the chance. Equality of opportunity is no guarantee of equality of outcome.

Yet our current educational arrangement hardly qualifies as meritocratic, and even equality of opportunity is elusive. Schools play a crucial role in perpetuating racial inequality and bolstering the class pyramid by ranking and tracking children from their earliest days, as most of us must know from personal experience. At my majority-black public high school in Georgia, all the "gifted" children were somehow white, disproportionately the children of professors at the local university. The revered *Brown v. Board of Education* Supreme Court decision overturning the doctrine of separate but equal did not pave the way for desegregation as hoped; to the contrary, classrooms are more racially and economically segregated than they were when the decision was issued in 1954.[4] Today, nearly half of all black students attend majority black schools, and poor black students are substantially more likely to attend those in high-poverty school districts than poor white students. At every level, the inequalities of our educational system couldn't be starker.

In the United States, much of the blame can be pinned on the decentralized model of funding schools through local property taxes, an arrangement devised by Puritan settlers in the 1640s. These public education innovators established laws compelling communities with fifty or more households to pool resources to guarantee that every child could read and write. At the time, communities didn't differ vastly in income, so the results were quite egalitarian.[5] But in our wildly unequal society, this method allows the amount of money spent per student to swing wildly from school to school, dramatically tilting the playing field in favor of the better off from the outset.[6] In some poor districts, budget-strapped teachers regularly beg for donations online; some have even taken to panhandling on the side of the road so they can purchase basic school supplies.

Studies show that class mobility in America has all but vanished and has even shifted into reverse for some populations. The already rich benefit from an education escalator that zooms upward, while people with less money find themselves stuck on a treadmill, racing to avoid a decline. Children with low-income parents, disproportionately children of color, are too often condemned to attend dilapidated institutions that are understaffed and lacking in basic items such as textbooks, while their more affluent brethren enjoy a wide range of course offerings taught by well-supported teachers in state-of-the-art buildings housing cutting-edge technology.

The disparities begin at a young age, even in preschool, meaning that the trajectory is fixed early on. So even when black and white or rich and poor students attend the same institutions—as in my Georgia high school—the sorting has already been done. The divide extends beyond good and bad facilities: poor kids are more likely to be denied arts, foreign languages, and sports programs, while rich kids not only enjoy all these but also benefit from costly after-school tutoring, private test prep courses, and professional assistance in composing their college application essays. (In America it seems you can't spell *enrichment programs* without the word *rich*.)

These inequities compound over time, culminating in college. The subset of high school juniors and seniors who make plans to attend illustrious universities with ample endowments and generous financial aid packages are vastly outnumbered by those who struggle to put themselves through community college while also working one or two jobs, not to mention the hundreds of thousands who annually get sucked into subprime, for-profit vocational programs that bury them in debt.[7] While American rates of college attendance are among the highest in the industrialized world, the nation's ranking plummets when it comes to the proportion of students who actually complete their degrees, primarily because low-income students do not get the support they need to finish. A small minority of privileged students attending prestigious institutions shape our image of the "college experience," but the millions of low-income students who have had to abandon their studies at far more numerous and less eminent institutions offer a more accurate if dispiriting representation of our deeply stratified system.

The biggest failing of the technocratic-meritocratic argument is not that those who ascend to the upper echelons aren't the most brilliant or skillful individuals available—no doubt some are quite smart and capable—but that so many are denied the chance to exercise their talents and develop their capacities.

This was made clear to me as I stood in a small barbershop located in a suburban shopping center north of Miami, talking to guys as they got fades and buzz cuts and had their beards and eyebrows trimmed. There I met Ellie Brett, one of the shop's most popular stylists, thanks to an introduction from a local radio host whose show addresses the ins and outs of the probation system. The host told me that Brett, a former prisoner turned barber and poet, was as much a philosopher as anyone she knew, and as the day progressed it became apparent that she was right. Brett's interest in spoken-word poetry lent him a unique eloquence that he kept up even while concentrating on the careful work of styling a customer's hair.

Thirty-two when we met, Brett had spent most of his twenties locked up after taking part in a botched armed robbery in North Carolina, his home state, that left the victim injured. In prison he had plenty of time to reflect on past mistakes. He'd learned his current trade through a correctional program and, in addition, like most other inmates, was assigned a job. He worked in the meat plant. The incarcerated workforce was paid what is known as an "incentive wage," exempt from minimum-wage requirements. Brett made forty cents a day. Enough, he said ruefully, to maybe get a Snickers bar from the prison commissary at the end of the week. The meat patties he produced on the job, he recalled with disgust, "consisted of a green powder, a red powder, and like twenty percent soy"—he had been surprised to learn that the food would be served in public school cafeterias.

School hadn't been Brett's top priority during childhood, but in prison learning helped him stay focused. He read whatever he could, studying authors ranging from Machiavelli to Cornel West, and kept up with current events at home and abroad. He studied the law so he could follow his own legal case and advise others on theirs, while also learning about the justice system in other countries. Brett researched places such as Norway, where inmates are afforded a degree of autonomy that he found unimaginable given his experience being collared and kept in solitary (known as "iso," for "isolation").

Then, out of the blue, the authorities cut off inmates' access to books and learning. "This lady came and she told us that no one can go to school anymore," Brett said. "Yeah, she came in and she basically was like, 'Y'all don't deserve to get an education.' So we stood up and fought." A group of prisoners, including Brett, rebelled by going on hunger strike to save the library. "And that'll be initiated like we'll pass notes and we'll get everything together, and then we just won't go to chow. They'll try to wake us up; we won't go," Brett said. "They drag you in, and they said they're not gonna change because they're saving money on food—that's what the officers will tell us. 'We don't care if y'all starve and die.'"

For Brett and others, the threat of closing of the library was the last straw, an indignity that cut deeper than being kept in a cage. It shattered the myth that incarceration had anything to do with rehabilitation or redemption of convicts; they were being kept down, held back. Brett connected this to his African American roots. "I know, for my heritage, it used to be illegal for us to read. So, I don't know if they're trying to go back to this, or what they're trying to do, like reverse all of this progress and things," he said, shaking his head. "But there's just no telling what type of laws are gonna be passed. It used to be illegal to read. I can't believe this. Maybe they're trying to do it again."

As I spoke to Brett, I thought of the conversations I'd had the day before, with kids at a youth center in Overtown, an inner-city neighborhood of Miami that was known as Colored Town during Jim Crow. The room where we met was painted with bright, inspirational murals, and included a quote from the rapper Nas— "I know I can be what I wanna be, if I work hard at it"—under an image of a black female tennis player, a black businessman, and a racially ambiguous astronaut. Over two sessions around a large table, the preteens and teenagers told me about attending some of the most financially strapped schools in the state, places where they hardly felt anything was possible.

When I asked the younger group what they would change in their school, they didn't miss a beat: the food. The problem wasn't that the meals often lacked taste, which is hardly surprising given the powder-based meat patty recipe Brett described, but the fact that the food was often cold. The kids told me that when they asked the adults to warm up their lunches, they were met with dismissiveness, which made them feel disrespected. Food without flavor was bad enough; cold food only added insult to injury.

They knew that, in theory, they had the right to protest for better treatment. But whenever they had tried to stand up for themselves, they were punished. "If you go against them, they take away something we like," a girl with long braids said, explaining the dilemma. The administrators, the kids continued, had already taken away the vending machines for an earlier rebellion over the quality of the lunchroom offerings. Another girl, who wore a large bow in her hair and couldn't have been older than twelve or thirteen, took the floor. The words came out in an impassioned rush, reflecting long-brewing frustration.

School is supposed to be your home away from home, where you are just getting an education. But I feel like if you just keep taking away stuff from us, that's not right. My mom won't take away my lunch and say, "Oh no, you can't eat." No, she won't do that. She's going to find a way for me to have a better environment. I feel like when you take away stuff from us, it's just like, "Why? Why are you doing this?" What's the point of taking away vending machines from children; some kids don't even eat breakfast. So, when seven fifteen hits and they haven't eaten breakfast, and you say, "We're not serving breakfast," that's a whole day they are not even thinking about school; they are thinking, "I'm hungry, I'm hungry, I'm starving, I'm not having a better environment." So, I just feel like, why do you take it away? Why not try to make it better? If you hear us saying something about it, you should be like, "That's a concern we'll put it on the board for our next meeting." Don't just try to push it under the rug and say, "No you're not going to do this" and try to beat us. I don't understand it.

As she spoke, the other students nodded their heads in agreement. By the end of her commentary, they broke into cheers. The adults, the young students agreed, didn't take their grievances seriously. Deep down, these students knew something was wrong with the picture, and they still held out hope that it could change. The slightly older group had similar complaints and yet seemed more resigned. They had come to accept that there wasn't much they could do to change their school, and that the best approach was to grin and bear it. "Whatever rules they establish, we just have to follow. There's nothing we can say to defend ourselves. We just have to do whatever they say," one boy said, and no one disagreed. All of them commented on the atmosphere of distrust and the presence of police in the school halls. (One of the young boys compared the school to prison, saying it was "like a jail without a cell," while another scoffed and replied, "You've never seen a real prison, then.")

Some were hurt that, when it came to teaching, there were teachers who appeared to be phoning it in; one participant appeared to be on the verge of tears as she spoke of a teacher who didn't seem to care if she understood the material or not. Strikingly, though, the students didn't blame their instructors for the sorry state of affairs. "I don't think we have a say at the school because it's run by people bigger than us and bigger than the school; there's a whole county," one girl explained. The teachers weren't free, either, as far as they could see.

Indeed, the students all understood that a complex hierarchy exists: the teachers are controlled by administrators, who are controlled by the county, which is controlled by the state, which is controlled by the federal government. If the presence of cops in the hallways made them feel like criminals, the curriculum was uninspiring, and the food was inedible (which they assured me it was), they felt it was likely because of a rule made far away, maybe in Washington, DC.

I asked whether they learned about democracy in school, and they said yes. "But it's about government, like different branches, things like that," the boy clarified. "They don't ask us, 'Oh, how do you feel about the school?'" Being invited to give their opinions on how the school was run, they all agreed, was unimaginable. "People inside the school should have something to say, but it's really not going to matter because, like I said, it's other people ruling it. One voice, my voice, is not really going to change nothing," one girl said.

Did they expect to have more freedom when they became adults? The group expressed skepticism. Their parents were also stifled and constrained. "I don't think people of higher power really want to hear a black mom that's poor in the ghetto. I don't think anybody cares what she's got to say," the same girl remarked. "It's like survival of the fittest," a boy said, picking up the thread. "Because if she speaks out and says what she wants to say, they might just find someone else who's better for the job that's probably not going to talk, because there's probably plenty of people who want that same job she has. So, it's better just to go out, do whatever you have to do, and get it over with."

This was a notable twist on Charles Darwin's theory. Elsewhere, a more privileged or entitled student might equate Darwinian ideas of survival with getting the highest grades and beating the competition. But this boy, in contrast, equated survival of the fittest with blending in and being obedient. It fit the overwhelming lesson that the Miami schoolchildren seemed to receive: follow orders. They were being trained in the servile arts, not liberal ones, and the teachings were perfectly suited to meet the needs of a boss at a low-wage job. When the younger group asked for their lunch to be heated up, the principal responded, "Food is food. Children in Africa don't get food, so you should just be grateful." The underlying message? Be grateful for crumbs, even cold ones, and if you dare ask for more, you will be penalized or, if you keep it up later in life, replaced.

This is what some scholars refer to as public education's "hidden curriculum," or the forms of consciousness, interpersonal behavior, and expectations that schooling fosters, and how those are consonant with the skills required for a deferential labor force. Modern schooling must manage and even dampen people's expectations, acculturating students to accept an economy of scarcity and competition and the inevitability of failure—a process sociologist Burton Clark, in his influential study of community colleges, called "cooling out."[8] It can sound conspiratorial, yet it's hardly a secret that schools serve to prepare young people for future employment and aim to integrate them into the labor markets; nor that the traits rewarded on the job are those generally encouraged in the classroom: punctuality, obedience, predictability, external motivation, and so on. No doubt there must be plenty of poor students who attend underperforming schools who are less weary and more optimistic than the kids I met that day. But I don't believe that those young people were outliers. Their experiences reflect the paradoxical, deeply contradictory role of education under capitalism, which facilitates the ascension of some while preparing a great many more for lowly positions.

That knowledge is power is a cliché because it's true. Throughout history, the only thing elites have feared more than the uneducated multitude is an educated one, which is why Brett was right to recall that there was a time not that long ago when a slave's merely learning to read was an offense punishable by the lash (teaching a slave to read was illegal as well). Brett's experience with the prison library highlighted a long-standing tension: while people are consistently reproached for their ignorance, the system works to deny them meaningful intellectual opportunity. Industrialists would have happily kept children out of school and toiling in the factories, as they still do in some countries, if labor organizers had not pressured them to cease that practice.

Americans may now view education as a basic entitlement, but it's easy to forget that it is nowhere mentioned in the Bill of Rights. The idea of free, universal lower education was initially a controversial goal, and one that gained traction slowly and on an ad hoc basis, state constitution by state constitution, building on the localized funding model established by the Puritans centuries prior. The effort took off only after antebellum reformers, including Horace Mann, tapped into widespread anxiety over rising immigration and the need to promote a unifying culture and values. (Compulsory schooling was also a way to keep the children of riffraff, freed from the factories, mines, and fields, off the streets.) The middle and upper classes, therefore, saw mass education as both a form of benevolent social uplift and a means of social control.

Though credit often goes to well-meaning reformers such as Mann, who sincerely believed in education as a "great equalizer," the fight for the right to learn has always been led from below. Consider one strand of this rich history. Throughout the nineteenth and twentieth centuries, radical party and labor union members were at the forefront of the push for public education. The lowliest workers struggled to find outlets to learn and share ideas. With few formal options available, people devised creative ways to nurture their intellectual capacities and expand their mental horizons outside traditional institutions of learning, such as the men and women in Cuban cigar factories who pooled their money to hire lectors to read aloud to them while they worked. While rolling tobacco, they listened to classic works of literature, took in the latest news, or learned about economic and political theory, often with a radical or socialist bent. In North America, laborers and artisans crowded into lyceum lecture halls, read newspapers, frequented libraries, and founded debate clubs. Edification was a form of popular entertainment.

Incorporating educational components into campaigns for social change has also been another historical strategy. Participants in the famed Paris Commune championed what they called "integral education," an endeavor aiming, in the words of chronicler Kristin Ross, to "overcome the division between head and hand."[9] Before they were violently stamped out, rebel workers took the unprecedented step of instituting free, secular compulsory schooling for all children on the grounds that all people, regardless of gender or class, have the right to an intellectual life. ("He who wields a tool should be able to write a book, write it with passion and talent . . ." one journal of the period pronounced.[10]) In the United States, grassroots movements have always had strong pedagogical components: the Knights of Labor attempts in the 1800s to promote civic virtue through self-education; the National Farmers' Alliance and Industrial Union, which employed more than forty thousand lecturers across the country; the public oratory and popular broadsheets of the abolitionists and suffragists;

the Freedom Schools of the civil rights movement; the political education programs of the Black Panther Party; the Vietnam-era antiwar coffeehouses; the feminist consciousness-raising circles of the 1970s; the volunteer-run libraries found at every Occupy encampment. As media scholar Jesse Drew has noted, the conceptual frameworks and theoretical perspectives driving these movements often get ignored in favor of "a narrative of pure self-interest and naiveté," which posits activists as reactive, not reflective.[11]

A particularly striking example of this phenomenon, Drew argues, is Rosa Parks, who is generally remembered as a tired, frustrated woman who spontaneously refused to give up her seat on a bus one afternoon. Parks did indeed launch the Montgomery Bus Boycott in an act of tremendous bravery, but the move was well planned: she was a dedicated activist, and had been part of the Highlander Research and Education Center, sometimes called the Highlander Folk School, an influential participatory educational institution founded in Tennessee in 1932 to support a range of labor and other radical causes. (Highlander still exists today.) Parks wasn't driven by emotion alone; it was her analysis of racism and the theory of change that spurred her to act.

Before Red Scare repression decimated the organized left, Communist, socialist, and anarchist groups offered an intellectual world for workers in urban and rural areas, often teaching illiterate people how to read and write (including in Alabama, where Parks lived[12]). Working-class educational development was seen as a vital part of building a robust movement that would challenge the status quo and usher in a fairer social order. Through speeches, soapboxing, debates, newspapers, study groups, and song, these political associations encouraged workers to be intellectuals, arguing that bosses preferred their laborers to be dumb and docile.

The ideal, witless, unquestioning laborer was exemplified by the figure of the blockhead, an image popularized by an Industrial Workers of the World—its members were known as Wobblies—cartoon character named Mr. Block, a man with an absurdly tiny top hat perched on his wooden head. Mr. Block represented the worker who let his employer do his thinking for him: "Mr. Block owns nothing, yet he speaks from the standpoint of the millionaire; he is patriotic without patrimony . . . he licks the hand that smites him and kisses the boot that kicks him . . the personification of all that a worker should not be." In one strip, anticipating the quote from Nas that would embellish the Overtown youth center, Mr. Block relaxes in his living room reading the *Saturday Evening Post*. "Here's a respectable paper. It says: Everybody can be successful if they only make up their mind. That's the dope." To avoid becoming Mr. Block, one had to use one's brain.

In pursuit of this aim, hundreds of workers' schools were opened across the country by the early 1930s. Learning, participants insisted, should not be a privilege enjoyed only by young people with parents wealthy enough to afford tutors. At the same time, unions cultivated a different sort of intellectual culture, one that affirmed the knowledge and capabilities of workers themselves, underscoring the fact that employees tended to know much more than their bosses liked to admit. From the earliest guild and craft unions to the Wobblies to modern-day democratically inclined unions fighting for their lives against conservative attacks on collective bargaining rights, these organizations have refused to see workers as ignorant simply because they performed manual or menial labor. The liberal arts—classically understood as the arts needed for free people, deriving from the Latin *liberalis,* or liberty—have historically been contrasted with the servile arts—the production of goods and provision of service—but the practitioners of the servile arts are not mindless.

Though we typically think of labor militants negotiating for better wages, benefits, and working conditions, an increase in free time used to be a core union demand. The struggle for the weekend and the eight-hour workday wasn't just about having time for relaxation and recreation: it was driven by a deeper craving for intellectual and cultural fulfillment that required time off the clock.[13] It was a yearning movingly expressed by the popular writer Anzia Yezierska in her 1920 short story about an immigrant girl whose night school principal disparages her hunger for knowledge and purpose.

> "I got ideas how to make America better, only I don't know how to say it out. Ain't there a place I can learn?"
>
> A startled woman stared at me. For a moment not a word came. Then she proceeded with the same kind smile. "It's nice of you to want to help America, but I think the best way would be for you to learn a trade. That's what this school is for, to help girls find themselves, and the best way to do is to learn something useful."
>
> "Ain't thoughts useful? Does America want only the work from my body, my hands? Ain't it thoughts that turn over the world?"
>
> "Ah! But we don't want to turn over the world." Her voice cooled.
>
> "But there's got to be a change in America!" I cried. "Us immigrants want to be people—not 'hands'—not slaves of the belly! And it's the chance to think out thoughts that makes people."[14]

Leading up to a wave of strikes between 1909 and 1917, the kinds of young women workers Yezierska would have known well "educated themselves any way they could—in night schools, in study groups, in collectives that pooled money to buy books," in the words of historian Annelise Orleck. Around the same time, the growing membership of the International Ladies' Garment Workers' Union (ILGWU) benefited from substantial and wide-ranging educational programs, though male officers bristled that education might inspire rank-and-file women to question male leadership—and they were right. Militant women wanted to remake the union into an "egalitarian and socially transformative community of workers where women shared power," overtures the men resisted mightily.[15]

Just as the male union bosses felt threatened by radical women, their business counterparts panicked at the prospect of a revolutionary working class, whatever its gender makeup. Since the antebellum period education reform has been fueled by fear of social unrest and of the strength of organized labor. In the nineteenth century, the slow spread of public schools tracked the geography of manufacturing with the aim of offering up a common curriculum that would, in the words of one influential study, "Americanize immigrant groups with a dangerous penchant for European radicalism and socialism."[16] Figures such as Carnegie and Rockefeller would also come to throw their weight behind educational measures to curb working-class consciousness and militancy. Proper instruction, the captains of industry hoped, would temper populist fervor and promulgate respect for social distinctions and private property.

In the early twentieth century, a mere 6 percent of Americans had a high school diploma. In a remarkably short period of time, high school became a mass institution, one designed to serve a society swiftly becoming more industrialized and complex. As the Progressive Era unfolded, industry-led groups tried to break the "common" curriculum model by creating two separate and unequal systems, one vocational and one academic (the National Association of Manufacturers deeming trade schools the best way to push back against the "withering blight of organized labor").[17] Workers fought the proposed split in turn, but won only a partial victory: vocational education was merely made into a distinct track within schools, paving the way for the system we have today, which is only superficially "common."

Even as schools shuttle young people along different tracks to varying heights of the class pyramid, education is perpetually held up as the solution to inequality and offered as a substitute for economic redistribution. Whenever working people have come together to demand material improvements and financial security, they have been advised to pursue instructional programs and specialized training instead, as though their lack of education were the sole cause of their destitution and distress. When President Lyndon B. Johnson told Congress in 1965 that "Poverty has many roots, but the tap-root is ignorance," his comment reflected this dynamic. Ignorance can indeed be ameliorated through access to education, and so the comment struck a note of hopeful humanism. At the same time, it cynically reinforced the view that poor people lack means because they lack smarts, not because of structural conditions stacked in rich people's favor.

At every juncture, the evolution of public education has been the outcome of class conflict and compromise. (Recent militant strikes against austerity by public school teachers in Illinois, West Virginia, California, and elsewhere demonstrate this is still the case.) Through a convoluted, push-and-pull process, we've come a long way and yet not nearly far enough. Progress has stalled, in part, because we now expect education to do too much; learning is extolled as the ultimate fix. We expect schools and teachers to open doors closed by prejudice, repair a lopsided economy, create jobs where there are none, and even heal our ailing democracy. These difficulties do not stem solely from a lack of learning, however. They are political and economic, and require solutions of an altogether different order.

At the same time, we've forgotten the world-turning ambitions of the people who pushed from below for the right to learn. Idealistic reformers once presented a vision of a world in which everyone who desired to participate in a broader, more fulfilling intellectual life might do so. They imagined an economy where exploitation had no place and where an educational system was democratic to the core, aimed at empowering every person as a whole human being, as a free, not servile, individual. Though we enjoy a system of public education the size and scale of which would have been unimaginable to a tenant farmer or coal miner trudging away in the late nineteenth century, they might nevertheless have been surprised to learn that most of our curriculum is geared more toward ensuring employability than encouraging general edification. What would a radical garment worker of yesterday have made of the fact that young people accrue tens of thousands of dollars of debt so they can find a job, and that being exploited by a boss is a privilege we increasingly pay for? Surely, her jaw would have dropped.

Over the years we have seen what education becomes in the context of rapid industrialization, postwar state investment and Cold War rivalries, and neoliberal marketization. But we have caught only brief glimpses of what education might become under a more fully democratic system. Under more robust conditions of economic democracy—where jobs are not scarce but guaranteed, work hours radically diminished, or a universal basic income provided—learning could be decoupled from career pressure and remade as a lifelong endeavor instead of something aimed at a terminal degree. (Primary and elementary schools, then, could also be released from strict adherence to the eight-hour day of the modern workweek, and the necessity of keeping children occupied for long hours while parents labor.) Expanding spaces of learning for people of all ages would foster social equality and cultivate the liberty inherent in the liberal arts, enabling the continual pursuit of knowledge self-rule requires. Only when schools are freed from the structural constraints that compel them to track and sort students (while telling them they deserve what they get) will the promise of universal education cease to be a lie, for only then could educators truly prioritize cultivating curiosity over imposing social control, firing up students instead of cooling them out. Until such a day the observation of one of the outspoken girls from the youth center in Overtown remains true: "Democracy's not really real, to be honest . . . If we have to constrain our opinions because we have people over us, that's not democracy. Because democracy is run by the people, for the people." That's not how people live, she concluded, and certainly not how her country or her school is run.

Philosophy has been a conscript in the battle over the role of education in democracy, and not always blamelessly. It began with Plato's *Republic*, a text that speaks to the democratic clash between the masses and the intellectuals. (It's worth noting that Plato's notorious elitism is conflicted, for the very style in which his texts are written, in dialogues that portray all characters as capable of reflection, is an inherently democratic form.) In one of *The Republic*'s most quoted passages, Plato imagines a ship where command of the helm has been seized by a gang of unqualified sailors, with the assistance of an unscrupulous but wealthy sponsor. They take the wheel by fraud, force, and flattery, instead of handing control to a navigator who can read the wind and the waters and actually comprehend the stars they see in the sky. Contemptuous of knowledge, the sailors denounce the capable guide as a "prater, a stargazer, a good-for-nothing"—in other words, a pedantic intellectual or irritating egghead.

The allegory still resonates. Many have interpreted this passage to mean that Plato thought experts should rule and the masses are too ignorant to recognize what's good for them. This is an oversimplification. The class of philosophically inclined rulers Plato dreamed of were not our kind of modern-day technocrats; philosophers, according to the classical definition, are lovers of wisdom, not facts or data. Plato objected to democracy not because the system denied technically proficient people the right to run things, but because he believed it inevitably marginalized the wise. (His hero, Socrates, was put to death, after all, not elevated to leadership.[18]) The political navigators he envisioned had their eyes set not on true north but on something more profound: truth itself, or what Plato called the "good," which he believed to be absolute, unchanging, and adequately appreciated only by an unconventional, out-of-step minority.

It's a strange metaphysical paradigm, to be sure. But one does not have to be a card-carrying Platonist to accept the idea that wisdom is not the same thing as cleverness, which involves mastery of specific subjects to demonstrate superiority. Transcending competence or utility, wisdom exists for its own sake, which is why it is threatening; unlike expertise, acquired at a price, wisdom is not for sale. Plato's beloved Socrates, the lover of wisdom and a questioner par excellence, was a paragon in this respect. He refused to charge a fee for his teachings, unlike the sold-out practitioners of sophistry he so despised because they sought only to sway what the Greeks called *doxa*, or "public opinion," instead of pursuing more timeless and transcendent aims.

In the aftermath of Donald Trump's victory, Plato experienced something of a resurgence. What other president so closely resembled the unqualified sailor puffed up by ill-informed passengers seeking a pleasure cruise? "I love the poorly educated," Trump declared on the campaign trail in Nevada. Liberals gasped and guffawed, roundly mocking the comment in the media. Here was definitive proof of Trump's shameless pandering to the proudly ignorant. But you couldn't blame him: on Election Day, he won white voters without college degrees by a wide margin. Lots of poorly educated white people loved Trump back and Plato suddenly seemed eerily prescient on the theme of democracy's inevitable decline.

The liberal reactions to Trump's comment contained more than a hint of snobbery, since not everyone should have to have a college degree to be appreciated by politicians. But what the haughtiness missed was that conservatives and business figures had been using the same playbook for decades, redirecting anger away from economic elites like themselves and toward so-called cultural elites. The living embodiment of Plato's definition of a demagogue (and the antithesis of his ideal of an indigent, propertyless, philosopher king), Trump successfully pulled off an old trick by signaling that he, a billionaire Ivy League graduate, stood with the common people—unlike the out-of-touch latte-sipping, politically correct, college green–dwelling "snowflakes."

A pervasive hostility to intellectuals aided his deceit. As Richard Hofstadter observes in *Anti-Intellectualism in American Life*, his Pulitzer Prize–winning study published in 1963, ridiculing cerebral types is a venerable democratic tradition. (In ancient Greece, Aristophanes's comedy *The Clouds* made fun of Socrates for having his head you-know-where.) The democratic ethos has often been tinged with a mistrust of book learning, however misplaced this suspicion may sometimes be. Even though the founding fathers were an undeniably erudite bunch, their scholarly pro-clivities were quickly brushed aside. In 1828, the choice for leader was between "John Quincy Adams who can write and Andrew Jackson who can fight," and we all know it was the "unlet-tered man of the West" who won.[19]

Hofstadter traces the source of this dismissal of erudition to a combination of primitivism (or what could be called rugged individualism, a conscious rejection of European high culture), evangelical religion, and profit-focused business practicality, all tendencies that are suspicious of the intellectual's critical, noncon-forming disposition. While industry and government depend upon intelligence, which can be harnessed for concrete ends, intel-lectualism has far less utility. (Hofstadter notes that intelligence is a trait that can be admired in animals, but your dog can never be an intellectual.) The intellectual temperament, not unlike that of the philosopher, treats learning with near-devotional status, liv-ing *for* ideas, not off them.

Fond as I may be of intellectuals, I cannot entirely blame people for their anger at the highly educated. The cultural elite, or what we might call the professional class, has often operated to protect its own limited interests, pulling the ladder up behind itself to stave off competition from below while invoking the cover of meritocracy. To pass on their privileges, the educationally advan-taged cluster in desirable school districts, enrolling their offspring in programs that nurture their passions and honor their individ-ual quirks and interests, or pay a premium for private schools designed to encourage a love of knowledge, or at least academic facility, from an early age, perpetuating what amounts to an edu-cational aristocracy. Most children are locked out.

The majority of young people, meanwhile, get their first introduction to the world of ideas in a setting where the resi-dent intellectual authority, the teacher, is also forced to be an authoritarian—the roles of schoolmaster and taskmaster discon-certedly blur. No matter their enthusiasm or good intentions, teachers are required to both introduce children to academic disciplines and also discipline them, issuing threats and punishments to keep attention focused and overcrowded classrooms in line. This categorical confusion, one that many people carry with them for the rest of their lives, inhibits curiosity and confidence and taints our culture's relationship to learning as a result. The more open and democratic the educational context, the easier it is to admire intellectual ability on its own merits instead of viewing it as a force of oppression, displeasure, or shame.

A health clinic I visited in Greece provides one example of what a more egalitarian relationship to expertise might look like, making it worth describing in brief, as it points to one way out of our present bind. The volunteer-run center is one of dozens of similar operations that popped up in and around Greece in the wake of the country's devastating economic collapse, which started in 2008 and led to massive budget cuts, hospital closures, and dangerous drug shortages that plague the country to this day. With poverty rising along with its attendant illnesses, citizens organized themselves to fill the care gap and put pressure on the state to provide adequate service.

"This is a clinic that will try to help the people on every level, especially the poorest, those who suffer from the crisis more, and who don't have the ability to visit the doctor or get their medications," Emmy Koutsopoulou, the resident psychologist, explained. "It will try to be a lesson, a democracy cell within the neighborhood, here in the community, and it will try to sow some modicums of a different meaning of medicine, a different meaning of community, as an answer to the financial crisis." She laughed at these grandiose ambitions. "As much as we can, anyway!"

The clinic is on a lower floor of a modest apartment building, and the volunteers were still building out some of the offices when I was there. I arrived on a Tuesday evening, just in time for the weekly meeting. Doctors, dentists, and nurses crowded into the main space with the rest of the team, who might run the front office, solicit donations, or help with construction or cleaning. "There is no leadership," a surgeon named Ioanna Dimou said as

I tried to process the chaos around me. "There is no pyramid." All the decisions are made democratically, by consensus, in a process that includes every volunteer no matter his or her background.

Like many such projects throughout the region, the clinic also aims to break down the hierarchy between health care provider and patient. Instead of approaching patients as clients passively receiving a service, even a charitable one, the clinic hopes to involve the people they treat in the project, so that they might help it grow, better provide for the community, and reach the political goal of a functioning, free, government-supported medical system. The doctors I spoke to in no way found the organizing model threatening to their expertise or status. Instead, they recognized that they were but one component in a larger enterprise. They could also learn from the patients and volunteers, without whom the clinic would not exist. This is why, when I asked to interview the gynecologist on duty, she invited the man building out the new rooms to speak at the same time. She didn't make a production of this inclusion: she and he played equally vital roles, though she was a medical professional and he was spackling and painting the area where she worked. They both deserved to have their say.

The volunteer clinics in Greece refuse to accept the traditional breakdown between mental and manual labor. That alone is worth remarking on. But even more striking is that they do so without denigrating the special knowledge that some people, including but not only doctors, possess. Training and technical skills are not resented but respected, even revered; everyone is considered and treated as an essential, equal participant. The general ethos is one of humility. Not everyone can be expert at everything. Even the most credentialed soul is part of the lowly, ignorant masses, in most respects.

Alongside these egalitarian healers, we should also take inspiration from the inmates heroically battling to keep their library and the children who, by recognizing that their teachers also don't have a say in how their school is run, challenge us to imagine what education would be like if students and teachers together, not administrators and privatizers, were in charge. Above all we must remember the militant workers who understood that there could be no separation between economic and intellectual liberation, who aimed for both the redistribution of wealth and the democratization of wisdom. They encouraged their fellows not to be "blockheads," bodies without minds to be easily exploited, and they envisioned a future where schooling was not a means of social division and control but an integral path toward collective enlightenment and social transformation. Knowledge is power, and that power can and must be shared.

"Every thinker puts some portion of an apparently stable world in peril, and no one can wholly predict what will emerge in its place," the great philosopher of education John Dewey wrote.[20] Thinking is, indeed, a dangerous act. This is why, since the 1950s, conservatives content with the status quo have been pointing the finger at "eggheads," those smug know-it-alls who, they say, want to tell people what to think, watch, and eat, and how to live their lives. This is only the latest tactic in a long war to keep the majority of people in deferential darkness that dates back to Plato's call for an exclusive and lofty group of philosophers to lead the mindless masses. Ordinary people have struggled defiantly in response, banding together against the odds to form a philosophical public, a public that may not have all the answers but that is unafraid to ask questions, learn, and rebel. This is one thing the knowledge-hungry workers of the past knew to be true, and it remains so today: democracy demands that everyone contemplate and deliberate, that all of us think and reason, even if there have always been some who would prefer that we didn't.

CHAPTER 7

NEW WORLD ORDER

(LOCAL/GLOBAL)

IN MAY 2011 thousands of Athenians took to Syntagma Square, the public plaza in front of the city's grand parliament building. Like the Indignados then amassing in Madrid's Puerta de Sol, the Greek protesters occupied the space and refused to leave—at least not until the police violently cleared the camp three months later. Echoing the Spanish call for "¡Democracia Real Ya!" they rallied under the slogan "Amesi Dimokratia Tora!"—Direct Democracy Now!

The crowd at Syntagma Square was angry. Greece was tumbling into an economic depression from which it has yet to recover. The banking crisis that began in the United States in 2008 spread, becoming a European debt crisis. Dramatic curbs on public spending only made matters worse: hospitals shut down and ran out of medicine and the value of the health sector's budget fell by half; schools operated without books or heat and teachers were laid off; hundreds of thousands of small businesses shuttered.[1] The unemployment rate shot up, exceeding 70 percent for young women, and pushed four hundred thousand citizens, mostly young and college educated, to emigrate, a huge number given Greece's population of around ten million. A third of the country now lives near poverty, according to the Organization for Economic Cooperation and Development.[2]

In early 2010, a Memorandum of Understanding granted tremendous power to the foreign authorities commonly known as the "troika"—the European Commission, the European Central Bank, and the International Monetary Fund—in return for an emergency loan of more than $100 billion. Polls showed that over 60 percent of Greek citizens were opposed to the deal. The loan came with steep interest on the repayments and sweeping austerity measures: cuts to already insufficient pensions and wages, diminished health care services and education spending, weakened labor protections. All the while taxes ballooned and public assets were privatized for sale to foreign investors.

Ordinary people were keenly aware of the enormous human cost attached to the Memorandum of Understanding. The economy was already in decline, and cuts to social spending had the potential to transform a difficult situation into a full-blown humanitarian disaster. Protesters at Syntagma Square, enraged that the will of the national majority had been thwarted by transnational power, demanded the resignation of Prime Minister George Papandreou, a scion of a liberal political dynasty who campaigned by downplaying the country's economic woes and covering up years of fiscal mismanagement. By the end of 2011 he stepped down, only to be replaced by Lucas Papademos, a former vice president of the European Central Bank. The international creditors managed to install one of their own.

Democracy means rule of the people. But where do they rule? Where do they exercise their democracy? And how many people can this space hold? Sometimes the space is a humble park inhabited by a few thousand idealists. The occupation of Syntagma Square was not only a demonstration against injustice and an indictment of those in power; it was also a utopian expression of what a just society might look like, and an attempt to put a more authentic vision of democracy into practice.

Invigorated by solidarity, the protesters organized themselves into working groups to coordinate the supply of food, medicine, and sanitation, while also offering education programs and handling communications. Music and art events were frequent—a dance troop performing with umbrellas resembled a bloom of jellyfish gently floating across the plaza at sunset. Aspasia Balta, nineteen at the time, was attracted by the energy, camaraderie, and wide cross section of people who were taking part. Young and old, working class and white collar, radical and liberal, citizen and foreigner gathered to talk at the evening meetings. Anyone could address the crowd, as long as they respected the rule that limited speakers to three minutes. "Every day was a public assembly," Balta told me. "It was a great experiment in direct democracy."

The great experiment worked, in part, because it was not in fact that great, at least in terms of its scale. It was limited to a specific space (a public square) and size (the people who could fit in the square). Where democracy is concerned the problem of scale is important. Self-rule is generally a place-based phenomenon, an action tied to a particular location and the people who inhabit it. At what size are territories and groups best suited for collective decision making and at what point does direct deliberation become impossible?

So many of our modern-day problems are planetary in scope: interconnected markets mean stock trades in London or the price of oil in the Middle East affects New York, Hong Kong, and Mumbai; ideas circulate through digital networks; climate change cannot be quarantined; and pandemics can spread with a single transcontinental flight. That we live in a globalized world is obvious, but that doesn't mean we have figured out the appropriate democratic response.

Greece's crisis is instructive because the country's woes were not wholly homegrown—the local economy faltered because the global economy crashed, the initial contagion emanating from Wall Street before spreading far and wide. Greece came to exemplify a profound contemporary conundrum. Financial markets, neoliberal trade regimes, and *Fortune* 500 companies are all transnational, but democracy remains bound to the nation-state. This disjunction escalates the tension between the local and the global—a tension felt in so many of our political problems. The pervasive sense that power has moved beyond the grasp of ordinary people is part of what has fueled the turn toward ethnonationalism in many countries, including Greece, where the fascist Golden Dawn party gained ground. Today, any democrat worth the name has to balance multiple democratic dynamics at once— local, municipal, national, regional, global—especially when they clash. And clash they did at Syntagma Square.

Distance tends to give an advantage to antidemocratic forces, not because a larger scale is inherently autocratic or corrupt, but because people cannot readily reach the individuals in power or the institutions that wield it. That said, I've been involved in enough tiny dysfunctional groups to know that one-on-one democracy is not necessarily more efficient or egalitarian. Devolving power to smaller units can advance antidemocratic objectives, as the history of "states' rights" in the racist areas of the American South shows. At the same time, international law, whether designed to protect human rights or the climate, can certainly enhance democracy. Small is not inherently better, and big does not have to be bad. Scale is best understood as a strategy, a means to achieve democratic ends, or, as we'll see, to undermine them.

In school students are typically taught that democracy is the invention of the West, a gift bestowed upon the rest of the world. Europeans, according to this narrative, inherited the ideal from the visionaries of Athens and Rome and began to perfect and enlarge it in the eighteenth century. In reality, the Greeks may have coined the word *democracy* but they did not invent the practice. Democracy sprung up in all sorts of places and times, taking a variety of forms: citizen assemblies in the ancient Middle Eastern city of Nippur, the Mesoamerican collective republic of Tlaxcallan, African village councils, Icelandic Althings, Swiss cantons, and so on. Anthropologists argue that human beings likely spent much of our early existence living in relatively egalitarian tribes and communities, groups that were tiny enough that everyone knew everyone else's name and business, and cooperation was key to survival. Size is the common thread. All of these democratic precursors came from comparatively small societies, not countries of tens or hundreds of millions, or many billions, of people.

In 1513 Machiavelli agonized over the question of scale. His *Discourses* weighs the virtues of small republics against colossal empires, specifically imperial Rome. A community small enough to govern itself as a republic, he observes, would likely be too small to organize its own defense. But, if large enough to effectively protect itself, such a republic would be plagued by internal "confusion" and "tumults" and would eventually slide into despotism. Growth and success, in Machiavelli's cutthroat account, lead straight to Ceasarism. He dubs expansion "poison" for republics, and yet decides one must drink it nonetheless.[3] With no satisfactory resolution in sight, Machiavelli abandons the republican cause to embrace "Roman greatness."[4] If small states were necessarily doomed, why not go out with an imperial bang?

In the eighteenth century, as the idea of representative democracy took hold, the question of scale resurfaced. "If a republic is small, it is destroyed by foreign force; if it is large, it is destroyed by internal vice," the thoughtful aristocrat Montesquieu observed, echoing Machiavelli. Large republics would be more diverse, "distracted by a thousand private views." Commerce would result in inequality, which would pave the way to tyranny. Unlike Machiavelli, however, Montesquieu hinted at possible solutions, devising the basis of the liberal notion of the tripartite "separation of powers" to constrain despotic influence. He also wrote approvingly of the possibility of a "confederate" or "federative" republic. The formation of an alliance was a potentially appealing way to scale up and strengthen small republics.

The drafters of the United States Constitution regularly quoted Montesquieu in their correspondence. Many saw the expansive geography of North America's eastern seaboard, not to mention the vastness of the continent, as a challenge for republican self-rule. But Madison, in particular, made it his mission to trounce the argument in favor of small republics. Larger territories and more diverse populations could actually be beneficial, he insisted. Dismissing the possibility of social unity, Madison wagered that it would be more effective to let a wide variety of social forces cancel each other out: the destructive power of factions could be mitigated by increasing their number, not by trying to force everyone into a state of concord. An "extended republic" would funnel power upward to what he believed would be a more worthy and capable class of men, weakening what he called the "spirit of locality."

This is how the proponents of federalism made their case: great, as in virtuous, republics also needed to be great as in vast. Quantity—of citizens and square miles—would be the handmaiden of quality. Expansion was reformulated not as a poison but a cure, a welcome antidote that would work its magic by diluting the influence of diverse people and their complicated, parochial attachments while diverting their attention toward the horizon.[5] Magnitude would serve a multifaceted purpose, diffusing social antagonisms. As America's border crept in the direction of the setting sun, citizens waged wars westward, against Indians, instead of directing their ire upward, at the nation's elites.[6]

Long before Montesquieu formulated his thoughts a formidable confederacy already existed in the northeastern corner of the so-called New World. The League of Six Nations, or the Haudenosaunee Confederacy, provided a living example, dating back to the fourteenth century, of communities forging a union to extend their collective power. After a long period of internecine warfare, five powerful nations—the Mohawk, Seneca, Onondaga, Oneida, and Cayuga—followed by the Tuscarora in 1722, came together under the Kaienerekowa, or Great Law of Peace, a groundbreaking constitution outlining the structure, rights, and duties of federation membership.

The historical record shows that many colonial figures came into close and often extended contact with Haudenosaunee people, and they were often impressed by the individuals whose lands they sought to steal and way of life they tried to eradicate. Benjamin Franklin, for one, felt that the Iroquois federation was an advanced entity: "It would be a very strange Thing, if six Nations of ignorant Savages should be capable of forming a Scheme for such a Union, and be able to execute it in such a Manner, as that it has subsisted Ages, and appears indissoluble; and yet a like Union should be impracticable for ten or a Dozen Colonies, to whom it is more necessary, and must be more advantageous."[7]

Franklin published the proceedings of a treaty conference that took place in Lancaster, Pennsylvania, in 1744, including the remarks of Onondaga chief Canasatego. The colonists were at war with France and needed to ally with indigenous nations, but they were also squabbling among themselves. Canasatego advised the men seeking his allegiance to follow the Iroquois example and adopt a federal system. Forming a union, he insisted, would increase their stability and strength. Three decades later, in August 1775, the Continental Congress appointed delegates to meet with the League of Six Nations representatives. The colonial emissaries paid tribute to "the advice that was given about thirty years ago, by your wise forefathers . . . when Canasatego spoke to us, the white people," in words that had "sunk deep into" the hearts of those who heard them.

> The Six Nations are a wise people, Let us hearken to them, and take their counsel, and teach our children to follow it. Our old men have done so. They have frequently taken a single arrow and said, Children, see how easily it is broken. Then they have taken and tied twelve arrows together with a strong string or cord and our strongest men could not break them. See, said they, this is what the Six Nations mean. Divided, a single man may destroy you; united, you are a match for the whole world.

Soon after, the image of the bundle of arrows was incorporated as part of the official seal of the United States. In the original design, they were worn on the back of a Native American warrior. In the final version, thirteen arrows are clutched in the right claw of an eagle.[8]

Originally an oral code that took days to recount, the Iroquois Confederacy's constitution, the Great Law of Peace, contained 117 clauses that were also recorded on wampum. Mixing rich symbolism with technical specificity, the law outlines the formation of what historian and political theorist Taiaiake Alfred calls a "truly democratic system of political organization and the first genuine North American federal system."[9] While incorporated into a larger whole, each nation remained autonomous and distinct. There was no Haudenosaunee state in the modern sense—the confederation was not a government that ruled by coercive force. Consensual agreement was central to Iroquois political philosophy and the league was bound by what Alfred describes as "the moral force of the community itself."[10]

The law established the League's Great Council, a convening of a total of fifty "sachems," or chiefs, with each nation allotted a specific number of representatives. The wampum codify the council's authority while also constraining its influence, dividing power and establishing checks and balances, detailing the rules of debate and a system to facilitate unanimity in decision making, and outlining a process to recall leaders. Freedom of assembly, speech, religion, and cultural difference were also protected. "Their whole civil policy was averse to the concentration of power in the hands of any single individual," wrote Lewis Henry Morgan in an early ethnography.

In the first English-language account of the Iroquois, published in 1727, Cadwallader Colden, a colonial official and Mohawk adoptee, marveled that the chiefs tended to be poorer than the average person. "There is not a Man in the Ministry of the Five Nations, who has gained his Office otherwise than by Merit; there is not the least Salary, or any Sort of Profit, annexed to any Office, to tempt the Covetous or Sordid." Later he noted that the community had "such absolute notions of liberty that they allow of no kind of superiority of one over another, and banish all servitude from their territories."

The chiefs, then, were not kings or autocrats. According to the Great Law their legitimacy was rooted in the community, which they were bound to engage in processes of discussion and consultation. The Law makes that much clear.

> Whenever a very important matter . . . is presented to the Council of the League and that matter affects the entire [Confederacy], the Sachems of the League must submit the matter to the decision of the people and the decision of the people shall affect the decision of the Council . . . This decision shall be a confirmation of the voice of the people.[11]

The wampum decree that these "mentors" of the people, tasked with representing everyone's interests, must be able to handle public scorn and the inevitable tribulations of political office.

> The thickness of their skin shall be seven spans, which is to say that they shall be proof against anger, offensive action, and criticism. Their hearts shall be full of peace and good will, and their minds filled with yearning for the welfare of the people of the League. With endless patience they shall carry out their duty. Their firmness shall be tempered with a tenderness for their people. Neither anger nor fury shall find lodging in their minds and all their words and actions shall be marked by calm deliberation . . . in everything they say and do they will think only of the [people] and not of themselves, thinking ahead not only of the present but also of the generations of unborn yet to come.[12]

If a thin-skinned or hotheaded sachem failed to meet his obligations and defend the welfare of the people, he could be impeached after two warnings by those who had empowered him—the women known as "clan mothers." These clan mothers were the matriarchs of the subtribes that made up each nation, and it was they who possessed the ultimate power to appoint, and depose—literally, "dehorn"—the sachems. The clan mothers, in turn, were themselves chosen by other adult female members of their extended family group. In stark contrast to the deafening silence of the American Constitution in regard to half of the human population, nearly one quarter of the clauses that compose the Great Law of Peace pertain explicitly to the power and role of women.[13] The domestic and democratic spheres were not severed as in settler society, where women were confined to private space while men dominated public life.

And so, hundreds of years before the concept of "women's rights" made an appearance in the English language Haudenosaunee society embodied a twentieth-century feminist slogan: "Democracy in the home, democracy in the country." At its apex, the confederacy spread across a vast territory including most of what is now New York State and also parts of Pennsylvania, Ohio, and the provinces of Ontario and Quebec, resting on a Great Law that paid attention to every level of social and political life, from family obligations to foreign policy. "Iroquois society was characterized by an extensive democracy," Alfred writes. ' The central concern of the federal system was to ensure the perpetuation of this popular sovereignty, and the entire mechanism was organized so that chiefs directly represented the will of their people."[14]

When the founders of the United States took inspiration from the League of Six Nations, they did so seeking an example of democracy on a grand scale. Focused on the question of forming a union that could bond people across a massive landmass, they ignored the Iroquois example of full democracy across the gender divide as well as their profound lessons about how to relate to the land itself—lessons that are at the core of a variety of indigenous traditions.[15] As the scholar and member of the Yellowknives Dene First Nation Glen Coulthard explains, indigenous land

claims are not exclusionary—land is a "relationship" to be cultivated, not a resource to be hoarded. "Stated bluntly the theory
and practice of Indigenous anticolonialism, including Indigenous
anticapitalism, is best understood as a struggle primarily inspired
by and oriented around the question of land," Coulthard writes
in *Red Skins, White Masks*. "[A] struggle not only for land in
the material sense, but also deeply informed by what the land as
system of reciprocal relations and obligations can teach us about
living our lives in relation to one another and the natural world
in nondominating and nonexploitative terms."[16]

In their long quest for sovereignty, First Nations offer a unique
understanding of the term—sovereignty not as territorial domin-
ion and the right to exploit but, instead, a mutualism between land
and people and the right to coexist. Coulthard quotes Philip Blake,
a Dene from Fort McPherson, Canada, who, in the early 1970s,
offered this insight to settlers, which he hoped they would accept
as a substitute for minerals:

> We do not believe that our society has to grow and expand and con-
> quer new areas in order to fulfill our destiny as Indian people....
> That is not our way. I believe your nation might wish to see us, not
> as a relic from the past, but as a way of life, a system of values by
> which you may survive in the future. This we are willing to share.[17]

Almost one year after the Syntagma occupation began, a seventy-
seven-year-old retired pharmacist went to the square. He told pass-
ersby he didn't want to pass his debts on to his children and shot
himself. Austerity measures had slashed his pension and he condemned the government in a suicide note: "I cannot find any other
form of struggle except a dignified end before I have to start
scrounging for food from the rubbish."[18] His death came to symbolize the suffering of the entire nation.

"In a global economic crisis like the one we are in, the first
thing that will be sacrificed is democracy, the power of the people,"

Despoina Koutsoumpa, an archeologist and well-respected political organizer, told me. "We have a contradiction between what
we live here with social movements, which are very democratic,
and our public affairs, which are not ruled by the people or even
by representatives of the people," she explained. "Today power is
not in the parliament or even in the European parliament. The real
power lies in institutions that are not controlled by people power,
like the European Central Bank, the European Commission, and
the Eurogroup," the assembly of Eurozone finance ministers. Key
positions in these centers of power are filled by technocrats who
are appointed, not elected.

The Athenians I met often described the lending program and
the harsh austerity measures it required as a coup or a form of neo-
colonialism—a takeover by global financial elites who used
"banks not tanks" to undermine popular sovereignty. In response,
millions of Greeks pinned their hopes on a relatively new left-wing
party called SYRIZA, or the Coalition of the Radical Left, which
gained in popularity following the social movements of 2011.
Under the leadership of the young and charismatic Alexis Tsipras, the coalition swept into office in 2014 promising an end, as
the prime minister–elect put it in his rousing victory speech, to the
"vicious cycle of austerity."

The country's creditors were not impressed by the electorate's
revolt. German minister of finance Wolfgang Schauble sought to
dampen expectations from the start. "Elections change nothing.
There are rules," he declared in early 2015. Troika leaders insisted
that the economic policy of austerity would continue, regardless
of voters' preferences. If the Greek people were allowed to extricate themselves from such agreements, what would stop the Portuguese or the Italians or the Irish—not to mention other indebted
nations such as Pakistan, Mexico, or Zambia—from doing the
same?

Under Tsipras, a bold human rights lawyer named Zoe Konstantopoulou became speaker of the parliament. Konstantopoulou had been active in the Syntagma occupation, where she had

joined forces with a group of protesters concerned about the government's lack of financial transparency. They demanded an audit. Carrying the project from the streets into the halls of power, Konstantopoulou established a Truth Committee on Public Debt.

Examining the evidence left no doubt that much of Greece's sovereign debt was both illegal and immoral. The official audit, submitted by Konstantopoulou to the parliament revealed that the vast sums, though portrayed as a "bailout" of the Greek economy, were actually used to save foreign banks, with approximately 90 percent of the funds going straight to the creditors without even passing through Greece. Lenders were paid back, with interest and service fees, while Greeks lost their sovereignty: as part of the deal, public officials handed over budgetary autonomy and key administrators to their creditors, who arrogated to themselves the right to veto the country's laws and appoint the officials overseeing the public revenue system, effectively superseding the legislature.

Digging deeper, the researchers found that Greece's debt spiraled not because of overspending on public services, as the media maintained, but because of the aftershocks of the 2008 global crisis, which led to the country being shut out of international financial markets.[19] Rising interest payments produced a "snowball effect" that accounted for two-thirds of the increase of debt between 1980 and 2007 (along the way, interest-rate swap machinations by Goldman Sachs added to the country's deficit while the investment bank raked in around $800 million for its services).[20] The Truth Committee also determined that IMF officials were aware that the Greek debt was unsustainable and that vulnerable populations—the poor, pensioners, women, children, the disabled, and immigrants—would suffer the most.

The memorandum agreements, Konstantopoulou told me, resemble rushed business deals more than carefully considered public policy. "You really feel like you're not talking about a country, but you're talking about a company, an enterprise, which is going bankrupt, and is being asked to fire its employees," she said. "Only it's not an enterprise, it's a sovereign country, and these are

not employees, these are the country's citizens. It is not legal, and
it is not acceptable, to ask a government and a country to kill its
society in order to pay back creditors." Many of the specific austerity
measures passed since 2009—including cuts to essential services,
privatization of public assets, suspension of collective bargaining
agreements, and relaxing the conditions under which workers
could be fired—forced the country to violate its own constitutional commitments and international human rights obligations.

To Konstantopoulou's grave disappointment, Tsipras was
reluctant to dispute the legality of the loans. He did not want to
risk getting Greece kicked out of the Eurozone, which would have
compounded the country's woes, at least in the short term. As
the months dragged on, it became apparent that even a modest
write down was too much to ask, and the country teetered on
the brink of default. As a result of the crisis, a new memorandum agreement was on the horizon. In June 2015 Tsipras appeared
on national television and called a referendum.

> Greek citizens, I call on you to decide—with sovereignty and dig-
> nity as Greek history demands—whether we should accept the extor-
> tionate ultimatum that calls for strict and humiliating austerity
> without end, and without the prospect of ever standing on our own
> two feet, socially and financially. We should respond to authoritari-
> anism and harsh austerity with democracy—calmly and decisively.
> Greece, the birthplace of democracy, should send a resounding
> democratic message to the European and global community. And
> I personally commit that I will respect the outcome of your demo-
> cratic choice, whatever it may be.

The country split—Yes versus No, Nai versus Oxi—in reaction
to the terms of the new agreement.

Leading up to the vote, banks shut down and capital controls
went into effect, limiting citizens' access to cash. For days the
international media broadcast images of long lines at ATM
machines and reported on the disaster that would befall the country

if it defied its creditors. Pundits believed the prospect of catastrophe would weaken the "no" camp's resolve, and polls predicted
a landslide victory for "yes." At Syntagma Square, the night before
the vote, a massive crowd gathered, the chants of "Oxi" ringing
out. Tsipras took to the stage. "Today democracy is celebrating.
Democracy is a celebration! Democracy is joy! Democracy is sal-
vation!" No matter what happened, he proclaimed, democracy
had already won. The next day the "no" vote triumphed, taking
62 percent of the vote. An overwhelming majority of the citizenry
rejected the troika's terms.

To Konstantopoulou, the referendum was a moment of crown-
ing importance, a repudiation of the country's recent history that
elicited powerful emotion from the public. Greece will forever be
associated with democracy through its ancient heritage, but it has
a deeply troubled past. Until 1974, a far-right military junta controlled the country with the Cold War backing of the United States.
Tsipras's referendum was the nation's first. "For the first time in
forty years, the people were given a say for their lives, for their dignity, for their future, for their destiny," Konstantopoulou explained.
When the outcome was announced, citizens rejoiced, believing the
vote would give the government useful leverage. Instead, eight
days later Tsipras followed in his predecessor Papandreou's footsteps and signed the very memorandum the people had decisively
rejected.[21]

In the aftermath of the referendum, Konstantopoulou and
many other SYRIZA party members either resigned or were forced
out of office. The average citizen was stunned by their once-
uncompromising prime minister's volte-face. "After all these
years of fighting we thought that a party that owed its loyalty to
the people would be an instrument to voice the concerns of the
people," Aspasia Balta, the young activist told me. "And oh, we
were so naive" (like so many of her peers, she eventually left
Greece, feeling she had no long-term prospects in the country she
loves). As one woman who briefly worked under Tsipras put it to
me, the Greek indignados had done everything they could. They

assembled, petitioned, went on strike, rioted, built a political party, took state power, and voted overwhelming in the country's first plebiscite. Yet they were no better off than they had been at the outset. Instead, she said with a shrug, they were poorer and more demoralized. Still, when Tsipras called snap elections in September 2015, he coasted into office once again, in part because most voters wanted to keep his rivals—particularly the fascist Golden Dawn party—at bay. Many voters were angry at SYRIZA, but the alternatives were worse.

The referendum made it clear that the tactics citizens commonly employ to advance democratic causes within the nation-state are woefully inadequate to the challenges of our time. "We can protest and volunteer and help each other—and we do it all the time—but at the end of the day, there's a wall, and we have to break the wall," Koutsoumpa said. The wall she referred to is neoliberal capitalism, a system that is able to transcend borders and that pits the global against the local in its boundary-crossing quest for profits.

Facing this great obstacle, the social movements Tsipras rode to power fractured in two directions. Some SYRIZA supporters turned away from national politics to the hyperlocal, focusing on immediate, grounded endeavors: running consumer cooperatives to supply food to struggling neighborhoods, volunteering at clinics to offer basic health services, providing tutoring to families in need, or aiding the hundreds of thousands of Syrian refugees who began arriving in Greece in 2014. They organized within their own communities without giving attention to parties or elections—to manifest direct democracy on a one-on-one scale, not through the impersonal, corrupt channels of the state.

The other camp turned its energies away from the local to the global dimensions of the crisis, tracing its roots to larger European and supranational institutions. Democracy had faltered at the domestic level because the antidemocratic forces were operating at a higher altitude. The Democracy in Europe Movement kicked off, and Europe's first transnational political party was founded with the aim of pushing for a continent-wide New Deal that would foster democratic solidarity among countries. The problem with most supranational institutions, this group argued, is not one of size but rather the specific policies promoted and special interests served. Representative democracy could still be redeemed.

The sympathies of George Papandreou, I learned, lay with these critics. Speaking in his office, he surprised me by sounding a lot like the protesters who had demanded his resignation. As Papandreou tells it, he was powerless after the global crash. The government couldn't take productive steps to improve the situation without foreign investors responding erratically. At one point, there was a baseless rumor that Greece might get an emergency loan from China. "The markets immediately reacted in a negative way. Then we said no, we're not doing this, it's not true, and they reacted even worse." In the absence of reforms, Papandreou predicts, the "contradiction between markets and democracy" will become only more pronounced.

Regulation is needed but Papandreou sees the challenge as one of scale. "When we talk about democracy, we're talking about human beings making decisions and so you have to have decisions at the human level. It's a very Aristotelian idea, everything to human measure. But we have created systems that are not too big to fail—they can fail—but too big to be accountable," Papandreou reflected. "If we're talking about democratizing our societies, we need to democratize globalization, and that means put some limits on these financial powers." The European Union has done exactly the opposite, placing tremendous authority in the hands of unelected central bankers and technocrats whose mandates demand they view social policy as a line item on a budget, something to be reduced or cut even when essential to people's survival.

In 1994, Prime Minister Andreas Papandreou—George's father—gave a prescient interview to *New Perspectives Quarterly*, calling attention to this failing. He reflected on the Maastricht Treaty, the 1992 agreement that created the European Union and laid the foundation for the euro by emphasizing stability-oriented banking criteria such as positive debt-to-GDP ratios, low budget deficits, and controlled inflation for member-states.

> We want a united Europe, but we have reservations. The goals of Maastricht are all financial. . . . The road toward unity ought to have targets that seek to reduce unemployment just as there are targets to reduce inflation. Clearly, without targets for a social Europe based on a strategy of growth, Europe is going to face socially explosive forces—xenophobia and ultra-right threats to democracy.[22]

Years later, millions of people faced the consequences of this warning going unheeded.

Today we have a "semblance of democracy," Papandreou said when I asked him who actually rules, but financial markets have almost unchecked power to shape public policy, regardless of citizens' preferences, and flows of global capital are not subject to effective democratic control. "We've deified the markets, and said they are the ones that make the decisions. We've given up power as societies, as citizens. We have undermined our own democracy by saying: 'We give the power to the markets to plan, to decide, to create confidence.'" There are "huge powers out there that are multiple times stronger than any government or any society" that can damage the economy of a country in an instant: single corporations possess cash holdings that dwarf the gross domestic product of many governments. "A small country like Greece, with a parliament of three hundred people making decisions to try to solve things—we don't have that power to be able to withstand these huge forces."

How did it come to this? How did we arrive at a situation where the will of a sovereign country can be overruled by remote financial interests?

The answer is too complex for a single chapter, but one piece of the puzzle lies in Geneva, Switzerland, an Alpine city uniquely positioned to represent the tension between the local and the global. Thanks to Jean-Jacques Rousseau, Geneva's impressive democratic reputation dates back more than two centuries. In his foundational writings, the philosopher made the Swiss city on the lake synonymous with his vision of popular sovereignty, in which common citizens—male heads of household—cooperated as equals for the good of the whole, with prosperity and peace the supposed result.

However, the work of Rousseau is not Geneva's only or most influential legacy.

In his excellent book *Globalists: The End of Empire and Birth of Neoliberalism*, historian Quinn Slobodian profiles a group of neoliberal economists he dubs the "Geneva School," who waged a multipronged battle of ideas to promote and strengthen markets, establish the rights of corporations and investors, and diminish the power of nation-states. These men—well-known academic figures such as Friedrich Hayek, Ludwig von Mises, and Wilhelm Röpke, as well as countless lesser-known lights—lamented the spread of "rabies democratica" after World War II (the phrase is from Röpke, a Swiss economist and author of a book called *A Humane Economy*, who also lent his expertise to the South African apartheid regime). As democracy advanced geographically and into new areas of social life, they sought to maintain economic and political hierarchies. Their goal was nothing less than an "economic constitution for the world," or what they called a "rules-based international economic order," that would protect capitalism from democratic demands.

For thinkers of the Geneva School, nations were the province of the fatal democratic flaw: empowered citizens who would insist on regulating or even running the economy for their collective benefit. These early neoliberals saw mass enfranchisement, workers' rights, national sovereignty, protectionism, and redistribution as part of the same disturbing democratic package. "A nation may beget its own barbarian invaders," warned Röpke, speaking specially of labor movements, which tend to be at the vanguard of the push for a more redistributive state. Their solution involved emphasizing larger and smaller scales while shrinking and constraining the democratic middle: at one extreme were the supranational corporate confederations, in the form of trade bodies and investment treaties; at the other there would be billions of tiny "sovereign consumers."[23] "Denationalism," as Slobodian calls the Geneva process, was aimed at harnessing the power of the state to insulate the economy from the very citizens it is supposed to serve, ensuring that markets, not people, rule.

The Geneva School's decades-long campaign culminated in the creation of the World Trade Organization, called "one of the most significant milestones in the realization of global capitalism."[24] The WTO, headquartered in Geneva and established in 1995, is a consortium empowered to regulate international commerce with the authority to supersede local law from a distance. Backed by more than 150 states, the WTO scales up the power and influence of corporations and private investors, representing greater than 98 percent of all international trade.[25]

Ironically, the initial foundation for the WTO, the Bretton Woods system, was laid in the aftermath of World War II by a very different school of economic thinkers—economist John Maynard Keynes assisted by veteran New Dealers. The men who gathered at Bretton Woods, New Hampshire, in 1944, under the leadership of the United States and Britain, had lived through not just a terrible war but also the Great Depression, and these experiences had chastened them. A new international monetary order was born, aimed at taming capitalism; it ushered in a period of cross-border economic collaboration, one that led to the establishment of the International Monetary Fund, the World Bank, and the GATT (the General Agreement on Tariffs and Trade, precursor to the WTO).

The new order rested on a monetary exchange system that pegged currencies to the fixed gold value of the U.S. dollar, which provided stability while allowing national governments wide political and economic berth, used by many to provide a robust safety net and pursue policies aimed at full employment. America bolstered the economies of its former rivals not out of altruism but out of anxiety and self-interest; no one wanted to see another 1929, this time on a global scale. They succeeded: a postwar recession was averted and a period described as the "golden age of controlled capitalism" set in, albeit a golden age predicated on American dominance and exploitation of natural resources and raw materials from "peripheral" Third World countries.[26]

At the same time, Geneva School thinkers saw worrying signs on the horizon: between 1945 and 1960 forty countries, or a quarter of the world's population, gained independence, and the United Nations, under the mantle of human rights, was embracing rights to things such as housing, education, and health care for all.[27] As decolonization spread, Geneva School advocates insisted that the rights of foreign investors should be paramount. Corporate interests had to be protected against any form of protectionism or national expropriation, even when undertaken with the democratic mandate or to provide for a nation's citizens.[28]

Unsurprisingly, the economists eventually found eager allies in bankers, businessmen, and lobbying groups including the International Chamber of Commerce. Seeking ways to dampen the democratic flame, they promoted a vision of a "Capitalist Magna Carta," an idea first hatched in the late 1950s by a coalition led by the Deutsche Bank chairman Hermann Abs, a former Nazi collaborator concerned with protecting overseas investments. Their cause was boosted by the fact that the Bretton Woods system was in trouble by 1971. The United States had shifted course when President Richard Nixon took the dollar off the gold standard and the period of stable monetary exchange collapsed, causing currency exchange rates and valuations to go wild and inflation to run rampant.

After 1989, when the Soviet Bloc began to crumble and capitalism reigned triumphant, the remaining controls came off as the IMF, World Bank, and other trade organizations pushed for deregulatory arrangements. Finance and trade fully internationalized, with foreign money flooding into Wall Street, and multinational corporations became even bigger. By 1998 foreign exchange markets processed a trillion dollars daily, a twenty-fold increase from the early 1980s; between 1947 and 2017, the total value of world trade exploded from $57 billion to $18.5 trillion.[29] Meanwhile, the international monetary order promoted "structural adjustment programs" in the global south, anticipating the loans and accompanying austerity regime that would eventually be foisted upon Greece.

The creation of the WTO in 1995 saw the principles of the Capitalist Magna Carta put into full effect. The WTO and its agreements greatly expanded the realm of the transnational market: whereas the GATT had been limited to trade in goods, the WTO covered trade in services and intellectual property, largely due to lobbying by the American financial and entertainment sectors.[30] The impact was immediate. By the 2000s, globalization had become an article of faith, one invoked to describe a reality, an aspiration, and an ideology. While the world was far more interconnected and entwined—economically, technologically, and culturally—globalization's most vigorous boosters envisaged an extreme erasure of boundaries, portending a new age, a "flattened" world, in which the rising tide of unfettered trade would trickle down to lift all boats and transnational consumer habits—people everywhere watching Hollywood movies and eating fast food—would lead to cross-cultural mutual understanding. (What American proponents of this process called "globalization" other countries called "Americanization.")

Even more, they insisted that globalization would spread democracy far and wide, as long as democracy was understood to mean formal elections and free markets. That the reality rarely rose to the ideal—multinational companies are often happy to do business with murderous dictatorships and the IMF and World Bank frequently bankroll countries where corrupt strongmen enrich themselves and leave the impoverished masses with the bill—did little to diminish enthusiasm. In his second inaugural address President Bill Clinton predicted: "The world's greatest democracy will lead a whole world of democracies."

In truth, the last thing the globalizers wanted was a true world democracy, where the planet's inhabitants might have some say over American political and economic policy—or even their own. In his 2000 best seller *The Lexus and the Olive Tree*, Thomas Friedman sang hosannas to globalization, praising what he called the "Golden Straightjacket"—"golden" for the supposed affluence produced and "straightjacket" for the politically constricting effect. "When it comes to the question of which system today is the most effective at generating rising standards of living, the historical debate is over. The answer is free-market capitalism," Friedman enthuses. "When your country recognizes this fact, when it recognizes the rules of the free market in today's global economy, and decides to abide by them, it puts on what I call the Golden Straitjacket."

"The Golden Straitjacket," Friedman continues, "is the defining political-economic garment of this globalization era. The Cold War had the Mao suit, the Nehru jacket, the Russian fur. Globalization has only the Golden Straitjacket. If your country has not been fitted for one, it will be soon." Once a country puts it on only minor adjustments are allowed: "political choices get reduced to Pepsi or Coke—to slight nuances of taste, slight nuances of policy, slight alterations in design. . . . Governments—be they led by Democrats or Republicans, Conservatives or Labourites, Gaullists or Socialists, Christian Democrats or Social Democrats— that deviate too far away from the core rules will see their investors stampede away, interest rates rise, and stock market valuations fall."[31] According to Friedman, this attire, however obligatory and oppressive, is fundamentally democratic, for it was designed and promoted by Margaret Thatcher and Ronald Reagan, who were voted into office. Greek citizens, who did not vote in British or American elections but still felt the pinch of the Golden Straightjacket, would most likely hold a different view.

Among other innovations of the WTO that drain nations of their sovereignty, the organization inaugurated new procedures for the settlement of disputes, establishing a WTO "judiciary." This judiciary exemplified a game-changing development: the rise of an extensive and largely invisible corporate legal system that operates on a supranational scale.

At the heart of this global judiciary sit what are called Investor-State Dispute Settlements, which are now included in more than three thousand bilateral and multilateral trade agreements, the most famous being NAFTA (a deal that industry spent upward of $50 million lobbying Congress to approve).[22] ISDS establish secretive tribunals in which foreign investors have the right to sue governments for lost profits, including the loss of "expected future profits"—that is, money the companies were counting in their revenue projections but had not yet made.[33] Thus one dispute tribunal awarded Houston-based Occidental Petroleum $1.8 billion after Ecuador canceled an oil-exploration contract, a sum approximately equal to the country's annual health budget.[34] Countless similar cases are currently playing out around the world: Transcanada is suing the United States for $15 billion in damages because the government, under overwhelming public pressure, declined to approve the company's plan to build the Keystone XL Pipeline; Lone Pine, an American company, is suing Quebec for passing a moratorium on fracking; a Swedish company called Vattenfall is suing Germany for the federal government's decision to phase out nuclear power.[35] Today, about 10 percent of foreign investors currently have access to ISDS to challenge United States policy decisions.

The Office of the United States Trade Representative argues that ISDS are vital because they "signal to potential investors that the rule of law will be respected."[36] The question is *which* rule of law, given that such provisions allow corporations to override domestic statutes. Moreover, these suits are adjudicated by private arbitration panels rather than in public courts. There is no central registry of ISDS disputes and also no transparency, due process, or conflict of interest guidelines. The individuals who serve on the tribunals may play the role of a judge one day and

lobbyist the next, yet they have the authority to award corporations vast sums that must be paid by taxpayers. There is no right
to appeals and losing governments must pay all legal costs. There
is also no reciprocity: governments cannot sue companies for
damages they cause to public health, security, or if they violate a
contract (thus nations cannot win a case, they can only not lose
one).[37] Though the number of ISDS suits is on the rise, countries
such as Bolivia and South Africa are trying to extricate themselves from all agreements that include ISDS provisions. It is easier said than done: so-called sunset clauses mean treaties remain
in effect for a decade or two even after they have been formally
canceled.[38]

In her book *Shadow Sovereigns*, activist and political scientist
Susan George notes that, where the United States is concerned, an
astonishing double standard is in effect. When the cause is human
rights, labor rights, or environmental protections, American representatives never sacrifice sovereignty. (The government has
refused to sign or ratify a long list of treaties including the Kyoto
Protocol, the International Criminal Court Statute, the Optional
Protocol to the Convention against Torture, the Comprehensive
Nuclear-Test-Ban Treaty, the Convention on the Rights of Persons
with Disabilities, the Convention on the Elimination of All Forms
of Discrimination Against Women, and even the Convention on
the Rights of the Child.) Yet Democrats and Republicans alike
have, for the most part, tripped over themselves to compromise
popular autonomy and subject citizens to binding international
rules if doing so "frees" investors and markets from restrictive federal and state regulations.[39]

In the process, they have strengthened power structures that
are remarkably antidemocratic and, in George's estimation, fundamentally illegitimate. Corporations are effectively granted permission to make international law, performing a quasi-government
function to defend their mutual interests, which often directly
conflict with the needs and desires of citizens. International trade

rules provide investors a suite of powerful tools they can use to get around "obstacles" or "trade irritants" such as domestic health, labor, environmental, and safety regulations (and also procurement practices, subsidies, tariffs, and price controls), allowing corporations to strong-arm governments into doing their bidding instead of being forced to comply with a nation's laws and decisions.

These sorts of tricks, so central to modern globalization, are only the latest chapter in an old story of cooperation between economic elites. Nearly a century before Geneva School economists fretted over how to maintain power as decolonization spread, European and American leaders set aside their grudges to meet in Berlin and carve up the African continent, drawing arbitrary borders in order to exploit land and people. Dividing up the spoils, they agreed to engage in free trade while also establishing a framework for negotiating future territorial claims.

We could go back further still. The "rules-based international order" of the modern era strongly resembles the Lex Mercatoria, or merchant law, of the Middle Ages. A set of standards developed by the international business community to guide commercial dealings, one of the core functions of merchant law was to protect private property at border crossings. The transatlantic slave trade relied on merchant law: "A slave trader could buy slaves in Africa, underwritten by a British, Portuguese, or Dutch merchant, for sale in America, knowing that his ownership of the human cargo would be respected and guaranteed by several governments as it crossed the seas, should the issue ever be raised in any court of law," writes journalist Robert Kuttner. "What was true of slaves was true of lesser commodities."

What is new—and alarming—in our international commercial law is that, departing from the norms of modern democracy, these laws are now the province of opaque, unaccountable supranational systems.[40] Equally troubling is that these systems are designed to protect not only property rights but, more specifically, the right of capital *mobility*.[41] The Office of the United States Trade

Representative calls this the "right to transfer capital," defined as "an assurance that investors will be able to move capital relating to their investments freely."

Mobility—not being tied to spaces of democratic accountability—is key to profits. In the 1940s, during that golden age of "controlled capitalism," national restrictions on currency exchange meant that capital could not flee countries as easily as it now can. (If it could, the British Labour Party would never have been able to establish a robust welfare state, nationalize various industries, or create a universal health care system.) Today, money can fly around the globe, free to take advantage of the world's uneven political and social geography in a variety of ways. We see the effects of this mobility day after day. Multinational companies outsource production in search of low-waged and nonunionized work forces, seek lax environmental and regulatory standards, threaten to flee if taxes are raised, and so on.

Similarly, the internationalization of finance has allowed banks to open offices offshore to circumvent domestic regulations including reserve requirements and interest rate ceilings.[42] The right of capital mobility also fuels the creation of offshore tax havens; through subsidiaries and shell companies, corporations take advantage of differences in tax codes, situating profits in a low-tax zone and losses in a high one to dodge collection. Experts believe companies and wealthy households hold around $8.7 trillion offshore, an astounding 11.5 percent of the entire world's GDP.[43] This is why, historically, it has been progressives who have pushed for the creation of some kind of global tax system, typically in the form of tax on financial transactions, or Tobin Tax, an idea first proposed in the early seventies that has never been implemented. Today there is no global tax collector and also no global antitrust enforcer, no global labor relations board, and no global environmental protection agency. Instead, the aim of corporate globalization is to avoid such accountability.

For a long time, that avoidance was achieved through promotion of the myth that capitalism was apolitical, an outgrowth of natural economic laws that acted of their own accord. The global financial crash of 2008 put an end to this laissez-faire lie. Overnight, old certainties disappeared along with $40 trillion of global equity. In the United States, 2008 saw 3.1 million foreclosures filed and 700,000 jobs shed every month.[44] By October of that year, Alan Greenspan, former chair of the U.S. Federal Reserve, sheepishly admitted that there was a "flaw in the model" he had taken for "how the world works."

The crash prompted people across the political spectrum to question the inevitability of neoliberal globalization and chafe against the constraints of the Golden Straightjacket. At one end, the progressive uprising in Syntagma Square helped propel SYRIZA to victory. At the other, aggressive right-wing forces have surged to power, a seemingly contradictory international coalition of ethno-nationalists achieving prominence. In 2017 a group of Republican lawmakers fed the fantasy that the country could cut itself off from the rest of the world by proposing the American Sovereignty Restoration Act, which would terminate its relationship with the United Nations and endanger programs including the World Health Organization, the World Food Program, and the High Commission on Refugees.[45]

By pinning the blame for domestic woes on external threats— on all-powerful "globalists" and vulnerable immigrants and refugees—ethno-nationalists frame economic and class conflicts as international and cultural ones, wrongly identifying the primary fault lines of global capitalism as running *between* states while ignoring the way they also always run *within* them. (The problem with foreign oligarchs isn't that they're foreign, but that they're oligarchs.) Nationalism covers up the fact that even though rich and poor may share common citizenship they live in very different worlds and have conflicting interests. The wealthy few own multiple properties and live off passive income from investments while others struggle to afford shelter or wind up homeless, living on the streets or in their cars despite being employed.[46] Patriotism, with all its patriarchal undertones, thus functions as a kind of fig leaf, covering up stark domestic divisions in ways that lets homegrown financial elites off the hook. The chimera of unity based in blood and soil obscures the truth that it is often domestic special interests that push for, and benefit from, a global economic order that undermines accountability, stability, and democracy at home.

As we understand them, nations are relatively recent inventions. Scholars typically trace their development to a series of European peace treaties in the 1600s that established state sovereignty over a specific limited territory. Yet nations play the trick of appearing eternal, as though bound by some spirit dating back to time immemorial, to promote myths of common origin and destiny. The nation, in this sense, is different from the state: more an essence than an apparatus. Or, as Benedict Anderson famously argued, a figment. A nation, he writes, "is imagined because the members of even the smallest nation will never know most of their fellow-members, meet them, or even hear of them, yet in the minds of each lives the image of their communion."[47]

The term *international* is an even newer concept, dating back to 1780. The utilitarian philosopher Jeremy Bentham devised the term to distinguish laws within a state from laws between states. The left adopted, and adapted, the concept, marking an explicit commitment to internationalism in the founding of the International Workingmen's Association, or First International, in 1864. Solidarity, internationalists of this stripe correctly maintain, must transcend borders, since exploitation is exploitation, regardless of whether a worker and a boss hold the same passport and live within the same national territory. Thus the famous motto of the *Communist Manifesto* implores workers of the world—not of individual countries—to unite.

Democratic agitators and rebels have long possessed a kind of global consciousness, infusing their local struggles and spontaneous acts of resistance with a more expansive perspective.[48] Predating Bentham's neologism and Marx and Engel's visionary manifesto by at least a couple of millennia, Diogenes the Cynic, the third-century BC slave turned philosopher, proclaimed himself a cosmopolitan, a "citizen of the world," and refused to kowtow to none other than Alexander the Great. By rejecting the group membership that was central to Greek male identity of the period, Diogenes invited a kind of exile upon himself while declaring allegiance to the wider human community.

Centuries later, in the 1640s in England, the ingenious Diggers preached an internationalist creed without using the word. Defiantly squatting on an abandoned mound of earth, sowing the hard ground with parsnips and beans, their humble experiment in communal, egalitarian self-sufficiency aimed at something far more epic and universal. A Digger manifesto that called for "equal rights, free elections, a commonwealth, and a just portion for every persons" was subtitled *A Discovery of The Main Grounds and Original Causes of all the Slavery in the World, but chiefly in England.*[49] Tilling the soil of St. George's Hill—which they renamed George's Hill, out of refusal to recognize the saints of the established church—the Diggers understood that the local and global were necessarily linked. In this respect they anticipated the Russian workers' councils, or soviets, of 1905 and 1917, anarchist strongholds in 1936 during the Spanish Civil War, the Hungarian uprising of 1956, the Zapatista rebellion that began in Chiapas, Mexico, after the implementation of NAFTA in 1994, and so on.

Cities are the most common sites of these cosmopolitan outbursts, the duality between the local and global intensified within the confines of urban space. Ancient and republican forms of democracy were, after all, the fruit of city-states, and cities have always been central to political philosophy and experimentation. Plato, though critical of Athenian self-government, still set about imagining his ideal city, and Aristotle upheld the city as the foundation of a good, or happy, life—as long as a stable middle class could be maintained. Over time, however, cities came in for a beating.

Rousseau's vision of self-rule, which required a bucolic setting, reached its apotheosis in America. Madison's embrace of continental vastness went hand in hand with the conscious cultivation of democracy as a rural phenomenon. The "freeholders of the country would be the safest depositories of Republican liberty," Madison proclaimed. Jefferson agreed: "When we get piled upon one another in large cities, as in Europe, we shall become as corrupt as Europe." Inland New England townships and remote yeoman farmsteads came to symbolize American democracy, not the bustling coastal cities with their artisans, day laborers, and sailors and the diversity that ports always bring.

Despite sustained outbursts of agrarian radicalism, such as the Populists of the late nineteenth century with their Farmer's Alliance and Industrial Union, the image of insurgent country folk has always been overshadowed by the specter of subversive city dwellers, the workers, immigrants, single women, and rioters who threaten the moral order. By 1910, cities in the United States had elected thirty-three Socialist mayors.[50] Socialist women from that period went further, proposing what historian Dolores Hayden called "a complete transformation of the spatial design and material cultural of American homes, neighborhoods, and cities." They built community associations, set up housewives' cooperatives, and advocated for housing projects with day care centers and public kitchens, pushing for an inclusive form of urban planning that would no longer cloister women away in isolated domestic domains.[51] The Red Scare dashed any hope that their bold designs would be broadly implemented.

Geared to promote what scholar Sonia Hirt calls "spatial individualism," the nation's zoning laws evolved to reinforce an anti-collectivist and anti-urban bias, promoting detached, single-family dwellings accessible mainly by car. The financial system is structured around homes serving as both shelter and a strategic investment financed through a mortgage, the peaceful single family homes with the white picket fence juxtaposed with images of racialized urban poverty and radical urban politics ("Communism can never win in a nation of homeowners," a prominent housing economist prophesized in 1966).[52]

One of the most famous democratic upheavals in history—the Paris Commune of 1871—helped cement the view of cities as hotbeds of socialist, feminist subversion that the system of suburban homeownership was designed to ward off. At the time Paris was Europe's biggest city, home to two million souls. In the spring of 1871 workingmen and -women led a remarkable insurrection that lasted seventy-two days. ("Women were the first to act," one eyewitness recalled.) In an unexpected consequence of a failed military conflict with the Prussians that left the French defeated and besieged, proud Parisians refused to stand down and turned on their own rulers, holding elections to establish an alternative legislative body that assumed power and went to work remaking the city as a cooperative enterprise.

A severe and brutal punishment would be their fate, but for a brief and inspiring flash the commune gave concrete expression to grandiose democratic aspirations. Communards rallied under the flag of a "Universal Republic" and boldly admitted foreigners to their ranks—"an audacious act of internationalism," as one participant put it.[53] They burned guillotines and destroyed the Vendôme Column, erected to glorify Napoleonic imperialist conquest, only to rename it "Place Internationale." In the words of historian Kristin Ross, "Under the Commune Paris wanted to be not the capital of France but an autonomous collective in a universal federation of peoples."[54]

In the final hour, French and German elites made a deal and the city's insurrectionaries were massacred by the tens of thousands. The universal federation of peoples was not to be, and the commune, a chaotic and doomed experiment, passed into the realm of myth, a tragic strategic failure (even sympathizers and participants admitted the Communards blundered tactically) transformed into a romantic symbol of a better society yet to be born. Years later the geographer and naturalist Élisée Reclus, who had fought in the commune's ragtag forces before going into exile, reflected that the word *commune* had come to be understood "in the largest sense," representing "a new humanity, made up of free and equal companions, oblivious to the existence of old boundaries, helping each other in peace from one end of the world to the other." The anarchist Peter Kropotkin expressed this development well: "for us, 'Commune' no longer means a territorial agglomeration; it is rather a generic name, a synonym for the grouping of equals which knows neither frontiers nor walls."[55]

But who was the "us" to which Kropotkin referred? Even before its blood-soaked end, the Paris Commune captivated political radicals far and wide: seven thousand London workers marched in solidarity with the commune when it was at its height, banners reading "Long Live the Universal Republic" held aloft, and American cities immediately began hosting annual commemorations of the protest (perhaps most famously in Chicago, where labor militants helped win the eight-hour day with the Haymarket riots of 1886).[56] Karl Marx immortalized the rebellion, emphasizing its socialist currents in his book *The Civil War in France*. But the disobedient Parisians found little support in the rural communities within their own country.[57] The metropolitan Communards were only weakly bound to the French peasantry, and while some attempted to bridge the gap, the lack of safe and reliable travel and communication channels made that difficult. Indeed, peasants from conservative regions staffed the French armies and slaughtered their fellow citizens.

While it hasn't reached Paris Commune proportions, today's urban-rural divide ominously yawns, with electoral results in numerous countries often dramatically split along a fissure that is as much psychological or cultural as geographical. Despite common economic interests (the need for affordable housing, health care, well-paying work, and environmental protection), metropolitan attitudes clash with small-town sensibilities, and in rather predictable ways: dense, diverse, cosmopolitan cities tend to lean liberal, while rural communities, less populated and more homogeneous and nationalistic, tilt conservative. In the United States, the Republican Party has an advantage in government at the state level, but the majority of the nation's largest cities are run by Democrats. In North Carolina a group of young Republicans I met shuddered at the mention of New York City, calling it a "cesspool of liberalism."

This philosophical divide is reflected in the rise of municipalism, a modern variation of the Paris Commune's dream of a federation of cooperative urban enclaves. In places like Jackson, Mississippi, and Richmond, California, city residents and their representatives are finding new ways to flex their political might, from the creation of people's assemblies to legal action against oil companies. Other forms of urban defiance include the spread of sanctuary cities, where municipalities protect migrants by refusing to cooperate with federal immigration authorities, and by making their own commitments to the Paris Accord on the environment. ("I was elected to represent the citizens of Pittsburgh, not Paris," Trump intoned, justifying his withdrawal from the climate compact, to which the mayor of Pittsburgh tweeted: "Pittsburgh stands with the world [and] will follow the Paris Agreement.")

Ultimately, more than 350 cities announced plans to break with national policy and honor the international accord. No longer advising people to go back to the land, environmentalists increasingly recognize the role cities must play if they hope to achieve sustainability. Several earths would be required for everyone to live in a suburban home with a two-car garage, which means dense cities—compact, efficiently designed, and public service rich—will be crucial to a livable low-carbon future.[58] "The ecological genius of the city remains a vast, largely hidden power," writes influential urbanist Mike Davis. "There is no shortage planetary 'carrying capacity' if we are willing to make democratic public space, rather than modular, private consumption, the engine of sustainable equality."

Municipalist activists in European cities, particularly Spain, have made more headway toward participatory democracy, entering government in numerous cities, including Barcelona. In May 2015, Barcelona en Comú (Barcelona in Common) won city council elections and installed as mayor Ada Colau, a prominent organizer who made her name leading a direct action campaign against foreclosures and evictions after the financial crisis. Like SYRIZA in Greece, Barcelona en Comú owes its success to the anti-austerity protests of 2011 (in Spain 80 percent of the population supported the Indignados assembled in the streets). Unlike SYRIZA, however, Barcelona in Common is not a traditional party, but an independent citizen "platform" that aims to "occupy" municipal institutions to bring about progressive change.[59]

Barcelona en Comú's guiding manifesto was devised through an intensive grassroots process involving thousands of residents, who met in large neighborhood assemblies and online. Rejecting standard leadership models, the platform has an executive board with eight people and a coordination team of forty, both of which must meet a minimum threshold of gender parity. It adopted strict ethics policies, term limits, and pay limitations for officials— Colau is paid less than a quarter than her predecessor as mayor.

"Democracy begins where you live," says one oft-quoted municipalist slogan. Barcelona en Comú takes the motto literally, placing a strong emphasis on housing policies, a fitting turn given Colau's background. According to the United Nations, housing is a human right, but housing insecurity remains a fact of life for many. After joining the European Union in 1986 and adopting the euro in 1999, the Spanish economy became increasingly driven by speculative and foreign investment in real estate and construction, which brought growth but also inequality and instability; market signals responded more to outside investors with short-term needs than full-time residents seeking shelter. In an attempt to make Barcelona more hospitable to its inhabitants, Colau and her administration made international headlines by putting restrictions on Airbnb and other tech companies that facilitate short-term rentals, a business model that hollows out neighborhoods and destroys communities. It has invested in pub-

lic housing while fining banks for unused empty dwellirgs, based
on the understanding that housing does not have to be a speculative asset to be valuable to a community and that if we want to
democratize housing we must decommodify it.

Barcelona en Comú also aims to democratize public space,
allowing community management of resources while also expanding who counts as a member of the community. "Public space is
the place, par excellence, for democracy: this space that belongs
to all of us," Colau told the *New Yorker*. "Therefore, this is also the
space of the most vulnerable people, which is what democratic
systems should prioritize. . . . If you have little private space, you
have more public space and public services—libraries, beaches,
parks. . . . It is a space where you can build up the city with others.
So, from that point of view, the more public space there is, and the
better its quality, the better the quality of the democracy."[60]

Municipalists, including Barcelona en Comú, offer a vision of
citizenship that is not a patriarchal birthright or exclusive privilege, not an ethnic identity or legal status, but instead is based on
residency and active participation (a particularly interesting formulation in a country where separatist nationalist movements
regularly threaten the country with secession). Kate Shea Baird,
one of Barcelona en Comú's most outspoken advocates, told me,
"The citizenship question . . . is about scale, in that at local scale,
communities can be real and based on daily human interaction,
while at larger scales, they're largely imagined."

Baird argues that localism is powerful in part because it is
pragmatic: small victories "can demonstrate than there are alternatives to the status quo." Yet the challenge, as we've seen, is that
local problems often have distant causes. As Baird acknowledges,
"one of the greatest limits of Municipalism is the difficulty it faces
in responding to forces and interests that cross borders." Consider
one example: when Barcelona en Comú crowdsourced its manifesto, the most popular proposal involved taking back public control of the city's water company.

Agbar, a subsidiary of a multinational company called Suez

Environnement, charges Barcelona's residents 91.7 percent more than the fees paid by neighboring municipalities that manage their own water supply. Agbar went on to use its inflated profits to launch a lawsuit opposing the inclusion of a question on an upcoming city referendum: "Do you want water management in Barcelona to be public, with citizen participation?"[61] After three years, the city remained locked in a battle with the company, which did not want to see its revenues diminished.

Such roadblocks may explain why Colau was an early supporter of the Democracy in Europe movement and Barcelona en Comú established an international committee linked to other "rebel" municipalities. They have engaged in transnational urban organizing addressing everything from migration to technology to international trade deals. But some organizers, including Baird, are skeptical that radical democratic experiments will ever be able to scale up to effect global or regional transformation, and whether that should even be a goal. For Baird, radical democracy and real community can only ever be local. She is convinced that the vital qualities of municipalism, the social, political, and ecological transformations that can occur on the local scale, diminish or even disappear at higher levels.[62]

The jury is still out as to whether the municipalist model can grow to take on problems that exceed city limits—or whether it even should—but this uncertainty and experimentation is key to the guiding ethos, part of a process Colau, Baird, and their collaborators call "feminizing" politics. For Barcelona's municipalists, feminization is an expansive concept, not limited to women's daily concerns or gender equity in representation, however important they might be. "Demasculinizing" politics—another term that is used—emphasizes building commonalities instead of deepening differences, promoting collective models of leadership over individualized ones, collaboration and consensus instead of winner-take-all conflict, and listening over pontificating. "You can be in politics without being a strong, arrogant male, who's ultra-confident, who knows the answer to everything," Colau has said. The principle of feminization says it is okay not to have the answers ready-made, especially when the situations are contingent and complex. Figuring things out together is what municipalists believe cities are for and what democracy is all about.

Where is the space of democracy? It may be a literal place, a nation's capitol, a neighborhood's streets, a cooperatively run workplace, or the home. Or it could be something more abstract and formal, such as the realm of international law and transnational associations and agreements.

One day the space of democracy may be space itself, far beyond earth's atmosphere. The Outer Space Treaty states that national claims of sovereignty do not apply to space: it can be explored but not owned. Nevertheless, some entrepreneurs see potential business opportunities in things like Mars tourism and asteroid mining and have begun to lay the foundations for such enterprises. There may come a time when outer space is treated like international waters, where the lack of sovereign domain facilitates exploitation, with the profits from rampant overfishing, contamination, and exploitation of labor funneled to a few. Or perhaps outer space will open up a new futuristic frontier of democracy without property rights and the creation of a "cosmic commons" that benefits all of humankind.[63] Should we ever end up having to consider democracy at the galactic scale, the global will begin to feel downright local.

Of course the space of democracy is already digital. In the 1960s media theorist Marshall McLuhan predicted the emergence of a global village through new technology. The Internet has certainly connected the world, but not unified it as early optimists hoped. Though the web makes it possible to engage with people and ideas thousands of miles away, studies have found that the average North American Internet user actually takes in less international media than the television and newspaper consumers of yore. (Meanwhile, communities around the world are flooded with content produced in wealthy countries, disproportionately in English.[64]) In another twist, American news consumption has also become less local. Instead of picking up an independent weekly or tuning in to a local television network, Americans read articles from national outlets or stream popular podcasts or shows. Some political scientists attribute increasing political polarization to this shift. Local and state elections are now decided according to national debates, formulations, and scandals, and not necessarily the issues that most affect the ordinary day-to-day life of a community, which tend to create the most opportunities for compromise.

More than anything, the digital realm is a space of democratic contradictions. First, while the Internet and social media have opened up new public spheres, this has occurred on privately owned platforms. Virtual space, overwhelmingly, is corporate space. With the exception of a handful of municipal Internet service providers, there is no such thing as truly public Internet in the United States (in more than twenty states telecom giants have lobbied successfully for rules that forbid municipalities from providing fast, low-cost, or free publicly funded broadband).

Second, the Internet may be global, but the profits are disproportionately localized. Many of the largest technology companies and most prominent start-ups—which are now among the biggest companies in the world run by some of the richest men—are based in the United States, often in Silicon Valley. These companies treat personal information from worldwide users as a resource to be exploited—"data is the oil of the twenty-first century," goes one common refrain—as revenue flows to a tiny corner of California. Third, our communications infrastructure is simultaneously highly personalized and imperial. Algorithms may cater our feeds to our individual preferences, but American companies also export standards and models of communication, determining what knowledge is available and visible.

As human rights activists have pointed out, this can be a matter of life or death. Facebook, in particular, has come under fire for censoring activists in some cases and facilitating threatening speech in other. Right now, Mark Zuckerberg, who has 50 percent voting rights at the company, and his employees, many of whom are low-paid contractors, effectively determine what constitutes free speech for more than two billion users who have different cultures, speak different languages, and live in wildly different contexts. The web extracts economic value while imposing the values of American technologists and businessmen, which is why media activists from the global south have launched a movement to decolonize the Internet.

Today there is a geographic opposition between what Spanish sociologist Manuel Castells has called "placeless power and powerless places," and the Internet is only the latest mechanism through which this dynamic plays out. Historically, capitalism began by dispossessing people of land, severing them from the soil that sustained them. ("England is not a free people till the Poor that have no Land, have a free allowance to dig and labour the Commons, and so lie as Comfortably as the Landlords that live in their Inclosures," the Diggers averred.) The mobility that capital demands both produces and profits from human movement, forcing people into precarious and transient states, which is how we must understand the four hundred thousand young Greeks compelled to emigrate after the economic crisis. People should have the ability to cross borders as easily as capital, and certainly freedom of movement is a right that must be protected. But in an age when so much migration is involuntary, people also need the freedom to stay put and to keep communities and cultures intact—to not have families separated and individuals scattered as a result of poverty, war and violence, or ecological destruction.

From the perspective of self-government, the existing "economic constitution for the world," which protects this free flow of money and goods while impeding the mobility of those who have been dispossessed and displaced, is illegitimate and should be dismantled on the basis that it was not ratified to begin with. The nations and individuals under its command never consented to be governed by markets. Tearing down the existing neoliberal order and replacing it with more accountable, inclusive, and equitable structures will require the creation of cross-border coalitions that can breathe new life into the old ideal of international solidarity. But to have a chance of success, this cosmopolitan effort must be built from the bottom up; it cannot begin at the global scale, creating change from the top down. Strategically linked social movements are democracy's best leverage, exerting pressure from below. There is no way to effectively challenge placeless power without powerful places.

That is not to say that the local is always more democratic than the global. Instead, my point is mundane: communities and individuals have more capacity to determine their destiny—and to influence international politics and economics in turn—when they are strongly grounded, embedded in the space in which they live. Barcelona en Comú's approach to the Internet is instructive. In an attempt to link the digital revolution to their democratic revolution, the city has called for "technological sovereignty" for its residents. This means treating data as a public good, and making citizens co-owners and co-creators of services that rely on their personal data.[65] Technological sovereignty involves connecting virtual to physical space, linking the Internet to a specific place and people to better serve their needs. Why should Google, Uber, or Airbnb be the technological and financial beneficiaries of information extracted from citizens in Barcelona, Manila, Johannesburg, New York, or Mumbai?

Local democracy means that a city can demand public control over a vital utility, including the Internet or water provision; that a country can compel a multinational company to pay taxes for business done in its jurisdiction; that urban neighborhoods can resist the displacement that often comes with gentrification; that First Nations can halt the opening of a river-poisoning mine or oil pipeline; that rural communities can fight for the creation of jobs instead of having to leave their homes and loved ones; that unionized workers have a voice or own the institutions that employ them instead of being threatened with outsourcing and layoffs. These are all examples of local democracy in action. But the local is never only local. Each small victory creates ripple effects, shaping the larger, global whole.

"Democracy begins where you live," the municipalist slogan insists. The space of democracy is the space you are in, wherever you happen to be at this very moment. At the same time, democracy always has a vital transnational dimension, the idea itself disseminated over vast distances and across borders, mutating and transforming as it travels. It's a paradox: while the democratic imagination is open and expansive, the practice has to be both bounded and grounded, embodied in particular populations and places. Only by taking root can democratic seeds spread.

CHAPTER 8

A RUIN OR A HABITATION

(PRESENT/FUTURE)

WHAT IF CLIMATE change is a violation of the constitutional rights of those yet to be born? That's what some concerned young people are arguing in court. Article I, Section 27 of Pennsylvania's state constitution guarantees "the right to clean air, pure water, and to the preservation of the natural, scenic, historic, and esthetic values of the environment." On this basis, a group of six plaintiffs not yet old enough to vote filed a lawsuit in 2015 in the Commonwealth Court of Pennsylvania against Governor Tom Wolf and six state agencies. The suit argued that the defendants had failed to take necessary action to regulate carbon dioxide and other greenhouse gases consistent with the commonwealth's duty and obligations as a public trustee. In the legal team's language, the state has a responsibility to "conserve and maintain public natural resources, including the atmosphere, for the benefit of present and future generations." The daily news of melting ice caps, sickly coral reefs, and starving polar bears clearly demonstrates that this legal responsibility is not being met.

While the Pennsylvania lawsuit ended after the Supreme Court upheld a prior dismissal, a similar case filed in Oregon was wending its way through the legal system with greater success. In *Juliana v. the United States*, twenty-one plaintiffs take aim at the federal government for violation of the constitutional rights not just of their generation but also of future ones. Now aged eleven to twenty-two, they accuse federal officials and oil industry executives of knowingly creating a national energy system that causes climate change, despite decades of evidence that carbon dioxide emissions from the burning of fossil fuels destabilize the environment. Officials did not merely fail to regulate and restrain bad actors, they argue, but actively facilitated their endeavors, thereby violating citizens' constitutional rights to life, liberty, and property while also jeopardizing essential public resources.

In *Juliana*, "future generations" are explicitly named, represented through their "guardian," Dr. James Hansen, a NASA scientist and activist, whose granddaughter is part of the suit. The federal government failed in its attempts to get the case dismissed on the grounds that the grievances are too broad. U.S. district judge Ann Aiken wrote, "I have no doubt that the right to a climate system capable of sustaining human life is fundamental to a free and ordered society." Noting that the case was not about whether or not climate change is real (for the "purposes of this motion, those facts are undisputed"), Aikens added: "Federal courts too often have been cautious and overly deferential in the arena of environmental law and the world has suffered for it." Should the children's lawsuit be allowed to move forward, it will be the first time the federal government has faced allegations in court that its climate policies violate citizens' constitutional rights.

Though their quest may seem quixotic, the people participating in these suits are part of a larger trend of climate litigation around the world. Citizens of countries as far flung as the United Kingdom, New Zealand, Ireland, Norway, Switzerland, Belgium, Pakistan, Ukraine, India, and Uganda are attempting to use the legal system to force governments to ensure citizens a habitable future, whether by halting oil drilling or cutting emissions.[2] In Colombia, twenty-five young people aged seven and older are suing on constitutional grounds to stop the continued deforestation of the Amazon.[3] In Portugal, seven children whose home district of Leiria was devastated by forest fires in 2017 are suing the member states of the Council of Europe, accusing them of failing to take necessary action to prevent climate disaster.

In the United States, in addition to the dozens of small towns boldly rewritting local legal codes to deny corporations person-hood to block fracking, municipalities such as New York City, San Francisco, and Richmond are suing fossil fuel companies for billions of dollars in damages for suppressing information about the hazards of carbon emissions and the impending hazards of sea level rise. Additionally, First Nations communities are invok-ing treaty rights to prevent the pipeline transport of fossil fuels over unceded indigenous territories.[4] The citizens behind these creative legal campaigns are trying to curb resource exploitation in the present to ensure we leave behind a place that is livable.

Rekha Dhillon-Richardson became one of the plaintiffs in the Pennsylvania lawsuit when she was fifteen. "The fundamental human rights and futures of children and youth are dispropor-tionately threatened by climate destabilization, even though we have had little to do with the production of the problem," she told me in an interview when I asked what had inspired her to join the suit. "Children across the globe have trusted the adults to make the right decisions—to lead us forward into a cleaner and more just future for everyone. We have been harmed by decisions that were made without our authorization."

Though Rekha was disappointed that the specific litigation she was a part of had not been allowed to progress, the experience had yielded some useful if difficult lessons. "This case made me real-ize that just because a law is created in theory does not mean that it is applied in reality," she reflected. "I have also learned that the court process is extremely slow; it is hard to make quick and sig-nificant changes through the courts. Those of us deeply concerned about issues of environmental injustice would be wise to explore multiple strategies to challenge the government."

The youth lawsuits added a unique dimension to the wave of legal challenges to the fossil fuel–guzzling status quo, dramatiz-ing a crucial aspect of the threat to democracy posed by climate change: the question of intergenerational responsibilities and ethical duties across decades and centuries. To put it another way, what is the relationship of democracy to time? This question may seem abstract but is actually foundational, for it cuts to the very heart of those constitutional rights the litigants are fighting to see upheld. The project of self-government invariably requires navigating the tension between short- and long-term thinking, our immediate circumstances and what is to come, the present and the future.

Every person, whether or not they have children, exists as both a successor and an ancestor. We are all born into a world we did not make, subject to customs and conditions established by prior generations, and then we leave a legacy for others to inherit. Nothing illustrates this duality more profoundly than the problem of climate change, which calls into question the very future of a habitable planet. The scientific consensus describes a world of inundated coastlines, worsening food shortages, wildfires, droughts, and ecosystem die-offs as soon as 2040, and by 2100 some estimate that up to two billion people, or one-fifth of the world's population, could have their lives turned upside down or lost as climate refugees.[5] Those of us who live in rich nations are heirs to a way of life soaked in fossil fuels, but it is clear that if we continue on the current path of unrestrained energy consumption, there will be tragic, even genocidal, consequences for many living now and nearly all who will follow in our footsteps.[6]

When we talk about democracy and time, the future matters as much the past, but it lacks the same level of influence over the present because the yet-to-be-born cannot bind the living in constitutional doctrines or legal precedents. When individuals like me take multiple flights a year and buy food imported from halfway around the world, we can rest assured that we won't meet the people who will, down the road, be most gravely affected by our carbon-intensive lifestyle. But don't we have democratic obligations to them regardless? If we expect justice from our predecessors, don't we owe this debt to future generations? Right now the world's relatively affluent are on the way to being bad ancestors, the kind who think only of themselves in the here and now.

If we're concerned for democracy then we must include the future in our thinking. While it is a cliché to talk of protecting the future "for the children"—which is one reason why young people suing adults for failing to do so is so striking—there is often an implicit assumption about what kind of children will inherit the earth, an image that is rarely representative of humanity's diversity. With this diversity in mind, we need to fight to ensure not just a sustainable world but also what disability theorist Alison Kafer calls an "accessible" one, inspired by her recognition that idealized versions of the society to come usually leave out people who look like her.[7] An accessible future invites difference: disabled children, queer children, black and brown children, Muslim and also indigenous children, who are often told that their cultures and ways of life are relics and fated for extinction. The paradox is that to reach this accessible future, to figure out how to balance the needs and desires of those who live now with those yet to come, we need to tap the wisdom of the past without getting trapped by it.

In a letter to James Madison, Thomas Jefferson posed the question of whether the dead should have the ability to rule from the grave. Jefferson's answer to himself was a definitive no. "The earth belongs always to the living generation," he wrote—to the present and not the past nor the future. "[T]he dead have neither powers nor rights over it." The planet's current inhabitants, he effectively proclaimed, are sovereign in time, not just space. But to prevent society from ossifying, he made a rather extreme proposal. After studying mortality statistics, Jefferson concluded that generations turn over every nineteen years. This, he believed, offered a natural limit for laws, which should have a clear expiration date. Short-lived statutes and regulations, renewed only when living citizens saw fit to keep them, would ensure relevance and vibrancy. Whatever one might think of the practicalities of such a scheme—and

I believe it to be untenable—I find Jefferson's proposition to be oddly admirable. Advocating for self-destructing legislation is a rather charitable, self-deprecating position for a founding father of the United States.

If the dead do not exactly have power or rights, per se, they do still have a seat at the table—Thomas Jefferson among them. In ways obvious and subtle, constructive and destructive, the present is constrained and shaped by the decisions of past generations. A vivid example is the American Constitution, in which a small group of men ratified special kinds of promises intended to be perpetual. Sometimes I imagine the Electoral College, which was devised to increase the influence of the southern states in the new union, as the cold grip of plantation owners strangling the current day. Even Jefferson's beloved Bill of Rights, intended as protections from government overreach, has had corrosive effects. The Second Amendment's right to bear arms allows those who plundered native land and patrolled for runaway slaves, who saw themselves in the phrase "a well regulated Militia," to haunt us. Yet plenty of our ancestors also bequeathed us remarkable gifts, the right to free speech, privacy, and public assembly among them.

Some theorists have framed the problematic sway of the deceased over the affairs of the living as an opposition between tradition and progress. The acerbic Christian critic G. K. Chesterton put it this way: "Tradition may be defined as an extension of the franchise. Tradition means giving votes to the most obscure of all classes, our ancestors. It is the democracy of the dead. Tradition refuses to submit to the small and arrogant oligarchy of those who merely happen to be walking about. All democrats object to men being disqualified by the accident of birth; tradition objects to their being disqualified by the accident of death."[8] Social progress, in Chesterton's account, can thus be seen as a form of disenfranchisement, the deceased being stripped of their suffrage. Over half a century before Chesterton, Karl Marx expressed sublime horror at the persistent presence of political zombies: "Men make their own history, but they do not make it as they please;

they do not make it under self-selected circumstances, but under circumstances existing already, given and transmitted from the past. The tradition of all dead generations weighs like a nightmare on the brains of the living."[9]

The most eloquent partisans in this transtemporal power struggle said their piece at the end of the eighteenth century. Edmund Burke and Thomas Paine had a furious debate that articulated the dichotomy between past and future, dead and living, tradition and progress.[10] A consummate conservative shaken by the postrevolutionary violence in France, Burke defended the inherited privilege and stability of aristocratic government that radical democrats sought to overthrow: "But one of the first and most leading principles on which the commonwealth and the laws are consecrated, is lest the temporary possessors and life-renters in it, unmindful of what they have received from their ancestors, or of what is due to their posterity, should act as if they were the entire masters; that they should not think it amongst their rights to cut off the entail, or commit waste on the inheritance, by destroying at their pleasure the whole original fabric of their society." Any revolution, Burke warned, hazards leaving those who come after "a ruin instead of an habitation" in which men, disconnected from their forerunners, "would become little better than the flies of summer."

The left-leaning Paine would have none of it. Better to be a buzzing fly than a feudal serf. "Whenever we are planning for posterity we ought to remember that virtue is not hereditary," he quipped. His critique, forcefully expressed in *Common Sense* and *The Rights of Man*, was not just an attack on monarchy. Rather, it was addressed to revolutionaries who might exercise undue influence over time by establishing new systems of government. "There never did, there never will, and there never can, exist a Parliament, or any description of men, or any generation of men, in any country, possessed of the right or the power of binding and controlling posterity to the 'end of time,'" he protested. Paine echoed his good friend Jefferson: "[I]t is the living, and not the dead, that are to be accommodated."

Uncompromising in his view, Paine saw the past as oppressive as well as irrelevant. "The vanity and presumption of governing beyond the grave is the most ridiculous and insolent of all tyrannies. Man has no property in man; neither has any generation a property in the generations which are to follow." In a world still shaking off the divine right of kings and nobility, the implications were radical: "Every generation is equal in rights to generations which preceded it, by the same rule that every individual is born equal in rights with his contemporary." His words seem intended to travel through time to buoy the spirits of the young climate change litigants: "The rights of minors are as sacred as the rights of the aged."[11]

In his pithy style, Paine popularized a commitment both to revolution and to novelty. "A nation, though continually existing, is continually in the state of renewal and succession. It is never stationary. Every day produces new births, carries minors forward to maturity, and old persons from the stage. In this ever-running flood of generations there is no part superior in authority to another." Given the onslaught of change, a constitution "must be a novelty, and that which is not a novelty must be defective." Never one for moderation, Paine advocated a decisive break with tradition, rejecting lessons from the past, castigating those who scoured records of ancient Greece and Rome for models or insights. What could the dead teach the living that could possibly be worth knowing? What mattered, for Paine, was something more transcendent than tradition: our inherent, natural rights that both precede and supersede human law.

Being a populist revolutionary in a time of monarchal rule made Paine menacing enough to the established order, but part of what made his analysis so challenging, as we have seen, was his commitment to economic egalitarianism. He understood that the hereditary system he wanted to help overthrow had multiple dimensions. The social status and titles passed by aristocratic fathers to sons also facilitated the transfer of property through family relations, material wealth accumulating over generations. Paine's proposal to fund a basic grant of income to all citizens financed by inheritance taxes, then, aimed at more than ensuring basic subsistence for the masses. It was also intended to break the financial grip of the past on the present by ending filial oligarchy, thereby ensuring a broad basis for democracy's survival.

Paine was on to something. As the French economist Thomas Piketty carefully documents in his 2013 best seller *Capital in the Twenty-First Century*, the passage of assets across generations is one of the major drivers of the dangerous levels of inequality we see today. We live in what Piketty calls an "inheritance society," an arrangement that allows ancestors to ensure their progeny have outsize influence over everyone else by virtue of their bank balance. The wealthiest 1 percent of households has not produced its wealth by the sweat of its brow. Rather, it has inherited 447 times more money than households with wealth below twenty-five thousand dollars.[12] Some estimates predict that by 2030 this elite fraction, the global 1 percent, will own two-thirds of the world's wealth.[13]

Because the return on inherited capital has, in recent years, been larger than the rate of economic growth, this unearned wealth balloons faster than the money earned by those who work for a living. As Piketty shows, wealth accumulated in the past grows faster than income and output, making new money less profitable than old. No wonder that the rich have led such vehement attacks on inheritance tax. What American conservatives have rebranded as a "death tax" is, more accurately, a tax to prevent the emergence of undemocratic dynasties. Today, an astounding 99.8 percent of estates go untaxed by the federal government.[14]

We can distill this insight even further and say that the mechanisms that define contemporary capitalism have a tendency to compound the power of the past over the present. This problem manifests in two primary ways: inherited wealth and personal debt. As wealth swells on one side, with investments yielding dividends and interest, debt balloons on the other, as more people bind their future selves in contracts that allow them to access cash today in return for paying it back, plus fees and interest, at a later date. Today, the majority of Americans is in hock, often for basic necessities. With no public option for health care, medical bills stack up; when higher education budgets get slashed, student borrowing skyrockets; inadequate paychecks mean Visa or payday lending fill the gap (contrary to stereotypes, credit cards and short-term loans are typically used for essentials such as rent and food).

Over the last forty-odd years, consumer access to credit has helped mask stagnating wages, perpetuating the illusion that prosperity is being widely shared when statistics show that it is actually being hoarded. This is due partly to the rise of neoliberal financialization, or the way debt in the form of complex financial instruments is increasingly central to the functioning of our economy—think of that edifice of risky derivatives that brought down the economy in 2008. Financialization is everywhere: cities and countries issue bonds, borrowing money from the rich instead of taxing them, to fund necessary infrastructure; the most prestigious private universities have become hedge funds with schools attached, playing Wall Street games of arbitrage to grow their endowments.[15]

This is not to say that debt cannot be a net positive for individuals and communities—under the right circumstances credit on fair terms can be a way of expanding possibilities. But under predatory or odious conditions, debt becomes an oppressive burden, a hole into which consumers and citizens slide. Here, though, is the rub: as long as default is avoided, the deeper the hole, the more profitable the contract is to the lender. One person's debt is always somebody else's asset, two sides of the same ledger.

I'll never forget one of the first days of Occupy Wall Street in New York City in 2011, when this intangible ledger was made visible. A young man stood with a long sheet of butcher block paper and shouted at the crowd in the manner of a carnival barker: "Step right up and write down what you are worth to the 1 percent!" I watched, astonished, as people lined up, marker in hand, and jotted down their age alongside a number and what their debt had been incurred for. People listed six figures' worth of medical debt, the insurmountable costs of underwater mortgages, and sums for student loans they had no hope of repaying.

During the early days of the Occupy movement, I was happy to see progressive people responding forcefully to the financial crisis. After the encampments were cleared, I joined with others to continue organizing around the issue of indebtedness, convinced that it had wide appeal. In 2012, we launched the Rolling Jubilee, a mechanism to buy consumer debts on the secondary market and abolish them, erasing tens of millions of dollars in predatory loans that belonged to thousands of strangers we would never meet. Our message was that the powerful walk away from their debts all the time—just look at the bank bailouts—while regular people are penalized if they can't pay. The Jubilee was an attempt to jump-start a public conversation about the morality of debt and to demonstrate that our monthly bills, which seem personal and private, are in fact the product of larger economic structures and government policies, from the legality of extortionate interest rates to the lack of public goods. (Medical debt, the leading cause of bankruptcy in the United States, does not exist in countries with universal health care.)

To extend the work of the Jubilee, we began to build a new kind of union, a debtors' union. Our group, the Debt Collective, is based on the premise that debt is a problem that millions of people share and, more important, an untapped form of leverage. Our riff on an old adage states it clearly: "If you owe the bank a hundred thousand dollars, the bank owns you. But if you owe the bank a hundred *million* dollars, you own the bank." Alone, our debts are a burden; together, if we organize, they can make us powerful. Thus, this country's soon-to-be two trillion dollars in student debt can be seen as a tool to fight for better terms and a different system.

Putting theory into practice, we launched the first student debt strike in history in 2015, fifteen people growing to one hundred and then two hundred. Within three years, working with a coalition of allies through various channels, we helped win over a billion dollars in debt relief and a change to federal law, making it possible, for the first time, for defrauded student borrowers to discharge their loans. That change is particularly significant because student loans are the only kind of debt that individuals cannot discharge in bankruptcy. (This is the result of reforms passed in 1998 and 2005 at the behest of lenders and their lobbyists.[16] Our members and allies whose debts were erased were spared paying them off for decades on end. Freed from this obligation, people said they felt they had gotten their futures back.

Indebtedness has been historically useful to the powerful as both a source of profit and also an instrument of social control. It has been a catalyst for rebellion, as well. This dynamic, as we've seen, goes all the way back to Solon, ancient Athens's enlightened aristocrat who was compelled to end the debt slavery of citizens to avert a social crisis. A century later in Rome, a plague of debt helped spur the Secession of the Plebs, the mass strikes by commoners that led to the creation of *tribuni plebis*, or tribunes of the people. In another age, various American colonies were a magnet for insolvent souls. The founder of my home state of Georgia, James Oglethorpe, an eighteenth-century social reformer, envisioned the colony as an economic utopia, a haven for those locked in Britain's debtors' prisons. Oglethorpe petitioned King George II to allow the country's worthy poor a second chance in an overseas settlement, and then instituted laws that sought to erase class distinctions while prohibiting alcohol and slavery. (The experiment lasted less than two decades, cut short by Spanish hostilities and resistance from Georgians who wanted to own slaves and drink rum.) Fifty-odd years later, Shays' Rebellion and other debtor revolts struck fear into the hearts of many of the American founding fathers, inspiring James Madison to rail against the "wicked project" of debt abolition in the *Federalist Papers* and leading to the creation of what some scholars have referred to as a "creditors' constitution."

More significant is the way debt has been strategically employed in service of shoring up white supremacy. Following the model of French authorities seeking to squash Haiti's antiracist democratic rebellion by imposing preposterous penalties, the World Bank and International Monetary Fund issued loans allowing powerful countries to impose austerity policies known as "structural adjustments" on emerging nations in the wake of anticolonial struggles. After slavery's abolition, similar tactics were used to target individuals in the United States. Landlords deployed debt through sharecropping and tenant farming arrangements to suppress the dream of black freedom while also creating a moral economy in which black people, instead of being owed reparations for the past wrongs, were in fact indebted to white benefactors who deserved credit for securing their emancipation.[17]

Ironically, one group did receive reparations: slave traders. After the abolition of the slave trade in 1833, Great Britain took out a massive loan (a sum equal to 40 percent of the state's yearly income, or some three hundred billion dollars today) to offset the losses of profiteers who had kidnapped and sold human beings into bondage. The loan was so great that British taxpayers only finished paying it off in 2015.[18]

When usury has no limits, debt can be a form of domination extended over time, as Jefferson knew well. In his famous letter to Madison about Earth belonging to the living, he fulminated about the ways in which debt may destabilize the present and encumber posterity. His advocacy for short-lived laws extended to short-term loans, payable within the span of a generation, and the abolition of debts unpaid after this "natural limit." Highlighting the connection between military hawks and the financiers who profit from foreign entanglements, Jefferson hoped that reducing the faculty of borrowing "would bridle the spirit of war, to which too free a course has been procured by the inattention of money-lenders to this law of nature, that succeeding generations are not responsible for the preceding." Debt, he believed, was too often employed as an undemocratic tool, a means for profiteers to fill their coffers and perpetuate their influence against the common will.

And yet, in a later letter addressed to Indiana's governor, Jefferson was eager to wield debt's destructive power to undermine Native Americans whose territory he coveted. "To promote this disposition to exchange lands," he wrote in 1803, "we shall push our trading houses and be glad to see the good and influential individuals among them run in debt . . . when these debts get beyond what the individuals can pay, they become willing to lop them off by a cessation of lands."[19] A proponent of progress for whom history unfolded in linear, enlightenment style, with America as the evolutionary pinnacle, Jefferson took comfort in his conviction that indigenous people were out of step with time itself, vestiges of the past awkwardly lingering in the present, a vanishing race destined for extinction clinging to tradition in an age of revolution and expansion. He may have professed that the dead have no claim over the living, but he did his best to ensure that the future belonged to men like him.

Democracy's relationship to time will always involve some conflict between the short-term preferences of people in the present and the future interests of our collective progeny. But under certain conditions, productive tension may become a recipe for disaster. Extreme inequality, more than any other factor, compounds the temporal antagonism. This is true in the case of inheritance and indebtedness just as it is with climate change.

On one level, we all have a long-term interest in greenhouse gases being reduced, particularly those who have children or grandchildren they would like to see thrive, or just survive. If the world were a more equitable place, perhaps we could find a relatively painless resolution, because at least the sacrifice demanded of everyone would be more or less the same. (Although even an egalitarian society could decide to live it up in the here and now, burning energy while future generations be damned.) As things stand, though, people in wealthy countries appear unprepared to make anything resembling the sort of sacrifice required to reach what could be called climate equity or justice in terms of per capita consumption—especially not if citizens of other relatively affluent countries or communities are going to keep the coal fires burning. (And burn they do: coal remains one of the main fuels powering the global economy, with an estimated 1,600 new plants in the works worldwide.[20])

Citizens of less industrialized countries will invariably bear the brunt of this intransigence and the shifting weather patterns that result, despite barely having contributed to global emissions. The concept of "climate debt" has emerged to account for these historical inequities; some researchers estimate that the United States owes developing nations over four trillion dollars for exceeding its carbon allotment.[21] Should people from poor places, in response, feel entitled to work toward burning more carbon to make up for not having consumed anything near their "fair share"? These complexities and countless others make climate change the greatest problem requiring collective action that humanity has ever faced.

Climate change raises core questions about how we ought to organize our societies and distribute the planet's limited resources. Since 1990, the Intergovernmental Panel on Climate Change, or IPCC, has warned that developed countries must make a radical break with fossil fuels, which means lowering consumption and switching to renewable energy sources while also shifting our diets away from meat and dairy (animal agriculture is a massive emissions source). A proposal for curbing emissions from the developed world so that the billion individuals who live without electricity can enjoy its benefits would probably pass in a landslide in a world referendum, but it would likely fail if the vote were limited to people in the wealthiest countries.

Still, the majority of people in those affluent countries believe climate change is an urgent threat that must be addressed.[22] Going against the grain, one contingent of citizens, disconnected from the repercussions of their actions, sees environmentalism as the real threat and takes solace in denialism. If it is too hard to face the fact that one's way of life will lead to planetary catastrophe, disavowal is a way to alleviate the cognitive dissonance: the experts are untrustworthy, the scientific research an elaborate hoax, the whole thing a conspiracy cooked up by liberals. Denial, though sometimes the result of ignorance, can also be an act of self-protection, a last-ditch defense of social privileges.

We cannot say we were not warned. In an 1847 speech, pioneering conservationist and congressman George Perkins Marsh identified processes that would later be understood as part of the greenhouse effect.[23] His popular 1864 book *Man and Nature: Or, Physical Geography as Modified by Human Action* reprimanded those who despoil the environment and recommended a course of resource management that would take the needs of future generations into account. "The earth is fast becoming an unfit home for its noblest inhabitant, and another era of equal human crime and human improvidence . . . would reduce it to such a condition of impoverished productiveness, of shattered surface, of climactic excess, as to threaten the depravation, barbarism, and perhaps even extinction of the species," he wrote. "But we are. even now, breaking up the floor and wainscoting and doors and window frames of our dwelling, for fuel to warm our bodies and seethe our pottage, and the world cannot afford to wait till the slow and sure progress of exact science has taught it a better economy."

A century later, two pioneering climate scientists issued the following statement in a 1957 coauthored paper, bolstering Marsh's case for urgent action with carefully marshalled evidence:

> Human beings are now carrying out a large scale geophysical experiment of a kind that could not have happened in the past nor be reproduced in the future. Within a few centuries we are returning to the atmosphere and oceans the concentrated organic carbon stored in sedimentary rocks over hundreds of millions of years.

This astonishing paragraph touches on the most elemental aspects of the relationship among the climate crisis, democracy, and time. Fossil fuels (the gasoline we pump into our cars, the oil with which we heat our homes, the ingredients that make the plastic bags in which we carry our lunch, a lunch likely grown with the help of petroleum-based fertilizers) are the product of photosynthesis reaching back hundreds of millions of years. They are the past condensed, the geological remains of once-living organisms. Every barrel of oil represents a swath of land and epoch of life concentrated down to its potent essence.

The discovery of coal seams, the accumulation of past energy, sparked a frenzy of exploitation. "In the abstract, mankind entered into the possession of a capital inheritance more splendid than all the wealth of the Indies," Lewis Mumford observes in his masterwork *Technics and Civilization*. But like "a drunken heir on a spree" industrialists began burning through humanity's bequest. "The psychological results of carboniferous capitalism—the lowered morale, the expectation of getting something for nothing, the disregard for balanced mode of production and consumption, the habituation to wreckage and debris as part of the normal human environment—all of these results were plainly mischievous."[24] Mischievous perhaps, but also profitable.

This extractive fever had unexpected consequences, leading us to another temporal dimension of climate change worthy of comment. Two hundred years after the fact we are finally beginning to comprehend the full implications of burning coal in nineteenth-century England. The atmospheric transformations we are witnessing are the consequence of human actions of decades or even centuries ago. "[G]lobal warming is sun mercilessly projecting a new light onto history," writes historian Andreas Malm. "If we wait some time longer and then demolish the fossil fuel economy in one giant blow, it would still cast a shadow far into the future: emissions slashed to zero, the sea might continue to rise for many hundreds of years."[25] Time motion is all mixed up, boggling the minds of humans who live second by second, day by day. When the awesome power of coal and petroleum was unlocked, who could have predicted that by burning up the past, we would imperil everything to come?

This focus on fossil fuels may seem like a digression in a story about democracy, but it's nothing short of essential. The history of liberal democracy and its intimate companion capitalism is inseparable from the discovery of these incredible energy sources. Coal, gas, and oil are power in a double sense: they are mechanical power and social power. Coal enabled the rapid technological innovation that drove the industrial revolution; coal and, later, oil allowed for the concentration of wealth and influence in the hands of the few who controlled the sources and supply chains.

While societies were once dependent on scattered energy resources—wood for fire, human and animal labor (that is, horse power), water, and wind—fossil fuels changed the game. Coal turned water into steam, which led to the development of trains, which crisscrossed the country and then the continent. Soon enough, aided and abetted by colonial projects, pipelines and ferries began carrying crude oil from the Middle East to distant locales. Throughout human history, energy had been bound to a specific place and moment; with the discovery of fossil fuel, it could be extracted, transported, and stored. Space and time, once natural, inherently local phenomena, became global and abstract.

Industrialization coincided with the proliferation of clocks, a symbol of a new market-driven organization of time and synchronization of labor. This abstract, linear, regimented time steadily replaced other ways of understanding the passage of one instance into the next. In an essay on time and work discipline, historian E. P. Thompson observes that his fellow Englishmen used to speak of a "pissing while," which he calls "a somewhat arbitrary measurement"—it depends on how badly you need to go. He invokes Madagascar, where time was measured by "a rice cooking" (about half an hour) or "the frying of a locust" (a moment), and shares that some native communities were said to speak of how a "man died in less than the time in which maize is not yet completely roasted" (less than fifteen minutes). Time, Thompson notes, was embedded in natural cycles (daylight, nightfall, shifting tides, and changing seasons) that led to periods of intense work or phases of idleness.[26]

Clock time, the measure of an industrial fossil fuel–powered economy, changed all this, but it also opened up access to the universal, nonhierarchical present that modern democracy requires, or what philosopher Mark Kingwell describes as "egalitarian secular time"—the same measure for all.[27]

If self-government is the goal, this egalitarian secular time must be flexible, both fast and slow. Democracy entails careful, unhurried deliberation, a measured, assiduous pace of proceedings, not to be confused with inertia. But haste is also needed for a quick response to crises. Our current system poses challenges to both speeds. On the one hand, there is never enough time for representatives to fully think things through (which partly explains why politicians lean so heavily on lobbyists, who provide free expertise and cheat sheets on complex issues, biased as their summaries and suggestions may be[28]). On the other hand, elected officials are not generally inclined to make rapid moves, even when catastrophe threatens.

Preoccupied by their limited turn in office and seeking reelection, they have an incentive to pass the buck to whoever occupies their seat next. As the young petitioner against the state of Pennsylvania observed, the court system moves slowly, too. (Let's not forget that *Brown v. Board of Education*, one of the most celebrated progressive legal victories of the twentieth century, demanded only that schools integrate "with all deliberate speed," a vague pace that may partly account for why schools remain distressingly segregated along racial lines.) The urgency of climate change demands swift and decisive action, but the delayed consequences mean that most officials have even less reason to act. Why should they sacrifice their careers on the altar of the unborn, who can't vote?

Society's sluggish resistance to change is exacerbated by the many obstacles thrown up by vested interests. No oil executive in thrall to the profit motive can leave the liquid money in fossil fuels lying fallow—it must be extracted and sold, even if it causes the permafrost to melt, wildfires to rage, oceans to acidify, droughts to kill crops, countries to sink, climate refugees to flee, and species to go extinct. Those privileged few who control the flow are committed to maximizing future profits, for that's what the market impels them to do.

As environmentalists Bill McKibben and Naomi Klein have demonstrated in detail, the world's largest, most powerful corporations are already in possession of untapped reserves of oil and natural gas that far exceed the limits we must observe if we are to mitigate the oncoming catastrophe. Companies would need to keep those reserves buried underground, in the process forfeiting approximately twenty trillion dollars in assets.[29] This is a prospect they cannot entertain, because conventional business models are beholden to the bottom line and short-term thinking. Their time scale privileges the present, which is profoundly out of sync with environmental realities and democracy itself. Today, the average stock is owned for a fleeting twenty-two seconds. Capitalism, it seems, lacks the attention span required for survival, let alone self-rule.

Worse still, the logic of maximizing profits prevents adequate investment in renewable energy solutions (while also encouraging outright sabotage of anything that might depress demand for fossil fuels[30]). Though the sun supplies the planet with more energy per hour than humans consume in a year, this abundance is unwelcome to people with substantial investments in the status quo.[31] So after a short and highly publicized burst of enthusiasm for solar energy, the big players quit the business. "We have thrown in the towel on solar," BP representative Bob Dudley told investors in 2013. "Not that solar energy isn't a viable energy source, but we worked at it for thirty-five years, and we really never made money."

Shell executives are on the record expressing similar frustration: "In the oil market, the prices are going up and down in cycles. The solar price is just going one way—it's going down."

The fact that solar energy is cheap and decentralized, that the sun shines energy everywhere, free for the harvesting, poses a significant challenge both to future profits and to the accumulation of social power, for it allows for far more local and potentially democratic modes of production. In one appealing possible future, everyone could have solar panels and harvest the energy they needed directly from the sky.

Given the physics of solar, a more decentralized, sustainable energy future is technically possible. But man-made laws, not physical or natural ones, stand in the way. The switch from a fossil fuel economy can happen only if there is massive, coordinated public investment. Companies may be loath to leave gas wells and tar sands untapped, but the state should have no such qualms. The cities and countries that are making strides in renewable energy tend to be places where the government has subsidized innovation, yet the efforts remain far too small. McKibben compared the necessary scale of government investment to the mobilization of national resources during World War II. What's required is "a wholesale industrial retooling." McKibben writes, "World War III is well and truly underway, and we are losing."[32]

Oil companies have known about climate change and its risks for decades, although executives hid this news from the public, spending millions to sow confusion and doubt when word finally got out. Now, when the industry concedes the coercive truth of nature's physical laws and acknowledges the impact of greenhouse gases, it promises painless solutions. Geoengineering will save us: carbon will be sucked out of the air, oceans will be fertilized with iron, reflective shields will be shot into space to deflect the sun's rays.

Rex Tillerson, the CEO of Exxon turned Trump's short-lived secretary of state, reluctantly admitted that global warming is real and then brushed it aside. "It's an engineering problem, and there will be an engineering solution," he insists. In the ultimate act of hypocrisy, these industrialists disparage any attempt at public investment as a dangerous revival of the Soviet Bloc style of economic planning. Yet they happily appoint themselves central planners of the climate, the future autocrats of a geoengineered epoch they want us to believe is our only hope.

I'd guess that most of us are more able to imagine an environmental apocalypse than a green utopia. Nuclear holocaust, cyber warfare, mass extinction, superbugs, fascism's return. and artificial intelligence turned against its makers—these conclusions we can see, but our minds struggle to conjure an image of a desirable, credible alternative to such bleak finales, to envision habitation rather than ruin.

This incapacity to see the future takes a variety of forms: young people no longer believe their lives will be better than those of their parents and financial forecasts give credence to their gloomy view; political scientists warn that we are becoming squatters in the wreckage of the not-so-distant liberal-democratic past, coining terms such as *dedemocratization* and *postdemocracy* to describe the erosion of democratic institutions and norms alongside an ongoing concentration of economic power. Meanwhile, conservative leaders cheer on democratic regression under the cover of nostalgia—"Make America Great Again," "Take Our Country Back"—and seek to rewind the clock to an imaginary and exclusive past that never really existed.

This is the motivation of those who, more than a century after the Civil War ended (indeed, well into the 1990s), still erected Confederate statues across the country. These monuments were built not to honor history but to pledge to the perpetuation of white dominance. In this sense, they were the inverse of those Communists who, under the cover of the Iron Curtain, kept the people in limbo, deprived of both liberty and equality justifying an unbearable present by invoking some perfect future that would never come to pass.

Some have given up on our planet altogether. A new breed of Silicon Valley billionaire is preparing to flee from the future.

Elon Musk, the former PayPal investor and founder of Tesla, the electric car company, occupies the progressive pole of this position, promoting renewable energy use while simultaneously plotting his rocket-fueled departure from the planet. Worried that life on earth may well be ecologically unsustainable, he is pursuing the possibility of establishing private colonies on Mars to serve as an escape hatch for those who can afford it. In 2018, Musk told an audience at the South by Southwest conference that his ideal Mars settlement would have everything from "iron foundries to pizza joints to night clubs. Mars should really have great bars." What's more, it will be run as a direct democracy, "where everyone votes on every issue." Musk's comment was soundly mocked, as his union busting at his factories back home was being reported in the media at the time—how democratic can a space colony be if owned by someone who denies collective bargaining rights on earth and then takes off in a spaceship, leaving most human beings on the planet to suffer? Still, his view represents those who are not ashamed to imagine a future that only the obscenely prosperous would live to see.

Peter Thiel, Musk's old business partner at PayPal, who also has plans to escape the reality he is creating, makes Musk look enlightened by comparison. An outspoken supporter of Donald Trump's presidential campaign, Thiel is also the founder of Palantir Technologies, a data-mining and surveillance company that works for the national security state. Like other members of what might be described as the "anxious affluent," Thiel has purchased property and citizenship in New Zealand, where he believes he and other elites can survive civilizational collapse.[33]

The idea to relocate to that remote island country came from an obscure but influential book published in 1997, *The Sovereign Individual: How to Survive and Thrive During the Collapse of the Welfare State*, which Thiel praised as one of his all-time-favorite tomes. The book's authors paint a bleak yet gleeful portrait of democracy's inevitable and welcome breakdown—welcome because wealthy citizens will no longer have to pay taxes to fund hospitals, schools, and roads for the impoverished masses. They herald the imminent rise of a new global "cognitive elite," the eponymous sovereign individuals. "The new Sovereign Individual," the book predicts, "will operate like the gods of myth in the same physical environment as the ordinary, subject citizen, but in a separate realm politically."[34] (Thiel, it's worth noting, also seeks biological sovereignty, or immortality, which is why he has made investments in life extension therapy involving the transfusion of blood from young people.)

Influenced by such a vision, Thiel proudly articulates antidemocratic sentiments. "Since 1920, the vast increase in welfare beneficiaries and the extension of the franchise to women—two constituencies that are notoriously tough for libertarians—have rendered the notion of 'capitalist democracy' into an oxymoron," he wrote in an essay for the Cato Institute, a prominent right-wing think tank. He made it more than clear that it was the democratic element that would have to be sacrificed.[35]

Democracy, a growing number of people seem to believe, is dying. The question for them is how best to mitigate or weather its decline. Against this kneejerk apocalypticism, this loss of faith in liberalism's prospects, this toxic longing for a whitewashed past and an oligarchical future, belief in democracy as a viable project of collective self-rule is, in itself, a radical act. Though it contradicts many of our modern shibboleths, the crusade for a more democratic future obliges us to look to the past. From those democratic innovators Jefferson and Paine we inherited an obsession with novelty, in daily life and in activism. This was groundbreaking in the eighteenth century, but in the twenty-first it has become orthodoxy. Our relentless presentism, encouraged by the 24/7 news cycle and social media, enjoins us to immerse ourselves in an eternal now, a state of amnesiac contemporaneity. It severs us from the past and the future—which serves the powerful just fine: the past contains many ideas they would rather see buried than revived, and reconfiguring our way of life to account for the future would entail a massive disruption of business as usual.

I came of age in the nineties and aughts, after experts declared that we were at the end of history. The message, received loud and clear through a kind of cultural osmosis, was that protest was over and the future would simply be more of the same. Though some brave souls tried to buck the trend, conventional channels tended to portray engagement in social justice as risible and démodé. Feminists were mocked for being frumpy artifacts, antiwar protesters ignored as a hippie hangover from the sixties, and union organizers dismissed as specters of a discredited socialist era, destined for the dustbin. I was schooled in a postmodern theory that celebrated apolitical pastiche, was told that Marxism was a defunct "metanarrative," and that faith in progress would lead only to tragic ends. Instead of caring about the world and what might happen next, we were encouraged to cultivate an attitude of ironic detachment.

A new cohort of progressive activists has upended these convictions. Citizens young and old have woken up to the realization that social movements, updated and evolved, are a life raft. They understand that social media is no magic bullet and that organizing today requires the same slow and steady work it always has. (Indeed, effective organizing may now involve more work, not less, to combat the negative behaviors that social media affords and incentivizes.) By harnessing digital tools to longstanding methods of organizing—marches, occupations, boycotts, strikes, riots, the formation of pressure groups, and party building—they are adding a contemporary twist to proven, effective tactics.

The resurgence of interest in traditional left-wing politics is a sign that times have changed. Union membership in the United States is historically low, and organized labor has been dealt some major blows, but young people are far more likely than their elders to have a favorable view of unions: three-quarters of those aged eighteen to twenty-nine versus half of respondents aged fifty and older.[36] In a remarkable reversal for citizens of the country that brought the world Amazon and Coca-Cola, more American Millennials now say they would prefer to live in a socialist society than a capitalist one, and this preference has helped send a slew of self-described democratic socialists to office at the local and state levels. Some might object that socialism can only represent a return to an ignominious Cold War past, not a viable horizon, yet the egalitarian principles that provide the heart of the socialist impulse are old but not passé.

Because democratic socialism has never been tried in the United States, it's no wonder that a political program centered on fulfilling a variation on Pericles's definition of democracy, on providing for the many, not the few, strikes young people as refreshingly novel. The next step, however, is expanding "the many" to somehow acknowledge and account for future generations, adding a new temporal dimension to our concept of social inclusion. If the combined descendants of the earth's human and nonhuman creatures, in all their diversity, are to have a chance of a decent life, those of us who live here and now must create a society that is not just equitable but sustainable.

Sustainability has become fashionable in recent years, but the concept is worth contemplation. In the dictionary definition, "sustain" means "to continue or be prolonged for an extended period"; its etymological roots in the Latin *sustinere* connote support, holding strong, something lifted "up from below." Thus a sustainable democratic society involves reorienting our relationship to time, allowing for drawn-out and deliberate public participation, but this can be achieved only by transforming society's underlying economic relations, as well.

Capitalism thrives on speed, novelty, consumption, obsolescence, and, above all, growth. True sustainability, then, is anathema to capitalism, which rests on the following precept: there must be more value at the end of the day than there was at the beginning. Contraction is a crisis for capital—indeed, without expansion there is no capital, for there is no profit. At bottom, the twin perils of inherited wealth and mass indebtedness, as well as the threat of ecological apocalypse, flow from an economic system predicated on greed and boundless accumulation.

"Debts are subject to the laws of mathematics rather than physics," the radiochemist Frederick Soddy observed in 1926. "Unlike [material] wealth which is subject to the laws of thermodynamics, debts do not rot with old age . . . On the contrary [debts] grow at so much per cent per annum . . . which leads to infinity . . . a mathematical and not a physical quantity."[37] Oblivious to the laws of physics, capitalism's commitment to compound expansion inevitably leads to environmental catastrophe, compelling the extraction of natural resources to meet escalating targets, forcing us to behave, in aggregate, like Mumford's "drunken heirs," ransacking our common inheritance, despite the fact an overwhelming majority of individuals believe that environmental protection is more important than economic growth.[38]

In contrast to ecologically attuned public sentiment, influential and esteemed economists provide the frenzied pursuit of gain with a glowing patina of respectability by maintaining that the insatiability of markets is perfectly rational and ultimately beneficial. Yale's William Nordhaus, for example, has made his reputation arguing that we should "discount" or delay climate adaptations until a hypothetical future date. His optimistic linear models predict that we will all be richer down the road, which means the necessary adaptations will then be comparatively cheaper, and thus less painful, to make. Of course the problem with paying later is that it may be too late, and that the monstrous growth projected to save us may be the cause of our demise.[39]

In response, environmentalists since the seventies have understandably promoted "degrowth" as an alternative to self-destruction. But while our collective footprint must be dramatically reduced and consumption reined in, not all growth is bad—the question, rather, is which areas should expand and which contract. The oil and gas sectors, along with meat industries and car manufacturers, must shrink dramatically or disappear to avert a worst-case scenario, while new infrastructure (efficient public transit, urban agriculture, the retrofitting of existing construction, wind and solar farms, reforestation and conservation projects, and more) must prosper. Creating a zero-carbon society will require trillions of dollars of investment and state action on an unprecedented scale. This presents an opportunity to experiment with democratic modes of investment and forms of growth propelled by public mechanisms. As we saw with solar energy, our current profit-driven model does not encourage capital to invest in the technologies and institutions needed to save the planet. There's no assurance that ecological sustainability will be guaranteed under a more socialist system, but subordinating our collective survival to the short-term imperatives of the market means we don't stand a chance.

The fact is, we're up against ecological limits, not monetary shortages; we are constrained by a carbon budget not a federal one, and we need to remake our economy to reflect this reality. Ample wealth exists to be reclaimed for collective benefit, and bringing finance under democratic control will mean that money will finally serve people, instead of the other way around. Nationalization and other forms of community ownership of energy suppliers and infrastructure will be crucial but must also involve genuine public oversight and control.

To finance a green transformation on the necessary scale, new forms of socially productive, as opposed to predatory, credit and debt are required. Credit and debt are promises, commitments between parties, and those bonds can inhibit or emancipate, expanding our horizons by enabling ventures that bear future benefit (in the absence of credit we are left with savings, the wealth stored up in the past). Lending need not involve usurious, compounding rates of interests that bloat beyond what a person, community, or ecosystem can reasonably repay.

As economist Ann Pettifor has noted, the pressure to increase income demands that *both* land and labor be exploited ever more intensely.[40] The degradation of soil, sea, and atmosphere comes from the same source as the day-to-day deprivations of our working lives, propelling the hand-to-mouth treadmill on which many find themselves stuck. Millions of people toil nights and weekends, juggling multiple jobs, with the rewards flowing to the already rich. (Since 1973 productivity rose 77 percent in the United States while wages stagnated, the rising tide lifting only the most luxurious yachts; since the same year, the average American works an additional five forty-hour workweeks annually.[41]) That the affluent few are able to live idly off of unearned dividends and interest while most find themselves enduring extended shifts for a reduced paycheck makes this much clear: it is not just wealth but leisure that must be fairly apportioned if a sustainable democracy is to be achieved.

Questions of labor and leisure—of free time—have been central to debates about self-government since peasant citizens flooded the Athenian Pnyx. Plato and Aristotle, unapologetic elitists, were aghast that smiths and shoemakers were permitted to rub shoulders with the Assembly's wellborn. This offense to hierarchical sensibilities was possible only because commoners were compensated for their attendance. Payments sustained the participation of the poor—that's what held them up—so they could miss a day's work over hot flames or at the cobbler's bench to exercise power on equal footing with would-be oligarchs.

For all their disdain, Plato's and Aristotle's conviction that leisure facilitates political participation isn't wrong. Throughout the nineteenth and twentieth centuries, radical workers agreed. They organized and fought their bosses for more free time, making substantial inroads until a range of factors, including the cult of consumption and a corporate counterattack, overpowered their efforts. A more sustainable, substantive democracy means resuscitating their campaign. Free time is not just a reprieve from the grindstone; it's an expansion of freedom and a prerequisite of self-rule.

A reduction of work hours would have salutary ecological effects as well, as environmentalists have noted. A fundamental reevaluation of labor would mean assessing which work is superfluous and which essential; which processes can be automated and which should be done by hand; what activities contribute to our alienation and subjugation and which integrate and nourish us. "The kind of work that we'll need more of in a climate-stable future is work that's oriented toward sustaining and improving human life as well as the lives of other species who share our world," environmental journalist and political theorist Alyssa Battistoni has written. "That means teaching, gardening, cooking, and nursing: work that makes people's lives better without consuming vast amounts of resources, generating significant carbon emissions, or producing huge amounts of stuff."[42] The time to experiment with more ecologically conscious, personally fulfilling, and democracy-enhancing modes of valuing labor and leisure is upon us, at precisely the moment that time is running out.

With climate calamity on the near horizon, liberal democracies are in a bind. The dominant economic system constrains our relationship to the future, sacrificing humanity's well-being and the planet's resources on the altar of endless growth while enriching and empowering the global 1 percent. Meanwhile, in America the Constitution exacerbates this dynamic, preserving and even intensifying a system of minority rule and lashing the country's citizens to an aristocratic past.

The fossil fuel and finance industries, alongside the officials they've bought off, will fight to the death to maintain the status quo, but our economic arrangements and political agreements don't have to function the way they do. Should democratic movements manage to mount a successful challenge to the existing order, indigenous precolonial treaty-making processes provide an example of the sort of wisdom a new, sustainable consensus might contain. The Gdoo-naaganinaa, or "Dish with One Spoon" treaty, outlines a relationship between the Haudenosaunee Confederacy and Nishnaabeg people. The dish symbolizes the shared land on which both groups depend and to which all are responsible; in keeping with the Haudenosaunee Great Law of peace, the agreement aims to prevent war, so there is only a spoon and no knife, to ensure no blood will be shed. The dish "represented harmony and interconnection," Leanne Betasamosake Simpson explains. "Neither party could abuse the resource."

> Nishnaabeg environmental ethics dictated that individuals could only take as much as they needed, that they must share everything following Nishnaabeg redistribution of wealth customs.... These ethics combined with their extensive knowledge of the natural environment, including its physical features, animal behavior, animal populations, weather, and ecological interactions ensured that there would be plenty of food to sustain both parties in the future. Decisions about use of resources were made for the long term. Nishnaabeg custom required decision makers to consider the impact of their decisions on all the plant and animal nations . . . [43]

Both Nishnaabeg and Haudenosaunee law dictated that leaders must take the needs of the next seven generations of their respective communities into account.

What comes next is an open question. Capitalism is in doubt. The patriarchy is trembling. White supremacy is sputtering. Borders are going up where they once came down. Technology may tip the balance of power toward an elite that owns the robots and controls the algorithms. The natural environment is on the brink of chaos. To combat the apocalyptic apparitions, we need to conjure alternative worlds, leaping forward *and* looking back. As Hannah Arendt observes in *Between Past and Future*, tradition does not have to be a fetter chaining us to dead matter; it can also be a thread that helps guide us toward something better and still unseen.

What kind of ancestors do we want to be? With every action or inaction, we help decide how the future will unfold. What principles and commitments do we want to adopt for a democracy that doesn't yet exist? How will we cast our votes for a society we won't live to see?

FROM FOUNDING FATHERS TO
PERENNIAL MIDWIVES

WHILE IMPRISONED BY Fascists in 1929, the Italian Communist philosopher and politician Antonio Gramsci wrote a searching letter to his younger brother Carlo from his cell, unaware that a fragment of the correspondence was destined to become a well-known slogan. Gramsci offered an assertion of bold if conflicted commitment to political transformation. "I'm a pessimist because of intelligence," he said, "and an optimist because of will."[1]

This resonant sentence was embedded in a paragraph grappling with war and hardship, a context more fraught and taxing than a twelve-word maxim can convey. Writing as a brother, militant, and prisoner, Gramsci confesses his hopes to "never again despair and lapse into those vulgar, banal states of mind that are called pessimism and optimism." Instead, he aims to synthesize and overcome them, holding the two emotions in tandem instead of letting one or the other keep him back (both can lead to disengagement, imagining outcomes, good or bad, to be practically preordained). This delicate balancing act, Gramsci continues, arms him with "unlimited patience, not passive, inert, but animated by perseverance." The tension produced is generative, helping him to endure conditions of terrible adversity.

Here is our final paradox, a duality central to democratic theory and practice: optimism and pessimism. Although they are present in all human lives, in our current political context, when the survival of our species, and many of our fellow creatures, is at stake, the two states take on special urgency. Hope and despair, confidence and doubt, suffuse our pursuit and practice of self-rule. Gramsci's letter articulates how these dueling forces can productively coexist.

Despite my reverence for Gramsci's insights, if I were to rewrite his famous words I'd be tempted to switch the polarity. When I look at all of the forces aligned to roll back and block democratic change—the concentration of wealth, the structures of minority rule, the market imperative of endless growth, the seemingly irrepressible appeal of racism, and the rapidity of climate change—I feel my will weaken. Given the magnitude of the task at hand, how can people like me possibly make a dent? The established order is so big and powerful, and a single individual so vulnerable and small. But when I engage my intellect, something approaching optimism is possible. The past is proof that it can be done.

I would never deny that history provides mountains of evidence to fuel a fatalist inclination to failure—our legacy brims with horrors. But the past abounds with counter evidence, deep veins of conviction and ample fodder to maintain morale, a second legacy of compassion, courage, tenacity, vision, solidarity, and strategy. Prior struggles and victories put the present in perspective. Who am I, writing these words on a portable computer (in my living room and not a prison cell, no less), to imagine the challenges we face as terrible and immutable? Countless nameless women before me were burned at the stake as witches, held as chattel, force-fed when they demanded the right to vote, and here I sit with rights some of them could never have dreamed of. In light of the sacrifices made by past rebels to secure our privileges, defeatism feels wrong, even trite.

Holding optimism and pessimism in equipoise, it seems to me, is the only way to proceed. The political status quo may be under assault, but it's impossible to say whether we are on the brink of catastrophe or perhaps democratic rebirth. For better and worse, on the right and the left, the failures of neoliberalism have opened up space long deemed off-limits, while galvanizing people who can broadly be defined as progressive most of all. Millions of Americans who never protested in their lives took to the streets after 2016, decrying cruel immigration policies, defending women's rights, and calling for gun control, with over twenty thousand demonstrations organized in a mere two years.[2] Conversations challenging half a century of free market consensus are now commonplace. Activists and officeholders are explicitly embracing socialism. Citizens are debating the antidemocratic structure of the American political system. While parts of the population have retreated to nationalism and xenophobia, they are outnumbered (though not outfunded or outorganized) by people who understand that acute inequality, global migration, and climate change demand a visionary response, not a nostalgic turn to the past.

A democratic flame has been lit. However intense, this fervor, like all democratic flares, might be snuffed out. There is a chance that nascent movements will lose momentum, failing to settle on an effective course of action or imploding from internal strife. High rolling adversaries with battalions of lawyers and lobbyists might exhaust activists' limited resources. Violent crackdowns and infiltration are possible should campaigns gain real strength. Incremental reforms, responding superficially to the clamor of the moment while keeping long-standing power imbalances in place, also pose a risk, for incrementalism can undercut more far-reaching demands by allowing representatives to appear responsive, impeding real change.

Whatever the method of subversion, many establishment figures, liberal and conservative, would like to see this resurgence of civic spirit extinguished. Writing in the *Atlantic*, Jonathan Rauch rallied to the defense of those in control: "Our most pressing political problem today is that the country abandoned the establishment, not the other way around," he complained. "Neurotic hatred of the political class is the country's last universally acceptable form of bigotry." Mass discontent, he concluded, is a "virus" that must be quarantined.[3] But what some take to be an affliction is better understood as a cure. People challenging the leaders, laws, and norms that have led to their dispossession is an indication of increasing democratic health, not its decline.

The real malady afflicting democracy today is not an excess of popular power but a lack of it. Despite frequent and egregious miscalculations—the disastrous Iraq War and devastating 2008 financial crisis; British prime minister David Cameron calling the Brexit referendum (while assuming that the vote would go the other way); and politicians and executives rooting for Trump's candidacy for private benefit ("It may not be *good* for *America*, but it's damn *good for CBS*," the network's then-CEO gloated)—elites as a class have been let off the hook. Instead of issuing mea culpas, they tarnish angry citizens on both sides of the political divide as "populists" while clinging ever more vehemently to a ruinous, oligarchic status quo. Over the last half century these oligarchs and their acolytes have entrenched their rule and wealth by attacking democratic gains: taxes have been eviscerated, unions and job security crushed, welfare gutted, education defunded, prisons packed to overflowing, voting rights curbed, and regulations repealed. What should terrify us is not the frustration of the people but the sources of their frustration, which have gone unaddressed for so long.

With wealth and power as concentrated as they are, and with the restraints on capitalism unleashed, realizing even relatively uncontroversial goals—such as allowing people to exercise the political rights liberal democracy claims to guarantee—would seem to require something of a revolution. If we have to battle for meager concessions from vested interests, we may as well aim for more ambitious and inspiring goals (deposing those interests should be at the top of the list).

Democracy, as we've seen, is a deceptively simple concept that requires a robust set of supports to enact. Going beyond the standard framework of periodic elections, civil liberties, legal equality, and education, self-rule could be reimagined to include

additional social and collective entitlements: an expansive commons and shared public wealth; access to dignified work and
plentiful leisure; the extension of democracy into domains including workplaces and schools; a guarantee of housing free from
the pressures of speculation along with political rights based on
residency and participation; a demos that takes nature and nonhuman animals into account and the assurance of a habitable
world for those to come. Such demands would surpass the social
democratic pacts central to countries such as Denmark, Canada,
and Sweden and widely regarded as a kind of democratic apex
(however admirable and fragile such pacts may be) in favor of
something more akin to democratic socialism, a system where,
in contrast to capitalist democracy, social power, not economic
or state power, prevails. This is a democracy that has never been
tried and is not yet in our sights.

Defining the contours of this still-unseen democracy is something we can do only collectively. Think and reason the mob must,
including thinking through democracy's abiding paradoxes. In
these pages I placed the insights of schoolchildren, doctors, former prisoners, workers, and refugees alongside the likes of Plato,
Locke, Rousseau, Madison, and Marx partly to underscore people's
tremendous and mostly untapped capacity for reflection—or what
W. E. B. Du Bois called "excluded wisdom," the knowledge possessed by everyday people he believed democracy desperately
requires. If figuring out how we want to live together entails the
kinds of inquisitiveness, imagination, and critical engagement that
comprise political philosophy then it too must be democratized.

Pessimism or optimism? As Gramsci knew, the answer is both
at once. The future to come might resemble a high-tech form of
feudalism or something that makes our nominal democracy
appear feudal in comparison; it might be an ecological wasteland
or an arcadia of sustainable, equitable abundance. The unsettling
fact is that ruling ourselves is not a predictable or stable enterprise,
but this is as much a cause for jubilation as despair. This seemingly fatal flaw is also the source of democracy's strength. Its

fragmentary, unfinished nature poses a challenge to all of us who want to be both equal and free.

If we refuse the task, progress will inevitably retreat. But if we rise to the occasion the tantalizing possibility beckons of improving our collective condition and ushering in a more just and gentle world. Change is a democratic constant, with no solid ground in sight. We inhabit what Gramsci called an interregnum, a "new world struggling to be born." Instead of founding fathers let us aspire to be perennial midwives, helping always to deliver democracy anew. Democracy may not exist and yet it still might.

NOTES

INTRODUCTION: LIVING IN THE TENSION

1. Jean-Jacques Rousseau, *The Social Contract or Principles of Political Right* (1762), book 3, chap. 15.
2. For a full account read Freedom House's "Freedom in the World 2018" report, available at https://freedomhouse.org/report/freedom-world/freedom-world-2018.
3. This is based on the *Economist* Intelligence Unit's Democracy Index, which rates 167 countries scored on a scale of zero to ten based on sixty indicators. See "Democracy Continues Its Disturbing Retreat," *Economist*, January 31, 2018.
4. David Adler, "Centrists Are the Most Hostile to Democracy, Not Extremists," *New York Times*, May 23, 2018.
5. Oxfam International, "Just 8 Men Own Same Wealth as Half the World," January 16, 2017, https://www.oxfam.org/en/pressroom/pressreleases/2017-01-16/just-8-men-own-same-wealth-half-world.
6. Oxfam International, "Richest 1 Percent Bagged 82 Percent of Wealth Created Last Year—Poorest Half of Humanity Got Nothing," January 22, 2018, https://www.oxfam.org/en/pressroom/pressreleases/2018-01-22/richest-1-percent-bagged-82-percent-wealth-created-last-year. A report from the Economic Policy Institute has data on stagnating wages: Lawrence Mishel, Elise Gould, and Josh Bivens, "Wage Stagnation in Nine Charts," Economic Policy Institute, January 6, 2015, available at https://www.epi.org/publication/charting-wage-stagnation/.
7. Board of Governors of the Federal Reserve System, "Report on the Economic Well-Being of U.S. Households in 2015," May 2016, https://

www.federalreserve.gov/2015-report-economic-well-being-us-house holds-201605.pdf.

8. Janelle Jones, John Schmitt, and Valerie Wilson, "50 Years After the Kerner Commission," Economic Policy Institute Report, February 26, 2018, https://www.epi.org/publication/50-years-after-the-kerner-commission/.

9. The fact-checking website Politifact verified these statistics after presidential candidate Bernie Sanders mentioned them during the PBS Democratic debate. Linda Qiu, "Sanders: African-Americans Lost Half Their Wealth Because of Wall Street Collapse," February 11, 2016, available at http://www.politifact.com/truth-o-meter/statements/2016/feb/11/bernie-s/sanders-african-american-lost-half-their-wealth-be/.

10. David Dayen, "Revenge of the Stadium Banks: Instead of Taking on Gun Control, Democrats Are Teaming with Republicans for a Stealth Attack on Wall Street Reform," *Intercept*, March 2, 2018, https://theintercept.com/2018/03/02/crapo-instead-of-taking-on-gun-control-democrats-are-teaming-with-republicans-for-a-stealth-attack-on-wall-street-reform/.

11. War and national security are other areas where there is quite a lot of bipartisan collaboration. Perhaps one of the strongest arguments against America's claim to be a democracy is the president's unilateral authority to launch nuclear warheads, a problem that long precedes Trump's boasting about his supersize "nuclear button." In 1976, the *New York Times* reported that two years prior, a drunken Nixon had boasted to two congressmen, "At any moment I could go into the next room, push a button, and twenty minutes later sixty million people would be dead." Terrifyingly, he wasn't wrong. That a solitary individual holds such enormous, sublime, and murderous power dispels any notion that we live in something resembling a democratic society.

12. Michael Savage, "Richest 1% on Target to Own Two-thirds of All Wealth by 2030," *Guardian*, April 7, 2018.

13. I recommend Ellen Meiksins Wood's work on this topic for those who want to learn more, particularly the first chapter of *Citizens to Lords* (Ellen Meiksins Wood, *Citizens to Lords: A Social History of Western Political Thought from Antiquity to the Middle Ages* [London: Verso Books, 2008]).

14. Rousseau, *The Social Contract*, book 2, chap. 7.

15. Karl Marx, "Critique of Hegel's 'Philosophy of Right,'" in Karl Marx and Frederick Engels, *Collected Works*, vol. 3 (New York: International Publishers Co., 2005), p. 29.

16. "Democracy, which is a charming form of government, full of variety and disorder, and dispensing a sort of equality to equals and unequals alike" Plato has Socrates say in book 8 of *The Republic* in Benjamin Jowett's

translation. The whole text is available at the MIT Internet Classics Archive at http://classics.mit.edu/Plato/republic.html.

1: FREE TO BE WINNERS AND LOSERS

1. Eric Foner, *The Story of American Freedom* (New York: W. W. Norton, 1998), p. 253.

2. Use of the word *democracy* (in general and also as the new moniker embraced by Jeffersonians and the common epithet against them) spiked in the United States in 1792–93, fueled by an association with France (James T. Kloppenberg, *Toward Democracy: The Struggle for Self-Rule in European and American Thought* [Oxford, UK: Oxford University Press, 2016], p. 569). Unsurprisingly, the word *equality* was eradicated from the French Republic's motto after Napoléon took over; it was changed simply to "liberté, ordre public" (liberty, public order).

3. The *Stanford Encyclopedia of Philosophy* calls equality "the most controversial of the great social ideals" in its entry on the concept. The exception to the general rule of equality not being hyped is art communist propaganda, in which equality, as a leveling down and destructive sameness, looms as the ultimate menace.

4. Paul Cartledge's *Democracy: A Life* (New York: Oxford University Press, 2016) offers one of many enjoyable accounts of why Athens stood apart. Ellen Meiksins Wood's *Peasant-Citizen and Slave: The Foundations of Athenian Democracy* (New York: Verso, 2015) makes a strong case that the inclusion of free laborers in the Assembly gave Athenian democracy a unique class composition that advantaged the working poor. We also probably shouldn't be too proud of ourselves in comparison to ancient Athenians. The liberty of citizens of today's industrialized democracies still depends on exploited labor, even if modern supply chains are far more difficult to trace than they were back in the days when slaves and free men mingled daily in the famed Agora, and we have yet to vanquish gender discrimination or imperial warfare.

5. Cartledge, *Democracy: A Life*, p. 1.

6. See Plutarch's *Parallel Lives* for his full account, but one additional reform merits noting: "Among Solon's other laws there is one very peculiar and unexpected one, which decrees the disfranchisement of any citizen who, in the event of revolution, does not take one side or the other. Solon's intention was evidently that men should not remain indifferent or apathetic to the public interest or safeguard their private affairs while congratulating themselves upon having nothing to do with the disorders and misfortunes of

their country; he wished instead to encourage them to attach themselves at once to the better cause, share its dangers, and give it their support, not to sit back in safety waiting to see which side would win."

7. Aziz Rana, *The Two Faces of American Freedom* (Cambridge, MA: Harvard University Press, 2010), p. 7.

8. Quoted in ibid., p. 10.

9. Ibid., pp. 89–90.

10. Quoted in Ta-Nehisi Coates, *We Were Eight Years in Power: An American Tragedy* (New York: One World, 2017), p. 67.

11. Foner, *The Story of American Freedom*, p. 87.

12. Yet the question remains, what are rights? Are they intrinsic and self-evident—"inalienable," in the language of the Declaration of Independence—or are they legal fictions, something we've created out of whole cloth? Are they properties we possess or claims we have to actively make? The political theorist Lida Maxwell, for example, argues that we don't have rights in the sense of possessing an object; rather, we have rights the way we have a meeting or a dinner party. In other words, rights must be exercised in order to exist. Marx, perhaps the world's most famous egalitarian, criticized rights for being egoistic, emphasizing individual liberty over collective liberation, which is why he advocated for a bespoke solution to inequity: "From each according to his ability, to each according to his needs."

13. L. A. Kauffman makes the case for the March on Washington as the first mass protest march in American history in the first chapter of *How to Read a Protest* (Berkeley: University of California Press, 2018).

14. Foner, *The Story of American Freedom*, p. 277.

15. On March 25, 1911, Perkins witnessed the Triangle shirtwaist fire and watched in horror as young women plummeted to their deaths to escape the flames. The New Deal, she would later say, was born on that day. For an engaging account of Perkins's contribution to the New Deal see Kirstin Downey, *The Woman Behind the New Deal: The Life and Legacy of Frances Perkins—Social Security, Unemployment Insurance, and the Minimum Wage* (New York: Anchor, 2010).

16. For one crucial account of why this was the case, see Ira Katznelson, *Fear Itself: The New Deal and the Origins of Our Time* (New York: W. W. Norton, 2013).

17. Kimberly Phillips-Fein, *Invisible Hands: The Businessmen's Crusade Against the New Deal* (New York: W. W. Norton, 2009), p. 32.

18. Milton Friedman, *Free to Choose: A Personal Statement* (Boston: Mariner Books, 1990), p. 138.

19. Ibid., p. 137.

20. Friedrich Engels, *Socialism: Utopian and Scientific* (New York: International Publishers, 1972).

21. Quoted in William Brandon, *New Worlds for Old: Reports from the New World and Their Effect on the Development of Social Thought in Europe, 1500–1800* (Akron: Ohio University Press, 1986), p. 6.

22. Ibid., p. 23.

23. Ibid., p. 13.

24. Jean-Jacques Rousseau, *Discource on the Origin and Basis of Inequality Among Men* (1754), part 2.

25. Rousseau's influence was diffuse and profound, but he had a direct influence on the founding fathers, including John Adams and James Wilson, who both kept copies of his 1762 work *The Social Contract* (Kloppenberg, *Toward Democracy,* pp. 421–22).

26. Karl Marx and Friedrich Engels, *The Communist Manifesto: A Modern Edition* (New York: Verso, 2012), p. 34.

2: SHOUTING AS ONE

1. I found other ways to carry on what I felt was significant about Occupy, namely its focus on economics, and built on the experience by organizing with and on behalf of debtors. The initiatives I've been involved with, including the Rolling Jubilee and the Debt Collective, have not operated by consensus and have made demands of corporations and the state.

2. Martin Gilens and Benjamin I. Page, "Testing Theories of American Politics: Elites, Interest Groups, and Average Citizens," *Perspectives on Politics* 12, no. 3 (September 2014): 564–81.

3. Astra Taylor, "Occupy the Media—and the Message," *Nation,* March 14, 2012.

4. "How Decisions Are Made at the UN," available at https://outreach.un.org/mun/content/how-decisions-are-made-un.

5. Jane J. Mansbridge, *Beyond Adversary Democracy* (Chicago University of Chicago Press, 1983), p. xi.

6. Richard Hofstadter, *Anti-Intellectualism in American Life* New York: Alfred A. Knopf, 1963), p. 21.

7. Richard Hofstadter, *The Idea of a Party System: The Rise of Legitimate Opposition in the United States, 1780–1840* (Berkeley: University of California Press, 1992), p. 4.

8. Quoted in Seth Ackerman, "A Blueprint for a New Party," *Jacobin,* November 8, 2016, available at https://www.jacobinmag.com/2016/11/bernie-sanders-democratic-labor-party-ackerman.

9. Omar Ali, "The Jim Crow of Bipartisan Rule," *The Public Professor*, November 1, 2010, available at http://www.thepublicprofessor.com/the -jim-crow-of-bipartisan-rule/.

10. L. A. Kauffman, "The Theology of Consensus," *Berkeley Journal of Sociology*, May 2015, available at http://berkeleyjournal.org/2015/05/the -theology-of-consensus/.

11. Quoted in L. A. Kauffman, *Direct Action* (New York: Verso: 2017), p. 55.

12. In *The Cult of the Constitution* (Redwood City, CA: Stanford University Press, 2019) legal theorist Mary Anne Franks lambasts the idea that the founders' decisions can be justified because they were "products of their time." They were revolutionaries and intellectuals, which means they were exposed to a range of radical ideas, from more economically egalitarian possibilities to women's equality, abolitionism, and what we would now call animal rights (through Benjamin Franklin's friendship with the intersectional radical Quaker activist Benjamin Lay).

13. John Nichols and Robert McChesney, *Dollarocracy: How the Money and Media Election Complex Is Destroying America* (New York: Nation Books, 2012), p. 31.

14. Emmanuel Sez and Gabriel Zucman, "Wealth Inequality in the United States since 1913: Evidence from Capitalized Income Tax Data," working paper 20625, National Bureau of Economic Research, October 2014.

15. Marcus Rediker, *Villains of All Nations: Atlantic Pirates in the Golden Age* (Boston: Beacon Press, 2004), p. 53.

16. Peter Linebaugh and Marcus Rediker, *The Many-Headed Hydra: Sailors, Slaves, Commoners and the Hidden History of the Revolutionary Atlantic* (New York: Verso, 2001), p. 162.

17. Ibid., 163.

18. Ibid., 162

19. Gallup Poll results compiled and available at https://www.crmvet.org/docs /60s_crm_public-opinion.pdf.

20. Sarah Leonard, "Good Jurors, Bad Laws," *Dissent*, Summer 2014.

21. Daniel Lazare, *The Frozen Republic: How the Constitution Is Paralyzing Democracy* (New York: Harcourt Brace, 1996).

3: REINVENTING THE PEOPLE

1. Tim Sullivan, "Bhutanese Reluctantly Stepping into World of Democracy," *New York Times*, March 21, 2008.

2. Somini Sengupta, "Line Up and Pick a Dragon: Bhutan Learns to Vote," *New York Times*, April 23, 2007.

3. "Bhutan Mock Poll Votes for Tradition," *Star* (Toronto), May 30, 2007.

4. Quoted in Sengupta, "Line Up and Pick a Dragon."

5. Quoted in Peter Foster, "Bhutan Heads Towards Democracy," *Telegraph* (UK), April 23, 2007.

6. "BKP's Challenge Is Changing People's Mindset," *Kuensel*, August 25, 2018, available at http://www.kuenselonline.com/bkps-challenge-is-changing-peoples-mindset/

7. "We Hold All Parties in Equal Esteem: DPT," *Kuensel*, August 25, 2018, available at http://www.kuenselonline.com/we-hold-all-parties-in-equal-esteem-dpt/.

8. "The Mood," *Kuensel*, August 18, 2018, available at http://www.kuenselonline.com/the-mood/.

9. "PDP Is Its Biggest Competitor," *Kuensel*, August 25, 2018 available at http://www.kuenselonline.com/pdp-is-its-biggest-competitor/.

10. Stephanie DeGooyer, "Democracy, Give or Take?," *Humanity: An International Journal of Human Rights, Humanitarianism, and Development* 5, no. 1 (Spring 2014): 93–110.

11. Maximillian Morch, "Bhutan's Dark Secret: The Lhotshampa Expulsion," *Diplomat*, September 21, 2016.

12. "Bhutan Mock Poll Votes for Tradition."

13. Jacques Derrida, *Rogues: Two Essays on Reason* (Redwood City, CA: Stanford University Press, 2005), p. 36.

14. James Miller, *Can Democracy Work?* (New York: Farrar, Straus and Giroux, 2018), p. 35.

15. Ellen Meiksins Wood offers a compelling discussion of the differences between slavery in the ancient and modern worlds and how capitalism, with its commitment to formal equality and freedom of contract, necessitated an ideology of dehumanization to justify holding individuals in bondage. *Democracy Against Capitalism: Renewing Historical Materialism* (New York: Verso, 2017), pp. 267–69.

16. Lynn Hunt, ed., *The French Revolution and Human Rights* (Philadelphia: University of Pennsylvania Press, 1996).

17. C. L. R. James, *The Black Jacobins: Toussaint L'Ouverture and the San Domingo Revolution* (New York: Random House, 1963), p. 38.

18. Adom Getachew, "Universalism After the Post-colonial Turn: Interpreting the Haitian Revolution," *Political Theory* 44, no. 6 (2016): 821–45.

19. Ibid., p. 823.

20. Michael Garcia Bochenek, "Guantanamo's Other Sordid Legacy," January 18, 2016, Human Rights Watch, available at https://www.hrw.org/news/2016/01/18/guantanamos-other-sordid-legacy.

21. Research by Giovanni Peri for the IZA World of Labor think tank looking at thirty years of empirical research shows little supporting evidence for the common view that immigrants suppress wages: "Most studies for industrialized countries have found no effect on wages, on average, and only modest effects on wage differentials between more and less educated immigrant and native workers. Native workers' wages have been insulated by differences in skills, adjustments in local demand and technology, production expansion, and specialization of native workers as immigration rises."

22. Edmund S. Morgan, *Inventing the People* (New York: W. W. Norton, 1988), p. 63.

23. Michael Mann, *The Dark Side of Democracy* (New York: Cambridge University Press, 2004).

24. Hannah Arendt, *The Origins of Totalitarianism*, rev. ed. (1951; repr., San Diego: Harvest, 1968), p. 299.

25. The most generous estimates put Jewish refugee immigration to the United States from 1933 to 1944 at about 250,000, a devastatingly small number.

26. According to the Pew Research Center, as of January 29, 2018, there are 3.4 million Syrians in Turkey, 1 million in Lebanon, 600,000 in Jordan, 250,000 in Iraq, more than 150,000 in North African countries including Egypt and Libya, and around 20,000 in the United States. For more information see: http://www.pewresearch.org/fact-tank/2018/01/29/where-displaced-syrians-have-resettled/.

27. NATO warships return migrants to Turkey, as Frontex, the EU's border agency, patrols the coastlines, while backroom deals have been cut with Libyan authorities. Europe's boundaries now reach well beyond the shoreline, stretching into what geographers describe as an "enforcement archipelago" of policing and detention. See Caitlin Chandler, "How Far Will the EU Go to Seal Its Borders?," *Dissent*, Summer 2018.

28. Deborah Amos, "The U.S. Has Accepted Only 11 Syrian Immigrants This Year," NPR.org, April 12, 2018.

29. I wrote about these issues in "Our Friends Who Live Across the Sea," *Baffler* 31 (June 2016). It's also worth noting that Bhutan offers an interesting and in many ways exceptional case. Tens of thousands of refugees from Bhutan were resettled in the United States between 2006 and 2008, during the administration of George W. Bush. It seems that Bhutanese refugees were accepted in high numbers partly because Bhutan is the rare country in which the United States has few strategic interests and Bhutanese refugees were seen as a "low risk" population to welcome. See Margaret Piper, "Refugee Resettlement: 2012 and Beyond,"

New Issues in Refugee Research, p. 31, available at http://www.unhcr.org /510bd3979.pdf; Matt O'Brien, "Bhutanese Refugees' Road to America Started in the Bush Administration," *San Jose Mercury News,* September 1, 2010; "A/S Sauerbrey Discusses Refugee Problem with Bhutanese Officials," Wikileaks Public Library of US Diplomacy, 07NEWDELHI5243_a, India New Delhi, December 7, 2007, available at https://wikileaks.org /plusd/cables/07NEWDELHI5243_a.html; "Chief Government Negotiator Optimistic About Summit Talks," Wikileaks Public Library of US Diplomacy, 06KATHMANDU2666_a, Nepal Kathmandu, October 6, 2006, available at https://wikileaks.org/plusd/cables/06KATHMANDU 2666_a.html; "Donor Countries Coalesce on Bhutanese Refugee Strategy," Wikileaks Public Library of US Diplomacy, 06THEHAGUE1303_a, Netherlands The Hague, June 9, 2006, available at https://w kileaks.org /plusd/cables/06THEHAGUE1303_a.html.

30. Susan Gzesh, "Central Americans and Asylum Policy in the Reagan Era," Migration Policy Institute, April 1, 2006.

31. Dylan Matthews, "The Case for Open Borders," *Vox,* December 15, 2014.

32. Will Kymlicka, "Territorial Boundaries: A Liberal Egalitarian Perspective," in David Miller and Sohail H. Hashmi, eds., *Boundaries and Justice: Diverse Ethical Perspectives* (Princeton, NJ: Princeton University Press, 2001), p. 270.

33. Ibid., 250.

34. Ibid., 270.

35. Ron Hayduk, "Why Non-Citizens Should Be Allowed to Vote," *Jacobin,* November 6, 2018, available at https://jacobinmag.com/2018/11 noncitizen -voting-undocumented-immigrants-midterm-elections.

36. Michael Gormley, "Teachout Would Give Undocumented Immigrants State Citizenship after 3 Years," *Newsday,* September 3, 2014.

37. Peter Spiro, "State Citizenship Has Roots in American History," *New York Times,* June 24, 2014.

38. Sarah Song, "Democracy and Noncitizen Voting Rights," *Citizenship Studies* 13, no. 6 (2009): 607–20.

39. Ayelet Shachar, *The Birthright Lottery: Citizenship and Global Inequality* (Cambridge, MA: Harvard University Press, 2009).

40. I was introduced to the concept in Keeanga-Yamahtta Taylor, "How Real Estate Segregated America," *Dissent,* Fall 2018.

41. James Baldwin, *The Fire Next Time* (New York: Random House, 1993), p. 89.

42. David FitzGerald and David Cook-Martin, *Culling the Masses: The Democratic Origins of Racist Immigration Policy in the Americas* (Cambridge, MA: Harvard University Press, 2014), p. 38.

43. Nell Irvin Painter, *The History of White People* (New York: W. W. Norton, 2011), p. 292.

44. FitzGerald and Cook-Martin, *Culling the Masses*, p. 334.

45. Ibid., p. 333.

46. It's worth noting that Alexis de Tocqueville might not have objected to the sort of hostility that bonds the demos against an external "other." For example, he advocated for the colonization of Algeria to provide his countrymen with common cause and a sense of honor and superiority. Democracy at home would depend on despotism abroad, civic equality on imperial conquest and exclusion. For an in-depth account see Jennifer Pitts, *A Turn to Empire: The Rise of Imperial Liberalism in Britain and France* (Princeton, NJ: Princeton University Press, 2005).

47. Niraj Chokshi, "75 Percent of Americans Say Immigration Is Good for Country, Poll Finds," *New York Times*, June 23, 2018.

48. Tom Gjelten, "The Immigration Act That Inadvertently Changed America," *Atlantic*, October 2, 2015.

49. That conservative was actually a Democrat, Rep. Michael Feighan of Ohio.

50. By no means was Hart-Celler an unmitigated boon to all groups—by imposing stringent limits on previously unrestricted Latino immigration, the act helped create the problem of "illegal" immigration over the Mexican border.

51. Stuart Soroka and Sarah Roberton, "A Literature Review of Public Opinion Research on Canadian Attitudes Towards Multiculturalism and Immigration, 2006–2009," Citizenship and Immigration Canada, March 2010.

52. Until January 1, 1947, there was no legal status of Canadian citizens, only British subjects. Some speculate that the relatively recent breakdown of Anglo-British identity may have made Anglo Canadians more open to further evolution in their collective sense of self.

53. Ken Lum, "Ken Lum on Canadian Cultural Policy," *Canadian Art*, Fall 1999.

54. Himani Bannerji, *The Dark Side of the Nation: Essays on Multiculturalism, Nationalism and Gender* (Toronto: Canadian Scholars' Press, 2000), p. 10.

55. Leanne Simpson quoted in Glen Sean Coulthard, *Red Skins, White Masks* (Minneapolis: University of Minnesota Press, 2014), p. 154.

56. For an interesting discussion of this issue see Kevin Bruyneel, *The Third Space of Sovereignty: The Postcolonial Politics of U.S.-Indigenous Relations* (Minneapolis: University of Minnesota Press, 2007), pp. 111–21.

57. Sid Hill, "My Six Nation Haudenosaunee Passport Is Not a 'Fantasy' Document," *Guardian* (UK), October 30, 2015.

58. Quoted in Ingrid Peritz, "Mohawk Community's 'Marry Out, Get Out' Law Ruled Unconstitutional by Quebec Court," *Globe and Mail* (Toronto), May 1, 2018.

59. Coulthard, *Red Skins, White Masks*, p. 3.

60. Chris Hayes," The New Abolitionism," *Nation*, April 24, 2014.

61. Adam Winkler, "'Corporations Are People' Is Built on an Incredible 19th-Century Lie," *Atlantic*, May 5, 2018. For a more detailed account see Adam Winkler, *We the Corporations: How American Businesses Won Their Civil Rights* (New York: Liveright, 2018).

62. Christopher Stone, *Should Trees Have Standing?: Law, Morality, and the Environment* (New York: Oxford University Press, 2010). p. 3.

63. Ibid., p. 8.

64. Darlene May Lee, "Town of Crestone, Colorado, Takes Bold Step by Recognizing the Inherent Rights of Nature," *Mother Earth News*, August 8, 2018, available at https://www.motherearthnews.com/nature -and-environment/crestone-colorado-recognizing-the-rights-of -nature-zbcz1808.

65. I wrote about this fight and the larger issue of the rights of nature for the *Baffler*, from which some of this material is drawn. Astra Taylor, "Who Speaks for the Trees?," *Baffler* 32 (September 2016).

66. Kalhan Rosenblatt, "Do Apes Deserve 'Personhood' Rights? Lawyer Heads to N.Y. Supreme Court to Make Case," *NBC News*, March 11, 2017, available at https://www.nbcnews.com/news/us-news/do-apes-deserve -personhood-rights-lawyer-heads-n-y-supreme-n731431.

67. Suzanne Monyak, "When the Law Recognizes Animals as People," *New Republic*, February 2, 2018.

68. Plato, *The Republic*, G. M. A. Grube, trans., C. D. C. Reeve, ed. (Indianapolis, IL: Hackett Publishing, 1992), p. 234.

69. Stone, *Should Trees Have Standing?*, pp. 64–65.

70. A May 2018 study published in the Proceedings of the National Academy of Sciences revealed that since the dawn of civilization, human beings have caused the loss of 83 percent of all wild mammals and half of plants. In September of 2014 the World Wildlife Fund and the Zoological Society of London found the number of wild animals on Earth had halved in the previous four decades alone. Scientists have also been warning of an imminent "insect apocalypse" that would have a dramatic, destructive impact on ecosystems and food chains.

71. Safiya Noble, *Algorithms of Oppression: How Search Engines Reinforce Racism* (New York: New York University Press, 2018).

72. Nikhil Sonnad, "US Border Agents Hacked Their 'Risk Assessment' System to Recommend Detention 100% of the Time," *Quartz*, June 26, 2018,

available at https://qz.com/1314749/us-border-agents-hacked-their-risk-assessment-system-to-recommend-immigrant-detention-every-time/.

73. Atossa Araxia Abrahamian, "Digital Citizenship in a Bordered World," unpublished lecture given to me by the author.
74. Quoted in Atossa Araxia Abrahamian, "We're All Data Subjects," *New York Times*, May 29, 2018, p. A23.
75. Quoted in Michael Specter, "Rewriting the Code of Life," *New Yorker*, January 2, 2017.

4: CHOOSE THIS, OR ELSE!

1. I wrote an opinion piece for the *Guardian* about this issue. "Want Police Reform? Charge Rich People More for Speeding Tickets," *Guardian* (UK), July 22, 2016.
2. Hannah Arendt, "Truth and Politics," *New Yorker*, February 25, 1967.
3. Thomas Hobbes, *Leviathan* (1651; repr., New York: Penguin Classics, 1982), chap. 15.
4. Ibid., chap. 14.
5. Carole Pateman, *The Sexual Contract* (Stanford, CA: Stanford University Press, 1988), p. 40.
6. John Rees, *The Leveller Revolution: Radical Political Organisation in England, 1640–1650* (New York: Verso, 2016), pp. 290–91.
7. Silvia Federici, *Caliban and the Witch* (Brooklyn, NY: Autonomedia, 2004), p. 130.
8. John Stuart Mill, *Principles of Political Economy: With Some of Their Applications to Social Philosophy*, Stephen Nathanson, ed. (Indianapolis, IL: Hackett Publishing, 2004), p. 292.
9. Ellen Meiksins Wood, *The Origins of Capitalism* (New York: Monthly Review Press, 1999), p. 6.
10. Sheldon Wolin, *Politics and Vision: Continuity and Innovation in Western Political Thought* (Princeton, NJ: Princeton University Press, 1960), p. 280.
11. "The fiction of the invincible yeoman thus embodied the same ambiguities as the larger fiction it supported: it sustained the government of the many by the few, even while it elevated and glorified the many" (Morgan, *Inventing the People*, pp. 156, 173).
12. Quoted in Lizabeth Cohen, *A Consumers' Republic: The Politics of Mass Consumption in Postwar America* (New York: Alfred A. Knopf, 2003), p. 24.
13. Quoted in Fred Turner, *The Democratic Surround: Multimedia and American Liberalism from World War II to the Psychedelic Sixties* (Chicago: University of Chicago Press, 2003), p. 216.

14. Zeynep Tufekci, "Beware the Smart Campaign," *New York Times*, November 17, 2012, p. A23.
15. Kim Phillips-Fein, *Invisible Hands: The Businessmen's Crusade Against the New Deal* (New York: W. W. Norton, 2010), p. 52.
16. Ibid., p. 34.
17. Christopher Mayer, "Democracy Is Coercive," *Mises Daily*, February 16, 2000, available at https://mises.org/library/democracy-coercive.
18. Ludwig von Mises, *Bureaucracy* (New Haven, CT: Yale University Press, 1945).
19. Phillips-Fein, *Invisible Hands*, p. 100.
20. February 20, 2018, Quinnipiac University Poll: "American voters support stricter gun laws 66–31 percent, the highest level of support ever measured by the independent Quinnipiac University National Poll, with 50–44 percent support among gun owners and 62–35 percent support from white voters with no college degree and 58–38 percent support among white men. Support for universal background checks is itself almost universal, 97–2 percent, including 97–3 percent among gun owners. Support for gun control on other questions is at its highest level since the Quinnipiac University Poll began focusing on this issue in the wake of the Sandy Hook massacre."
21. "Public Support for 'Single Payer' Health Coverage Grows, Driven by Democrats," Pew Research Center, June 23, 2017.
22. Justin Sink, "Congress Less Popular Than Colonoscopies, Root Canals, Poll Finds," *The Hill*, January 18, 2013. The low approval rating is consistent across a range of recent polls, including Gallup (https://news.gallup.com/poll/1600/congress-public.aspx) and YouGov (https://today.yougov.com/topics/politics/articles-reports/2018/04/10/dismal-ratings-congress-though-democrats-are-less-).
23. Michel J. Crozier, Samuel P. Huntington, and Joji Watanuki, *The Crisis of Democracy: Report of the Governability of Democracies to the Trilateral Commission* (New York: New York University Press, 1975), p. 37.
24. He made his comments on Fox News February 17, 2018.
25. Cass Sunstein, "When Crowds Aren't Wise," *Harvard Business Review*, September 2016.
26. For an informative historical account of how public choice economics rose to prominence see S. M. Amadae, *Rationalizing Capitalist Democracy: The Cold War Origins of Rational Choice Liberalism* (Chicago: University of Chicago Press, 2003).
27. Quoted in Nancy MacLean, *Democracy in Chains: The Deep History of the Radical Right's Stealth Plan for America* (New York: Viking, 2017), p. xxii.

28. Leon Fink, *The Maya of Morganton: Work and Community in the Nuevo New South* (Chapel Hill: University of North Carolina Press, 2003).

29. Mary Beard, "Democracy, According to the Greeks," *New Statesman*, October 14, 2010.

30. Martin Luther King Jr., "The Montgomery Bus Boycott," 1955, available at https://blackpast.org/1955-martin-luther-king-jr-montgomery -bus-boycott.

5: IS THIS WHAT DEMOCRACY LOOKS LIKE?

1. Miller, *Can Democracy Work?*, p. 43.

2. The press release can be accessed online at https://us2.campaign -archive.com/?u=f3100bc5464cbba2f472ddf2c&id=e4b9a8fb19.

3. Patrick Kingsley, "Taking an Ax to Democracy as Europe Fidgets," *New York Times*, February 11, 2018, p. A1.

4. Cited in Greg Grandin, *The End of the Myth: From the Frontier to the Border Wall in the Mind of America* (New York: Metropolitan Books, 2019), p. 107.

5. Cited in David Runciman, "Destiny v. Democracy," *London Review of Books* 35, no. 8 (April 25, 2013).

6. Sydney Worth, "Indian Country Moves to Secure Voting Rights," *Yes! Magazine*, November 16, 2018.

7. "Securing Indian Voting Rights," *Harvard Law Review* 129, no. 6 (April 2016): 1736.

8. The nonprofit watchdog Open Secrets tracks reelection rates, updated here: https://www.opensecrets.org/overview/reelect.php. For approval ratings see Gallup's "Congress and the Public," posted at https://news .gallup.com/poll/1600/congress-public.aspx.

9. Daniel Lazare's work on this topic is unparalleled. "In 1810, thanks to the bedrock principle of equal state representation, it was possible to cobble together a Senate majority out of states representing just 33 percent of the total population. Today candidates can achieve the same thing with states that account for just 17.6 percent of the population. By 2030 that figure will drop to 16.7. The proportion needed to mount a successful filibuster—i.e. forty-one senators from twenty-one states—will drop to just 11 percent over the same period, meaning that just one person in nine will be in a position to bring government to a halt," writes Lazare in "A Constitutional Revolution," *Jacobin*, January 3, 2017, available at https://www.jacobinmag.com/2017/01/constitution-trump-democracy

-electoral-college-senate. For a more in depth account see Lazare, *The Frozen Republic*.

10. Morgan, *Inventing the People*, pp. 204–5.

11. This is according to a Harvard-Harris Poll conducted August 2017.

12. Drew DeSilver, "U.S. Trails Most Developed Countries in Voter Turnout," Pew Research, May 21, 2018.

13. Waleed Aly, "Voting Should be Mandatory," *New York Times*, January 19, 2017.

14. Thomas E. Cronin, *Direct Democracy: The Politics of Initiative, Referendum, and Recall* (Cambridge, MA: Harvard University Press, 1989), p. 54.

15. Owends Davis, "Uber, Lyft Lose Austin, Texas, Referendum After Spending Millions to Change Ride-Hailing Rules," *International Business Times*, May 7, 2016.

16. Alex Samuels, "Uber, Lyft Returning to Austin on Monday," *Texas Tribune*, May 25, 2017.

17. Referenda outcomes from Ballotopedia.

18. Douglas J. Amy, "A Brief History of Proportional Representation in the United States," published by Fair Vote, a nonpartisan nonprofit devoted to electoral reform and available at its website www.fairvote.org.

19. Quoted in Clyde Haberman, "The California Ballot Measure That Inspired a Tax Revolt," *New York Times*, October 16, 2016.

20. Thomas B. Edsall and Mary D. Edsall, *Chain Reaction: The Impact of Race, Rights, and Taxes on American Politics* (New York: W. W. Norton, 1992), p. 131.

21. Quoted in Michael Foley, *Front Porch Politics: The Forgotten Heyday of American Activism in the 1970s and 1980s* (New York: Hill & Wang, 2013), p. 241.

22. Adam Clymer, "Reagan Urges Party to Support Tax Cuts," *New York Times*, June 25, 1978, p. 27.

23. Isaac Martin's work on tax revolts and political movements led by the upper classes in the United States is excellent, and this point is one he argues convincingly: while people's attitudes toward taxes did shift, what was really significant was the change in how political parties approached taxes. (Either you are for taxes or against them!) See Isaac Martin, *The Permanent Tax Revolt: How the Property Tax Transformed American Politics* (Redwood City, CA: Stanford University Press, 2008); and Isaac Martin, *Rich People's Movements: Grassroots Campaigns to Untax the One Percent* (New York: Oxford University Press, 2013).

24. What if the legitimate fears people had about ballooning housing costs

had been addressed in another way? Left-wing responses to the revolt's initial grievances were (and still are) possible. Proposals could have included different tax rates for people with fixed incomes; anti-speculation laws to curb skyrocketing housing prices, capping price increases instead of property taxes; more quality, affordable public housing could be built to ease fears about displacement, and so on.

25. Foley, *Front Porch Politics*, p. 242.

26. Taxes are a brilliant lever for conservatives who are "made sick at heart" by the operation of the machinery of the state—a machine that regulates corporations, sets labor standards, provides health care to people, educates kids whose parents don't have money to pay for private tutors, and protects the environment—not just to make it grind to a halt, but to completely transform its functioning. "Starve the beast," "drown it in a bathtub"—these are their slogans. The wealthy have been on a long and extremely successful tax revolt for a trajectory with deep historical roots that I don't have the space to explore here.

27. This assumption, however, turns out to have been based on a misunderstanding, or, rather, a mistranslation: the origin of the concept of "self-organization" can be traced to the field of cybernetics, the scientific study of systems that rose to prominence after World War II. Early cyberneticians looked at nature and mistakenly assumed they were observing a neatly self-regulating, stable system. (In doing so, they founded the discipline of ecology, which would come to understand nature as something far more complex and erratic.) As John Duda has convincingly demonstrated, the term *self-organization* was imported from cybernetics into the translation of classic left-wing political texts in the 1970s, where it had no precedent, establishing the concept as a core part of the progressive political vocabulary.

28. Roslyn Fuller, *Beasts and Gods: How Democracy Changed Its Meaning and Lost Its Purpose* (London: Zed Books, 2015), p. 88.

29. Quoted in David Van Reybrouck, *Against Elections: The Case for Democracy* (New York: Seven Stories Press, 2018), p. 93.

30. John Gastil and Erik Olin Wright, eds., *Legislature by Lot* (New York: Verso, 2018).

31. Reybrouck, *Against Elections*, p. 152.

6: A SOCRATIC MOB

1. Andrew Sullivan, "Can Donald Trump Be Impeached?," *New York Times*, March 18, 2018, p. 1 of the *Sunday Book Review*.

2. Lee Drutman, "Will Trump Break American Democracy?," *Vox*, March 20, 2018.

3. Michael Young, "Down with Meritocracy," *Guardian* (UK), June 29, 2001.

4. It's important to note that *Brown v. Board of Education* can be understood only in the context of the Cold War and the negative imagery and evidence of hypocrisy projected by Jim Crow, which undermined American authority abroad. James Baldwin put it this way: "Most of the Negroes I know do not believe that this immense concession [*Brown v. Board*] would ever have been made if it had not been for the competition of the Cold War, and the fact that Africa was clearly liberating herself and therefore had, for political reasons, to be wooed by the descendants of her former masters. Had it been a matter of love or justice the 1954 decision would surely have occurred sooner; were it not for the realities of power in this difficult era, it might very well not have occurred yet."

5. Alana Semuels, "Good School, Rich School; Bad School, Poor School," *Atlantic*, August 25, 2016.

6. Unlike their white counterparts, black boys raised in relatively well-to-do areas earn less in adulthood and are significantly more likely to become poor than their white counterparts, who tend to stay in the upper class. Emily Badger, Claire Cain Miller, Adam Pearce, and Kevin Quealy, "Extensive Data Shows Punishing Reach of Racism for Black Boys," *New York Times*, March 19, 2018.

7. Propped up by taxpayer dollars through the Department of Education's lending program, these for-profit educational companies are the top producers of black graduates, even though the programs are often fraudulent, the degrees practically worthless, and the debt loads sky high.

8. Burton R. Clark, "The 'Cooling-Out' Function in Higher Education," *American Journal of Sociology* 65, no. 6 (May 1960), pp. 569–76.

9. Kristin Ross, *Communal Luxury* (New York: Verso, 2016), p. 39.

10. Quoted in ibid., p. 43.

11. Jesse Drew, "Commons Sense," in Cal Winslow, ed., *Rivers of Fire: Commons, Crisis, Imagination* (Arlington, MA: Pumping Station Press, 2016).

12. The Communist Party was famously active in Alabama in the decades leading up to Parks's world-changing protest. In the days of the Great Depression, party members believed that black people had the right to self-determination in the Deep South and helped them organize around a range of grievances, from lynchings to wage theft. Though she never joined the party, Parks attended numerous official meetings, and like many others who became prominent activists in the region she no doubt learned

some of the basics of political organizing and benefited from the infrastructure the Communist Party had helped lay down for what would later be the civil rights movement. The work in Alabama was not isolated nor an aberration, but part of a wider strategy to build power for poor people. See Robin D. G. Kelley, *Hammer and Hoe: Alabama Communists During the Great Depression* (Chapel Hill: University of North Carolina Press, 1990).

13. Benjamin Hunnicutt's books *Work Without End: Abandoning Shorter Hours for the Right to Work* (Philadelphia: Temple University Press, 2010) and *Free Time: The Forgotten American Dream* (Philadelphia: Temple University Press, 2013) are both excellent resources on this topic. Also see Drew, "Commons Sense."

14. Anzia Yezierska, *Hungry Hearts* (Boston: Houghton Mifflin, 1920), pp. 169–70. The story is discussed in Annelise Orleck, *Common Sense and a Little Fire: Women and Working-Class Politics in the United States, 1900–1965* (Chapel Hill: University of North Carolina Press, 1995), p. 39.

15. Orleck, *Common Sense*, p. 169.

16. Samuel Bowles and Herbert Gintis, *Schooling in Capitalist America: Educational Reform and the Contradictions of Economic Life* (New York: Basic Books, 1975), p. 186.

17. Ibid., p. 193. A complementary version of this history is recounted in Andrew Hartman, *Education and the Cold War* (New York: Palgrave Macmillan, 2008), p. 19.

18. He also thought it marginalized the virtuous.

19. Hofstadter, *Anti-Intellectualism in American Life*, p. 159.

20. John Dewey, *The Later Works of John Dewey, 1925–1953*, vol. 1, *1925, Experience and Nature,* Jo Ann Boydston, ed., (Carbondale, IL: Southern Illinois University Press, 2008), p. 172.

7: NEW WORLD ORDER

1. Stathis Kouvelakis, "Borderland," *New Left Review* 110 (March/April 2018): 25.

2. Liz Alderman, "Greece's Bailout Is Ending. The Pain Is Far from Over," *New York Times*, August 20, 2018, p. B1.

3. Niccolò Machiavelli, *Discourses on Livy*, tr. Harvey C. Mansfield and Nathan Tarcov (Chicago: University of Chicago Press, 1998), p. 22.

4. Ibid., p. 23.

5. Jacob T. Levy, "Beyond Publius: Montesquieu, Liberal Republicanism and the Small-Republic Thesis," *History of Political Thought* 27, no. 1

(Spring 2006); Christopher Wolfe, "The Confederate Republic in Montesquieu," *Polity* 9, no. 4 (Summer 1977): 427–45.

6. Grandin's *The End of the Myth* is an extended argument for this case.

7. When Benjamin Franklin published *A Narrative of the Late Massacres* in 1764, it was settlers, not natives, who committed the massacres he decried. Franklin condemned members of the notorious Paxton Boys gang for killing indigenous neighbors who were from tribes that were members of the Haudenosaunee Confederacy.

8. While the precise degree of influence remains the topic of intense scholarly debate, in 1988, the United States House and Senate passed a concurrent resolution acknowledging "the contribution of the Iroquois Confederacy of Nations to the development of the United States Constitution." The "confederation of the original Thirteen Colonies into one republic was influenced by the political system developed by the Iroquois Confederacy as were many of the democratic principles which were incorporated into the Constitution itself," the official recognition states. In the final instance, however, what is clear is that even if the Constitution was directly inspired by the democratic example of the Haudenosaunee, as some historians maintain, the influence did not go deep enough. Had the aboriginal forerunner been taken as a literal prototype the American Constitution would have expanded democracy in two directions at once—not just up to the federal level but also into the family, extending the freedom to participate politically to women.

9. Taiaiake (Gerald) R. Alfred, *Heeding the Voices of Our Ancestors: Kahnawake Mohawk Politics and the Rise of Native Nationalism* (Don Mills, ON: Oxford University Press Canada, 1995), pp. 77–78.

10. Ibid., p. 80.

11. Ibid., p. 78.

12. I've combined two quotations from books by Taiaiake (Gerald) Alfred. The first half appears in *Peace, Power, and Righteousness: An Indigenous Manifesto* (Don Mills, ON: Oxford University Press Canada, 1999) p. 41, and the latter in Alfred, *Heeding the Voices of Our Ancestors*, p. 79.

13. Women at least merit a fleeting remark in the *Federalist Papers*, in the form of a warning of the political risks of courtesans and mistresses, as Renée Jacobs points out in her fascinating essay, "Iroquois Great Law of Peace and the United States Constitution: How the Founding Fathers Ignored the Clan Mothers," *American Indian Law Review* 16, no. 2 (1991): 497–531. For more on gender politics in Haudenosaunee society see Barbara Mann, *Iroquoian Women: The Gantowisas* (New York: Peter Lang Publishing, 2006).

14. Alfred, *Heeding the Voices of Our Ancestors*, p. 78.

15. While some colonial men seemed dimly aware of the elevated political status of women in Iroquois society (Franklin, for example, reported on it as a matter of fact), the phenomenon was usually either ignored or deplored. One account rued that native women "exercised an influence but little short of despotic, not only in the wigwam but also around the council fire"—an observation that echoed John Adams's famous dismissal of his wife Abigail's request that he and his collaborators "remember the ladies" in their new legal code: "Depend upon it. We know better than to repeal our Masculine systems . . . which would compleatly subject Us to the Despotism of the Peticoat." (Operating in a similar mode, Jefferson sneered about the French women he met while traveling overseas who he believed overstepped their station by expressing curiosity about political affairs.) The fear of female despots was, of course, pure projection. It was the male settlers who ruled as tyrants on the home front, even as they conspired to overthrow a monarch overseas. In colonial America, women were property of their husbands with virtually no privileges or freedoms to call their own. In the eyes of the law, women were civilly dead. They could not sue, enter contracts, control property, or vote, and husbands could legally beat and rape them. Not so in Haudenosaunee society, which was matrilineal.

16. Coulthard, *Red Skin, White Masks*, p. 13.

17. Ibid., p. 57.

18. Renee Maltezou, "Greek Pensioner Kills Himself Outside Parliament," Reuters, April 4, 2012.

19. Truth Committee on the Greek Public Debt, "Preliminary Report," June 18, 2015, available at http://www.cadtm.org/Preliminary-Report-of-the-Truth.

20. Robert Reich, "How Goldman Sachs Profited from the Greek Debt Crisis," *Nation*, July 16, 2015.

21. Konstantopoulou and others who had front row seats to the drama, including former finance minister Yanis Varoufakis, believe that Tsipras assumed that the polls were correct and that "yes" would win, allowing him to agree to the new bailout with some semblance of dignity intact. He was caught off guard and had no plan B.

22. This reference was brought to my attention through personal correspondence by Stan Draenos, Andreas Papandreou's former assistant and biographer.

23. Quinn Slobodian, *Globalists: The End of Empire and the Birth of Neoliberalism* (Cambridge, MA: Harvard University Press, 2018), p. 118.

24. Sam Panitch and Leo Gindin, *The Making of Global Capitalism: The Political Economy of American Empire* (New York: Verso, 2012), p. 229.

25. This comes from the "History of Trade" section of the WTO website, which comes under the heading, "History of the Multilateral Trading System," available at https://www.wto.org/english/thewto_e/history_e/history_e.htm.

26. Yanis Varoufakis, *The Global Minotaur* (New York: Zed Books, 2011), p. 80.

27. FitzGerald and Cook-Martin, *Culling the Masses*; Slobodian, *Globalists*, p. 124. Samuel Moyn's *Not Enough: Human Rights in an Unequal World* (Cambridge, MA: Harvard University Press, 2018) provides a useful account of this history.

28. Slobodian, *Globalists*, p. 124.

29. Panitch and Gindin, *The Making of Global Capitalism*, p. 244; and Manfred B. Steger, *Globalization: A Very Short Introduction* (New York: Oxford University Press, 2017), p. 42.

30. Susan George, *Shadow Sovereigns: How Global Corporations Are Seizing Power* (Malden, MA: Polity, 2015), p. 97. The daily workings of the WTO (like its partner organizations the IMF and World Bank) take place behind closed doors, far removed from the prying eyes of regular people who might be partial to such protections. There are no clearly defined public rule-making processes, and citizens cannot use Freedom of Information requests to understand what happened and why.

31. Thomas Friedman, *The Lexus and the Olive Tree: Understanding Globalization* (New York: Picador, 2012), pp. 104–6.

32. Panitch and Gindin, *The Making of Global Capitalism*, p. 228.

33. "ISDS: Important Questions and Answers," United States Trade Representative Archives, available at https://ustr.gov/about-us/policy-offices/press-office/blog/2015/march/isds-important-questions-and-answer, accessed December 26, 2018.

34. ISDS are, in the words of the *Economist*, "a special privilege that many multinationals have abused" ("The Arbitration Game," *Economist*, October 11, 2014). For more extensive accounts see Claire Provost and Matt Kennard, "The Obscure Legal System That Lets Corporations Sue Countries," *Guardian* (UK), June 10, 2015; and Haley Sweetland Edwards, *Shadow Courts: The Tribunals That Rule Global Trade* (New York: Columbia Global Reports, 2016).

35. George, *Shadow Sovereigns*, pp. 87–91; Robert Kuttner, *Can Democracy Survive Global Capitalism?* (New York: W. W. Norton, 2018), pp. 199–200.

36. "ISDS: Important Questions and Answers," United States Trade Representative Archives.

37. George, *Shadow Sovereigns*, pp. 77–78. According to Edwards in *Shadow Courts*, "From the 1960s to 2000, corporations brought fewer than 40 disputes, but in the last fifteen years, they have brought nearly 650."

38. Provost and Kennard, "The Obscure Legal System That Lets Corporations Sue Countries."

39. I owe this point to Robert Kuttner (Kuttner, *Can Democracy Survive Global Capitalism?*, p. 255).

40. Kuttner, *Can Democracy Survive Global Capitalism?*, p. 241.

41. Ibid., p. 145.

42. Robert Z. Aliber, Federal Reserve Bank of Boston, quoted in ibid. p. 89.

43. Gabriel Zucman, "How Corporations and the Wealthy Avoid Taxes (and How to Stop Them)," *New York Times*, November 10, 2017.

44. Varoufakis, *The Global Minotaur*, p. 1; Les Christie, "Foreclosures Up a Record 81% in 2008," *CNN Money*, January 15, 2009, available at https://money.cnn.com/2009/01/15/real_estate/millions_in_foreclosure/.

45. The irony, given their jingoistic aspirations, is that ethno-nationalists are part of a self-consciously global movement: their parties hold international conferences, representatives speak at each other's political rallies, and followers cross-promote memes and misinformation on the borderless World Wide Web.

46. Carlito Pablo, "Two Out of 10 Homeless People in Metro Vancouver Have Jobs," *Georgia Straight* (Vancouver), September 26, 2017. For an in-depth exploration of the growing number of employed people who have no choice but to live in their vehicles, see Jessica Bruder's excellent *Nomadland: Surviving America in the Twenty-First Century* (New York: W. W. Norton, 2017).

47. Benedict Anderson, *Imagined Communities: Reflections on the Origin and Spread of Nationalism* (New York: Verso, 2006), p. 6.

48. For a genealogy of the term *activism*, see Astra Taylor, "Against Activism," *Baffler* 30 (March 2016).

49. Cited in Linebaugh and Rediker, *The Many-Headed Hydra*, p. 101.

50. New York City had ten Socialist state assemblymen, seven Socialist city councilmen, one Socialist municipal judge, and one Socialist congressman (Painter, *The History of White People*, p. 294).

51. Quoted in Silvia Federici, *Wages for Housework* (Brooklyn, NY: Autonomedia, 2017), p. 12.

52. Even as urban living becomes increasingly popular, "real America" still means rural America. As we've already seen, the American political system is structured to give substantial advantage to sparsely populated rural areas, which will continue to punch above their weight in national and state electoral contests even as they hemorrhage residents. Rural areas also tend to receive substantially more in federal funds per tax dollar paid than their urban counterparts, which further cements Republican advantage. That being true, it should also be noted, however, that it hasn't only been conservatives who have bashed cities. From Progressive Era reformers through the 1960s back-to-the-land counterculture, liberals and radicals of various stripes have also bemoaned the urban as chaotic, unclean, and inauthentic.

53. Ross, *Communal Luxury*, p. 11.

54. Ibid., p. 12.

55. Ibid., p. 124.

56. James Green, *Death in the Haymarket: A Story of Chicago, the First Labor Movement and the Bombing that Divided Gilded Age America* (New York: Pantheon, 2006), p. 88.

57. Ross, *Communal Luxury*, p. 95.

58. Daniel Aldana Cohen, "The Urban Green Wars," *Jacobin*, December 11, 2015, available at https://www.jacobinmag.com/2015/12/this-changes -everything-naomi-klein-climate-change/; Mike Davis, "Who Will Build the Ark?," *New Left Review* 61 (January/February 2010).

59. Ross, *Communal Luxury*, p. 3.

60. All quotes from Ada Colau taken from Masha Gessen, "Barcelona's Experiment in Radical Democracy," *New Yorker*, August 6, 2018.

61. Luke Stobart, "Reclaiming the City," *New Internationalist*, May 25, 2018, available at https://newint.org/2018/05/01/feature/reclaiming-the-city; Laia Bertran, "The Rising Tide for the Democratic Control of Water in Barcelona," *openDemocracy*, March 16, 2018, available at https://www .opendemocracy.net/can-europe-make-it/laia-bertran/rising-tide-for -democratic-control-of-water-in-barcelona.

62. Baird reflects on these issues at length on her personal website in a post titled "Municipalism: An Icarian Warning," June 14, 2018, available at https://katesheabaird.wordpress.com/2018/06/14/municipalism-an -icarian-warning/.

63. Meehan Crist, Atossa Araxia Abrahamian, and Denton Abel, "Mining the Sky," *Logic* 4 (n.d.); and Sarah Fecht, "Do Earth Laws Apply to Mars Colonists?," *Popular Science*, September 27, 2016.

64. Mark Graham and Anasuya Sengupta, "We're All Connected Now, So

Why Is the Internet So White and Western?," *Guardian* (UK), October 5, 2017.

65. One of the many challenges for Barcelona, or any other similarly minded municipal government, is that companies such as Google, Facebook, and Uber dwarf cities in terms of their budgets, technological infrastructure, human resources, and overall reach and are thus able to build on economies of scale that give them a tremendous advantage.

8: A RUIN OR A HABITATION

1. While the case garners regular media coverage, the best place for up-to-date information about the case is the website of Our Children's Trust, the organization behind the litigation: https://www.ourchildrenstrust.org /us/federal-lawsuit/

2. Dana Drugmand, "Citizens Sue to Hold UK Government Accountable for Climate Goals," *Climate Liability News*, March 7, 2018; and Damian Carrington, "Can Climate Litigation Save the World?," *Guardian* (UK), March 20, 2018.

3. The Greenpeace website has information about the case. See "Twenty-five Young Colombians Are Suing the Government over Climate Change," June 2, 2018, available at https://unearthed.greenpeace.org/2018/02/06 /young-colombians-suing-government-climate-change-amazon/.

4. This is a particularly notable development given that the pipelines were devised to disempower labor militants. "In fact, oil pipelines were invented as a means of reducing the ability of humans to interrupt the flow of energy. They were introduced in Pennsylvania in the 1860s to circumvent the wage demands of teamsters who transported barrels of oil to the rail depot in horse-drawn wagons," writes Timothy Mitchell in *Carbon Democracy: Political Power in the Age of Oil* (New York: Verso, 2013), p. 36.

5. Charles Geisler and Ben Currens, "Impediments to Inland Resettlement under Conditions of Accelerated Sea Level Rise," *Land Use Policy* 66 (July 2017): 322–30.

6. David Wallace-Wells, "UN Says Climate Genocide Is Coming. It's Actually Worse Than That," *New York*, October 10, 2018.

7. As Kafer points out, the standard optimistic vision of the future is often devoid of disabled people, sick people, and sometimes even old people (or at least we will get old more slowly and the effects of aging will be better hidden). This means resources are funneled into potential cures for disability or disease, or into youth- and life-extension therapies, instead

of planning for the reality of continued human vulnerability, illness, and interdependence. Alison Kafer, *Feminist, Queer, Crip* (Bloomington: Indiana University Press, 2013).

8. G. K. Chesterton, *Orthodoxy* (New York: John Lane Company, 1909), p. 85.

9. Karl Marx, "The Eighteenth Brumaire of Louis Bonaparte" (1852), available at https://www.marxists.org/archive/marx/works/1852/18th -brumaire/ch01.htm.

10. The battle of words played out mainly in Burke's *Reflections on the French Revolution* (1790) and Paine's *Rights of Man* (1791). Yuval Levin's *The Great Debate: Edmund Burke, Thomas Paine, and the Birth of Right and Left* (New York: Basic Books, 2013) provides an entertaining and insightful account of their rivalry and its political significance.

11. Thomas Paine, *Dissertation on First Principles of Government* (1795; repr., Ann Arbor: University of Michigan Library, 2011), p. 7.

12. The progressive think tank Demos posted a discussion about this statistic on its website: Matt Bruenig, "In Reality, the Wealthy Inherit Ungodly Sums of Money," January 21, 2014, available at http://www .demos.org/blog/1/21/14/reality-wealthy-inherit-ungodly-sums -money.

13. Savage, "Richest 1% on Target to Own Two-thirds of All Wealth by 2030."

14. Center on Budget and Priorities, "Ten Facts You Should Know about the Federal Estate Tax," available at https://www.cbpp.org/research/federal -tax/ten-facts-you-should-know-about-the-federal-estate-tax.

15. Astra Taylor, "Universities Are Becoming Billion-Dollar Hedge Funds with Schools Attached," *Nation*, March 8, 2016.

16. As I write, the Trump administration is seeking to illegally roll back these gains.

17. Saidiya V. Hartman has more to say on this dynamic in her trenchant *Scenes of Subjugation: Terror, Slavery, and Self-Making in Nineteenth-Century America* (New York: Oxford University Press, 1997), p. 131.

18. Kris Manjapra, "When Will Britain Face Up to Its Crimes Against Humanity?," *Guardian* (UK), March 29, 2018.

19. For a broader account of this strategy see Grandin, *The End of the Myth*, p. 43.

20. Hiroko Tabuchi, "As Beijing Joins Climate Fight, Chinese Companies Build Coal Plants," *New York Times*, July 2, 2017, p. A10.

21. H. Damon Matthews, "Quantifying Historical Carbon and Climate Debts among Nations," *Nature Climate Change* 6 (2016): 60–64.

22. The Yale Climate Opinion Maps 2018 poll reports that a majority of

Americans believe that climate change is true, support investment in renewables, want CO_2 to be regulated and for fossil fuel companies to pay a carbon tax, believe schools should teach about global warming, and more. See Yale Climate Opinion Maps 2018, available at http://climate communication.yale.edu/visualizations-data/ycom-us-2018/.

23. Leo Hickman, "The 1847 Lecture That Predicted Human-Induced Climate Change," *Guardian* (UK), June 20, 2011.

24. Lewis Mumford, *Technics and Civilization* (New York: Harcourt, Brace, 1934), pp. 157–58.

25. Andreas Malm, *Fossil Capital: The Rise of Steam Power and the Roots of Global Warming* (New York: Verso, 2016), p. 8.

26. E. P. Thompson, "Work-Discipline, and Industrial Capitalism," *Past & Present* 38 (December 1967): 56–97.

27. Mark Kingwell, *Democracy's Gift: Tradition, Time, Repetition* (n.p.: Blurb, 2016).

28. See Lee Drutman, *The Business of America Is Lobbying* (New York: Oxford University Press, 2015), for an excellent account of how this dynamic plays out.

29. Bill McKibben, "Global Warming's Terrifying New Math," *Rolling Stone*, July 19, 2012.

30. Ruth Sherlock, "Barack Obama Accuses Pro–Fossil Fuel Businesses of Sabotaging Solar Energy," *Telegraph* (UK), August 25, 2015; and Hiroko Tabuchi, "Kochs Finance High-Tech War Against Transit," *New York Times*, June 19, 2018, p. A1.

31. Naomi Klein, *This Changes Everything* (New York: Simon and Schuster, 2014), p. 367.

32. Bill McKibben, "A World at War," *New Republic*, August 15, 2016.

33. Mark O'Connell, "Why Silicon Valley Billionaires Are Prepping for the Apocalypse in New Zealand," *Guardian* (UK), February 15, 2018.

34. Quoted in ibid.

35. Peter Thiel, "The Education of a Libertarian," *Cato Unbound*, April 13, 2009, available at https://www.cato-unbound.org/2009/04/13/peter -thiel/education-libertarian.

36. Michelle Chen, "Millennials Are Keeping Unions Alive," *Nation*, February 5, 2018; and Shiva Maniam, "Most Americans See Labor Unions, Corporations Favorably," Pew Research, January 30, 2017, available at http://www.pewresearch.org/fact-tank/2017/01/30/most-americans -see-labor-unions-corporations-favorably/.

37. Quoted in Ann Pettifor, *The Production of Money: How to Break the Power of the Bankers* (New York: Verso, 2017), p. 45.

38. The Yale Climate Opinion Maps 2018 poll found that 70 percent of respondents agreed that environmental protection is more important than economic growth.

39. I owe this insight to Alyssa Battistoni and her work on the ecological crisis in *Jacobin* magazine, including, "How Not to Talk About Climate Change," *Jacobin*, August 3, 2018, available at https://jacobinmag.com/2018/08/new-york-times-losing-earth-response-climate-change.

40. Pettifor, *The Production of Money*, p. 46.

41. "The Productivity–Pay Gap," Economic Policy Institute, August 2018, available at https://www.epi.org/productivity-pay-gap/; and Juliet Schor, "The (Even More) Overworked American," in John de Graaf, ed., *Take Back Your Time: Fighting Overwork and Time Poverty in America* (San Francisco: Berret-Koechler Publishers, 2003), p. 7.

42. Alyssa Battistoni, "Living, Not Just Surviving," *Jacobin*, August 15, 2017, available at https://jacobinmag.com/2017/08/living-not-just-surviving/.

43. Leanne Simpson, "Looking after Gdoo-naaganinaa: Precolonial Nishnaabeg Diplomatic and Treaty Relationships," *Wicazo Sa Review* 23, no. 2 (Fall 2008): 29–42.

CONCLUSION: FROM FOUNDING FATHERS TO PERENNIAL MIDWIVES

1. Antonio Gramsci, *Letters from Prison*, vol. 1 (New York: Columbia University Press, 1993) p. 299. While Gramsci made it famous, the phrase was actually inspired by the French writer Romain Rolland (1866–1944) who had used a similar formulation elsewhere.

2. L. A. Kauffman, "Dear Resistance: Marching Is Not Enough," *Guardian*, July 7, 2018.

3. Jonathan Rauch, "How American Politics Went Insane," *Atlantic*, July/August 2016.

ACKNOWLEDGMENTS

Writing a book is not exactly a democratic enterprise, but neither is it the solitary process the sole name on the cover misleadingly implies.

When I first spoke to my wonderful agent, Melissa Flashman, about this book, I already had the basic structure outlined in my mind. I had briefly toyed with the idea of organizing my 2018 film *What Is Democracy?* along the lines of the chapters in this volume. It was too abstract an organizing principle for the screen, but I had a sense it could work on the page.

Though certainly its own creation, this book is an outgrowth of *What Is Democracy?* in myriad ways. The experience of making that film expanded my horizons and transformed my worldview, first by granting me the opportunity to seriously delve into political theory and second by leading me to many of the people who appear in the preceding pages. Sincere thanks are due to every single person who worked on the film (formally and informally), who allowed me to interview them for it, or who offered feedback at some stage, no matter how small or fleeting their role. I won't repeat the credit sequence in its entirety here, but I would be remiss if I did not acknowledge the National Film Board of Canada, the institution that funded the movie's creation and supported its Canadian release. An institution unique in the world, I can confidently say that no other arts organization would have gotten on board with my proposal, especially in 2014 when the Board green-lit the film.

Lea Marin, my producer, is simply one of the most brilliant, compassionate, and capable human beings I have ever met and I thank my lucky stars every day to count her as a collaborator and dear friend. *What Is Democracy?* was a true labor of love for both of us and would be nothing without her contribution. Our executive producer Anita Lee cheered and cajoled us when we needed it, and her cinematic discernment and unflagging commitment vastly improved the final product. Michelle van Beusekom was a rock, helping us keep the big picture in mind, offering her wisdom when we needed it and never losing faith. It was an honor to work with all three of these women.

I want to extend my sincere appreciation to many at the NFB and beyond: Robert Kennedy, Sanjay Mehta, Maya Bankovic, Lawrence Jackman, Denia Safari, Christos Giovanopoulos, David McCallum, Patricia Boushel, Heather McIntosh, Jacques Laroche, Aleksandra Perisic, Martina Radwan, Michael Galinsky, Jeremy Barnes, Heather Trost, Kevin Riley, Marcus Matyas, Chris Goll, Kate Vollum, Jane Gutteridge, Jennifer Mair, Katja De Bock, Melissa Wheeler, Donna Cowan, Mark Wilson, Élise Labbé, Éric Séguin, and Danielle Viau, and finally Emily Russo and Nancy Gerstman of Zeitgeist Films. I learned so much from every person in the film but Silvia Federici, Salam Magames, Abid Muhajir, Cornel West, Efimia Karakantza, Eleni Perdikouri, and Wendy Brown deserve special mention.

If this book was born of the film, the film was born of my political activism, especially my work with the Debt Collective over the last seven inspiring, tumultuous, and ultimately satisfying years. My cofounders Laura Hanna, Ann Larson, Thomas Gokey, Hannah Appel, and Luke Herrine are my heroes and I'm proud of what we have accomplished together. Our scheming got me thinking about the interconnections of debt and democracy and about finance more generally but it also inspired reflections on the broader challenge of building democratic power in an age of oligarchic control. Boundless gratitude goes to the Shuttleworth Foundation—to Helen Turvey, Karien Bezuidenhout, Jason Hudson, and Ryan George—who supported the Debt Collective at a critical juncture while bringing me into fellowship with people working to make positive change around the world. Leah Hunt-Hendrix, Brenda Coughlin, Will Meyer, and Jesse von Doom have also been crucial allies and champions of our seemingly quixotic efforts.

This is my second round with the incredible team at Metropolitan Books, a publisher I respected and admired from afar long before I became one of their authors. I shudder to imagine the prospect of writing a book with anyone else but my remarkably gifted editor Riva Hocherman to guide me. I never doubt Riva's judgment, and I have benefited enormously from her erudition, skill, and impressive grasp of how books work, and also from her political conviction, acuity, and empathy. (All the errors and shortcomings that remain are mine, of course.) My admiration and appreciation extend to Sara Bershtel and the rest of the Metropolitan team, including Connor Guy, Grigory Tovbis, Chris O'Connell, and Brian Lax. Sincere thanks, as well, to Declan Taintor and everyone on the postproduction side of things. Kelli Anderson was extremely kind to step in and help with the cover despite the pressure of Other deadlines.

I owe a huge thank-you to the *Baffler*, where I first tested out and published some of the material that made it into this book (a handful of paragraphs almost verbatim). It was there that I initially wrote about the Republic Windows cooperative in Chicago, the issue of the rights of nature and nonhuman personhood, the refugee crisis in Greece, the difference between activism and organizing, and the challenge inherent in representing "the people." Thank you to Lucie Elven, John Summers, Noah McCormack, the inimitable Chris Lehmann, and the rest of the current *Baffler* team. I also want to thank Bonnie Honig for inviting me to present at the "Riot, Refuge, Refusal" panel at Brown University, which gave me the opportunity to begin to write about the history of the Free Speech Movement and its relationship to the Prop 13 Tax Revolt.

Outside of official editing channels, other astute and generous souls helped me wrangle the manuscript into shape. I'm so happy the intuitive and inquisitive Patricia Boushel stayed on with me from the film through the writing process, sharing her insights and research acumen while also providing critical commentary and beneficial pep talks. Will Meyer was both a research assistant and partner in crime, mixing his reports with always-enlivening commentary. Will Tavlin dug up academic articles and summarized complex issues with speed and grace. Troy Vettese provided helpful notes at an early stage. The ever perceptive Stephanie DeGooyer championed both the film and the book every step of the way; she pushed me to think more deeply about citizenship and rights, led me to the example of Bhutan, and was even willing to read an entire messy draft of the manuscript, a favor I won't soon forget. I am grateful beyond words to my Debt Collective comrades Ann Larson and Luke Herrine for providing illuminating and incisive comments on various chapters. Alyssa Battistoni's feedback was discerning and essential, pushing me during the final stretch to stake out my own position more forcefully and to think through some difficult philosophical dilemmas more deeply. Lida Maxwell boosted my morale when it was flagging. Though she did not read the book until it was complete, I have learned so much about the art of writing from my two-decade-long friendship with Rebecca Solnit.

No doubt my interest in the perplexities of self-rule can probably be traced back to my family and our unusual household where "child-led" and "noncoercive" frameworks were the norm. I'm not able to adequately express how grateful I am to my parents, Ethan and Maria Taylor, who trusted their offspring completely and truly encouraged us to question authority, even theirs. As a tiny child I never doubted that my opinion counted and that I was worthy of respect. My parents, siblings, and extended family are my anchor and inspiration: Sunaura Taylor, Alexander Taylor, Nye Taylor, David Wallace, Sylvia Mangum, Melissa Colbert, Sebastian, Isadora, and Leonara (aka "Badger"). It also must be said that it was my mother who first suggested I make a film about democracy, in an email she sent me back in 2013. So an extra hearty thank-you goes to her for planting the seed that would sprout and grow to consume my life for nearly five years.

My final and most profound thanks is to my partner Jeffrey Mangum, who encouraged me to think about writing a book at a moment I was deeply immersed in other projects and commitments. His support and patience made the research and writing possible. His love and friendship make life worth living. I will forever treasure our democracy of two.

INDEX

ABOUT THE AUTHOR

ASTRA TAYLOR is the author of *The People's Platform* (winner of the American Book Award) and has made three documentary films, *What Is Democracy?*, *Zizek!*, and *Examined Life*. Taylor's writing has appeared in *The New York Times*, *The Washington Post*, *n+1*, and *The Baffler*, where she is a contributing editor. She lives in New York City.